ECONOMICS

ECONOMICS

Bibliographic Guide to

Reference Books and Information Resources

PETER MELNYK

1971

LIBRARIES UNLIMITED, INC. • LITTLETON, COLORADO

Library of Congress Card Number 71-144203
Standard Book Number 87287-021-9

LIBRARIES UNLIMITED, INC.
P. O. Box 263
Littleton, Colorado 80120

TABLE OF CONTENTS

ACKNOWLEDGMENTS
INTRODUCTION

CHAPTER ONE
ECONOMIC THEORY
(Systems and History of Economic Thought)

GUIDES TO ECONOMIC LITERATURE 15
BIBLIOGRAPHIES (CURRENT) 15
BIBLIOGRAPHIES (RETROSPECTIVE) 18
DICTIONARIES AND ENCYCLOPEDIAS 25
BIOGRAPHICAL DIRECTORIES 27
INDEXES AND ABSTRACTS 28
HANDBOOKS AND YEARBOOKS 29
MONOGRAPHIC TREATISES 30

CHAPTER TWO
ECONOMIC CONDITIONS IN VARIOUS COUNTRIES
(Economic Development — Underdeveloped Areas)

GUIDES TO ECONOMIC HISTORY 47
BIBLIOGRAPHIES (CURRENT) 47
BIBLIOGRAPHIES (RETROSPECTIVE)..................... 48
DICTIONARIES AND ENCYCLOPEDIAS 53
DIRECTORIES AND HANDBOOKS 53
GENERAL SURVEYS 54
ECONOMIC DEVELOPMENT IN VARIOUS COUNTRIES 60

CHAPTER THREE
PRIVATE AND PUBLIC FINANCE
(Banking, Currency and Money; Insurance; Investments;
Stock Markets; Taxation)

BIBLIOGRAPHIES (CURRENT) 90
BIBLIOGRAPHIES (RETROSPECTIVE)..................... 90
DICTIONARIES AND ENCYCLOPEDIAS 95
DIRECTORIES 97
HANDBOOKS 99
REPORTS AND YEARBOOKS 101
STATISTICS 102
MONOGRAPHIC TREATISES 104

CHAPTER FOUR
COMMERCE AND MARKETING

GUIDES TO INFORMATION 111
BIBLIOGRAPHIES (CURRENT) 113
BIBLIOGRAPHIES (RETROSPECTIVE) 114
DICTIONARIES AND ENCYCLOPEDIAS 118
DIRECTORIES 119
HANDBOOKS 120
INDEXES 121
ATLASES 121
STATISTICS 122
MONOGRAPHIC TREATISES 123

CHAPTER FIVE
INTERNATIONAL ECONOMICS
(Foreign Trade and Exchange: Exports, Imports)

GUIDES TO INFORMATION 125
BIBLIOGRAPHIES (CURRENT) 126
BIBLIOGRAPHIES (RETROSPECTIVE) 127
DICTIONARIES AND ENCYCLOPEDIAS 128
DIRECTORIES 129
HANDBOOKS 131
REPORTS AND SURVEYS 132
STATISTICS 134
MONOGRAPHIC TREATISES 136

CHAPTER SIX
AGRICULTURAL AND LAND ECONOMICS;
ECONOMIC GEOGRAPHY

GUIDES 139
BIBLIOGRAPHIES (CURRENT) 140
BIBLIOGRAPHIES (RETROSPECTIVE) 141
DICTIONARIES, ENCYCLOPEDIAS AND HANDBOOKS 143
INDEXES AND ABSTRACTS 143
SURVEYS AND STATISTICS 144
MONOGRAPHIC TREATISES 145

CHAPTER SEVEN
INDUSTRY AND TRANSPORTATION

Industry

GUIDES TO INFORMATION 147
BIBLIOGRAPHIES (CURRENT) 148

BIBLIOGRAPHIES (RETROSPECTIVE) 148
DICTIONARIES AND ENCYCLOPEDIAS 151
DIRECTORIES 151
SURVEYS AND STATISTICS 153
MONOGRAPHIC TREATISES 154

Transportation
(Communication; Public Utilities)

GUIDES TO INFORMATION 157
BIBLIOGRAPHIES (CURRENT) 158
BIBLIOGRAPHIES (RETROSPECTIVE) 158
DICTIONARIES, ENCYCLOPEDIAS AND HANDBOOKS 161
DIRECTORIES 161
ATLASES 163
SURVEYS AND STATISTICS 163
MONOGRAPHIC TREATISES 163

CHAPTER EIGHT
LABOR ECONOMICS

GUIDES 165
BIBLIOGRAPHIES (CURRENT) 165
BIBLIOGRAPHIES (RETROSPECTIVE) 167
DICTIONARIES AND ENCYCLOPEDIAS 174
DIRECTORIES 174
HANDBOOKS 176
INDEXES AND ABSTRACTS............................. 176
SURVEYS AND STATISTICS............................ 178
MONOGRAPHIC TREATISES 179

CHAPTER NINE
POPULATION AND STATISTICS

Population

GUIDES TO RESEARCH................................ 186
BIBLIOGRAPHIES 186
INDEXES 188
SURVEYS AND STATISTICS 188
MONOGRAPHIC TREATISES 190

Statistics

GUIDES AND REFERENCE SOURCES..................... 191
BIBLIOGRAPHIES (CURRENT) 192
BIBLIOGRAPHIES (RETROSPECTIVE) 192
DICTIONARIES 194

DIRECTORIES AND HANDBOOKS   195
YEARBOOKS AND SURVEYS   195
STATISTICAL REFERENCES AND REPORTS IN VARIOUS
COUNTRIES AND AREAS   196

CHAPTER TEN
PERIODICALS

PERIODICALS   207

INDEX   220

ACKNOWLEDGMENTS

I am indebted to many friends and institutions for helping me in preparation of the bibliography. The scene of work has been libraries of University of Victoria, B.C., University of British Columbia, University of Alberta, University of Washington, and University of California, Berkeley.

I wish to express my thanks and appreciation to Mrs. Wilma MacDonald for her dilligent typing and retyping of the difficult manuscript.

And finally many thanks belong to the members of my family for having patience with my absenteeism from and "disorderly conduct" at home.

INTRODUCTION

The compilation of a comprehensive bibliographical guide to reference materials in economic theory and its applications is not an easy task. First, it should be noted that, speaking about English language publications, the only existing guide on this subject is *A Selective Bibliography of Economic Reference Works and Professional Journals* (Johns Hopkins University, 1956. 50p.) that of necessity is highly selective, and by now rather dated. Arthur Maltby's guide *Economics and Commerce* (Archon Books, 1968. 239p.) is a more recent work but, again, as it is in the case of several standard reference sources pertaining to business literature, the emphasis is primarily business literature with almost a total exclusion of foreign titles in economic theory and related subjects. In this respect the student of economic theory might be even better served by somewhat older guides to business literature, e.g. E. T. Corman's *Sources of Business Information* (2nd ed. 1964) or even some of the more specialized reference works, e.g. Paul Wasserman's *Information for Administrators: A Guide to Publications and Services for Management in Business and Commerce* (1956). There is also a good chapter on economics in Carl White's *Sources of Information in the Social Sciences; a Guide to the Literature* and, obviously, in such highly selective universal guides as Winchell, Walford, and more comprehensive Malclès.

Thus, this guide might serve as the first attempt to cover the existing gap in our reference literature, offering, within its limitations, a rather substantial coverage of materials in the area of economic theory and its implications at the same time, not limiting itself only to works published in the English language. The reason for doing this is rather simple. Speaking about economic theory as well as economic conditions in various countries, a number of western European publications together with some eastern European countries, (esp. the Soviet Union, Poland and Czechoslovakia) provide a rather substantial contribution in this discipline. Therefore, we decided to include them on a selective basis, emphasizing bibliographies and some handbooks that should be found in most academic libraries in this country. Nevertheless, in comparison to the foreign reference titles, the bulk of the reference material is in English including the bibliographies and bibliographical guides, dictionaires, handbooks, encyclopedias and some monographic works (on a highly selective basis) that contain extensive bibliographical apparatus and, thus, may also serve as ready reference tools.

The emphasis in this guide is on economic theory covering in separate chapters such topics as economic systems and the history of economic thought, history of economic development (including under-developed areas), private and public finance, international economics, agricultural economics and industrial development, transportation and communication, labor economics, and (on a highly selective basis) population and statistics, and major reference works in commerce and marketing. Works in business administration have been, for the most part, omitted, since they are adequately covered in guides to business literature and information sources. Excluded also are bibliographies of more general nature (some of them with separate sections on economics) because they can be easily found in many standard guides.

This work is divided into ten chapters within which the listings are arranged alphabetically by type of reference material, starting with guides and current and retrospective bibliographies. Regarding country or area treatment, the emphasis is given to the United States, followed by Great Britain, Canada, western Europe, eastern Europe, Latin America, Asia and Africa. The entries provide as much as possible full bibliographical description, foreign titles are also translated into English and most important entries are briefly annotated. In order to keep this guide current periodic supplements are planned and the author will appreciate critical comments and suggestions to improve this first edition.

CHAPTER ONE

ECONOMIC THEORY
(Systems, and History of Economic Thought)

GUIDES TO ECONOMIC LITERATURE

1. Andreano, Ralph L. **The Student Economist's Handbook; a Guide to Sources.** by Ralph L. Andreano, Evan Ira Farler and Sabron Reynolds. Cambridge, Mass., Schenkman Pub. Co., 1967 169 p.

Intended for undergraduate students.

2. Leamer, Laurence E. and Guyton, Percy L. **Suggestions for a Basic Economics Library;** a Guide to the Building of an Economics Library for School, Classroom, or Individual. New York, Joint Council on Economic Education, 1965. 58 p.

Emphasis is on basic materials, including textbooks.

3. Library Association. County Libraries Group. **Readers' Guide to Books on Economics.** 2nd ed. London, 1967. 47 p. (Its Readers' Guide, New ser., no. 97.)

Covers primarily British imprints.

4. Maltby, Arthur. **Economics and Commerce; the Sources of Information and their Organization.** London, C. Bingley. 1968. 239 p.

This is a valuable introductory guide to literature in economics for students and librarians. Describes reference sources such as: guides, bibliographies, dictionaries, directories, handbooks, manuals, indexes, periodicals, yearbooks, etc. in economics, commerce and statistics. Emphasis is on British material describing British economic and commercial libraries, their organization, administration and functions.

BIBLIOGRAPHIES (CURRENT)

5. Associated University Bureaus of Business and Economic Research. **Bibliography of Publications of University Bureaus of Business and Economic Research.** v. 1 —   1951/56 —   Eugene, Ore.

6. **Bibliografie Ekonomicke Literatury.** roč. 1-3, 1961-63. Praha. Monthly.

A monthly publication of bibliography of economic literature. Superseded by Novinky Literatury. Společenske Vědy Rada II. Bibliografie Ekonomicke Literatury. roč. 4— 1964—

7. Buenos Aires. Universidad Nacional. Instituto de Economia. **Bibliógrafia Sobre Economia Nacional.** 1950 — Buenos Aires.

8. Colegio de Doctores en Ciencias Economicas y Contadores Publicos Nacionales, Buenos Aires. Biblioteca. **Catalogo Metodico.** Buenos Aires. 1950. 235 p. Suplemento 1 — Buenos Aires, 1950 —

9. **Cumulative Bibliography of Economic Books.** Annual ed. Edited by Dept. of Economics, University of Pittsburgh. v. 1 — 1954-62 —
This is a cumulative bibliography of all publications which appeared in the Series I and II issued by the Dept. of Political Economy at Johns Hopkins University, between 1954-1962, and current issues of both series. The citations (without annotations) contained in the Hopkins E.L.S. series are used. Also letters of rating for recommended library purchase in parenthesis are added. The items are alphabetically arranged under seventeen topics.

10. **Economics Library Selections. New Books in Economics.** Pittsburgh University, Dept. of Economics, 1963/64-65. Supersedes Economics Library Selections: Ser. 1. New Books in Economics, issued in 1954-62. Superseded by International Economics Selections Bibliography. Series 1: New Books in Economics, which later changed to Economics Selections: an International Bibliography. Series 1: New Books in Economics.
This is an annotated bibliography. See no. 37.

11. **Economics Selections;** an International Bibliography. Series I: New Books in Economics. Mar. 1966 — Pittsburgh, Dept. of Economics, University of Pittsburgh.
Title varies: 1966, International Economics Selections Bibliography; Series 1: New Books in Economics. Supersedes a similar subseries of Economics Library Selections.

12. European Coal and Steel Community, High Authority. **Bibliothéque: Catalogue Analytique du Fonds Plan Schuman — CECA, Conserve a la Bibliothèque de l'Assemblèe Commune.** Luxembourg, 1955 —

13. Hamburg. Welt-Wirtschafts—Archiv. **Bibliographie der Wirtschaftspresse.** 1949 — Hamburg. Monthly. Title translated: Bibliography of economic serials.

14. **Internationale Bibliographie der Fachzeitschriften für Technik und Wirtschaft.** 1st — München-Pullach, Verlag Dokumentationen der Technik. (Handbuch der Technischen Dokumentationen und Bibliographie, 6 Bd.) Translated title: International Bibliography of Technological and Economical Periodicals.

15. **International Bibliography of Economics. Bibliographie Internationale de Science Economique.** London, Tavistock, 1955 — v. 1 — Annual. Publisher varies: v. 1-8, Paris, UNESCO; v. 9— 1960 — In English and French.

Worldwide in scope this bibliography includes monographs, pamphlets, serial articles, reports, and government documents in various languages. Only items of scholarly quality are listed. Each volume has author and subject indexes. "The principal criterion for selection is the true scientific character of a text" (Foreword). Included material is divided into 15 subject groups.

16. **International Economics Selections Bibliography.** Ser. 1: New Books in Economics, 1954—

First published by the Dept. of Economics, Johns Hopkins University (1954-1962) and starting in 1964 has been issued by the Dept. of Economics, University of Pittsburgh. This is an annotated and classified list of newly published literature in economics. Superseded by Economics Selections: an International Bibliography.

17. International Monetary Fund and International Bank for Reconstruction and Development. Joint Library. **List of Recent Periodical Articles.** Washington, 1947 — Monthly. Mimeographed.

Contains: 1. Economic theory; 2. Descriptive economics; 3. International Monetary Fund.

18. Joint Council on Economic Education. **Annotated Bibliography of Materials in Economic Education.** 1955 — New York. Annual. Title varies: 1955-57, Bibliography of Free and Inexpensive Material for Economic Education.

19. Keizagaku Bunken Kihō. **Quarterly Bibliography of Economics.** Compiled by Keizai Shiryo Kyogikai (Association for Documentation in Economics) Tokyo, Yuhikaku, 1956 — v. 1, no. 1 — Quarterly.

The most valuable current Japanese bibliography which includes periodical articles in Japanese, Chinese, English, French, German, Russian, etc. Supplements Bibliography of Economic Science, published in Tokyo, 1934-39 in 4 volumes.

20. **Novaia Inostrannaia Ékonomicheskaia Literatura.** Moskva. Monthly. 1934 —

Issued by Fundamental ´naiâ biblioteka obshchestvennykh nauk Akademii nauk S.S.S.R., 1934 — Transl.: New foreign economic literature.

21. **Novinky Literatury. Společenské Vědy. Řada II: Bibliografie Ekonomické Literatury.** roč 4 — 1964 — Praha. Monthly.

Supersedes *Bibliografie Ekonomicke Literatury,* and continues its volume numbering.

22. Organization for European Economic Cooperation. Library. **Ouvrages et Documents Nouveaus Catalogués á la Bibliothèque.** New Books and documents catalogued at the library. 195 — Paris. Monthly.

23. **Przeglad Bibliograficzny Piśmiennictwa Ekonomicznego.** r. 1 — 1947 — Warszawa, Polskie Wydawn. Gospodarcze.

Frequency varies. Title varies. Translated title: The bibliographical review of economic literature.

24. **Quarterly Check-List of Economics & Political Science; an International Index of Current Books, Monographs, Brochures and Separates.** Darien, Conn. American Bibliographic Service. 1958 — Quarterly.

Each number contains an alphabetical survey of recent publications in economics and political science giving the physical description of item, its price and publisher's address.

25. Zagreb. Ekonomski Institut. **Bibliografija Ekonomske Literatury.** Zagreb, 1962 —

Yugoslavian periodical publication of bibliography of economic literature.

BIBLIOGRAPHIES (RETROSPECTIVE)

26. Allen, David E. comp. **Business Books Translated from English, 1950-1965.** Reading, Mass., Addison-Wesley Pub. Co., 1965. 414 p.

This is a selective bibliography of English books translated into foreign languages. The arrangement is topical based on the Library of Congress classification. Included are: directory of publishers alphabetically arranged by country, indexes by author, language and subject.

27. Batson, Harold Edward. **A Select Bibliography of Modern Economic Theory, 1870-1929.** With an introd. by Lionel Robbins. London, G. Routledge, 1930. xii, 224 p. (Studies in Economics and Political Science, Bibliographies, no. 6).

The scope of this bibliography is modern economic theory, excluding economic history and descriptive economics. The book has two parts: part 1 covers various branches of theory in an alphabetical subject arrangement; in part 2 entries are listed alphabetically by author in three separate sections, one for English and American authors, one for German and another for French authors.

28. Bordeaux. Chambre de commerce. Bibliothèque. **Catalogue de la Bibliothèque.** Bordeaux, Palais de la Bourse, 1955. 644 p.

29. Bordeaux. Chambre de commerce. Bibliothèque. **Tables Alphabétiques par Noms d'Auteurs et par Matières.** Paris, Palais de la Bourse, 1955. 244, 46 p.

30. Chamberlin, Edward. **The Theory of Monopolistic Competition; a Re-orientation of the Theory of Value.** 8th ed. Cambridge, Harvard University Press, 1962. 396 p. (Harvard Economic Studies, v. 38).

This study is an outgrowth of author's thesis in Harvard University, 1927. The theme is much wider than the title indicates. The whole theory of value under various conditions is discussed. Bibliography p. 319-390.

31. Chlebikova, M. **Aplikácia Matematiki v Ekonómii; Výber Literatúry.** Bratislava, Ustredná ekonomicka kniźnica, 1968. 401 leaves (in portfolio)

An application of mathematics to economics; selected literature.

32. Coman, Edwin Truman. "Economics" **Library Trends,** April, 1967.

Also: Downs, R. B. and Jenkins, F. B. Bibliography: Current, State, and Future Trends. Urbana, Ill., 1967. p. 263-277. Reviews and evaluates over one hundred most important titles of current economic reference literature.

33. Cossa, Luigi. **Saggi Bibliografici di Economia Politica.** Pref. di Luigi Saggi. Bologna, A. Forni, 1963. xxii, 452 p. (Bibliografie e opere classiche di economia politica, no. 1)

Italian bibliography of political economy.

34. Cruz, Salviano. **Bibliografia da Ciencia Economica.** Rio de Janeiro, 1949. 112 p.

35. Cruz, Salviano. **Teoria de Methodologia e Bibliografia de Pesquisas Econômicas;** critica bibliográfica da ciência econômicas. Rio de Janeiro, Instituto de Pesquisas e Análises Econômics, 1949. 324 p. (Coleçào de Pesquisas Econômicas e Socials).

36. **L'economia Degli Stati Italiani Prima dell' Unificazione.** v. 1 — Milano, Feltrinelli, 1962 — (in progress).

At head of title: Instituto Giangiacomo Feltrinelli. v. 1. Stati Sardi di Terraferma, 1700-1860, has a chronological arrangement with an author index.

37. **Economics Library Selections. Series 1: New Books in Economics.** Baltimore, Johns Hopkins University, Dept. of Political Economy. no. 1-35, Mar. 1954 — Fall 1962. Publication suspended with no. 35 in 1962.

Resumed publication in Feb./Mar. 1964 — by the Dept. of Economics, University of Pittsburgh under a new title, "Cumulative Bibliography of Economic Books." Annual edition.

38. **Economics Library Selections. Series 2: Basic List in Special Fields.** Baltimore, Johns Hopkins University, Dept. of Political Economy. no. 1-7, Mar. 1954-1962/63.

Ceased with no. 7, 1962/63. Resumed 1964 by the Dept. of Economics, University of Pittsburgh under a new title: "Cumulative Bibliography of Economic Books."

39. European Coal and Steel Community. High Authority. Bibliothèque. **Systematischer Katalog der Bücher, 1952-1962.** Catalogue Systematique des ouvrages, 1952-1962. Cataloguo sistematico dei libri, 1952-1962. Systematische catalogus van boeken, 1952-1962. Luxembourg 1964. 2 v. (1285 p.)

40. FitzPatrick, Paul Joseph, and Dirksen, Cletus F. **Bibliography of Economic Books and Pamphlets by Catholic Authors, 1891-1941.** Washington, Catholic University of America Press, 1941. 55 p. (The Catholic University of America, Studies in Economics, v. 7).

     Originally undertaken as thesis (M.A.) by Dirksen at the Catholic University of America. It consists of two parts: 1. Books and 2. Pamphlets; both arranged in alphabetical order by author.

41. **French Bibliographical Digest, Science, Economics.** Prepared by Pierre Tabatoni. New York, Cultural Division of the French Embassy, 1956. 103 p. (Its Series II, no. 17).

     Lists books, theses, articles and other publications which appeared in France during the years 1950-1955. Includes abstracts in English for books.

42. Germain-Martin, Henry. **Cours de Documentation et de Méthode Economiques, Centre d'Etudes Supérieures de Banque.** Paris, Cours de droit, 1950-51. 2 v.

43. Great Britain. British Council. **Economics; a Select Book List.** London. Longmans, Green, 1963. 60 p.

     Useful for comparatively recent material, emphasizing British publications.

44. Hall, Laura Margaret and others. **A Bibliography in Economics for the Honour School of Philosophy, Politics, and Economics.** 2nd ed., Oxford, Oxford University Press, 1959. 82 p.

     A selective list of monographs for undergraduate and graduate students of economics. Divided into 8 sections: Economic principles, economic organization, economic and social history, statistics, currency and credit, public finance, economics of underdeveloped areas, and mathematics for economics. Entries are very brief containing author's surname with initials, a short title and the year of publication.

45. Harvard University. Graduate School of Business Administration. Baker Library. **Kress Library of Business and Economics. Catalogue; with Data upon Cognate Items in Other Harvard Libraries.** Boston, 1940-67. 3 v. and 1 Suppl.

     Presents a chronological list of economic works in many languages from 15th century to 1846. Over 30,000 items have been collected. Many entries contain contents notes. The general arrangement is chronological, and alphabetical under each year. A detailed author-title index is provided. Intended to serve as a basic reference source to scholars and researchers in economic history.

46. Higgs, Henry. **Bibliography of Economics, 1751-1775.** Prepared for the British Academy. Cambridge, University Press, 1935. 742 p.

This comprehensive bibliography is chronologically arranged and partially annotated. The entries under each year are divided into the following headings: (1) General economics, (2) Agriculture, etc., (3) Shipping, Navigation, etc., (4) Manufactures, (5) Commerce, (6) Colonies, (7) Finance, Banking, Money, etc. (8) Transport, (9) Social Conditions, (10) Topography, (11) Miscellaneous. Indexes of authors and anonymous titles are appended.

47. Hollander, Jacob Harry. **The Economic Library of Jacob Hollander.** Compiled by Elsie A. G. Marsh. Baltimore, 1937. Detroit, Gale Research Co., 1966. 324 p.

Includes 3860 titles in chronological arrangement, in five parts: part 1, 1574-1750; part 2, 1751-1797; part 3, 1798-1936; part 4, Portraits; part 5, Personalia: manuscripts, letters, autographs, etc.

48. Joint Council on Economic Education. Materials Evaluation Committee. **Study Materials for Economic Education in the Schools. Reports, October, 1963.** New York, Business-Education Committee, Committee for Economic Development, 1963. 1 v. (Committee for Economic Development, Supplementary paper no. 12).

Designed as a supplementary reading list in economics for high school students. Includes 162 books and pamphlets, entries are annotated.

49. Kiel. Universität. Institut für Weltwirtschaft. Bibliothek. **Behördenkatalog. Catalog of Administrative Authorities.** Boston, Mass., G. K. Hall, 1967. 10 v. Added t.p. in English, preface in German and English.

This is one of the Library's catalogs of the Institute of World Economy at Kiel University. The library is world-wide in scope; recently was officially acknowledged as a central library in economic sciences in West Germany. It provides literature for comparative international studies in economics and the related fields. The Behördenkatalog covers all entries issued by administrative authorities, and official government agencies under the name of the regional unit. (i.e., U.S., Canada, Chicago, Toronto, etc.).

50. ————————. **Körperschaftenkatalog.** Boston, Mass., G. K. Hall. 1966. 13 v.

Covers all kinds of corporate bodies, organizations, associations, conferences, etc. as authors. Arrangement is alphabetical by name, listing writings by and about a corporation.

51. ————————. **Personenkatalog.** Boston, Mass., G. K. Hall, 1966. 30 v.

Arranged alphabetically by name, lists works by a person and about a person.

52. Kiel. Universität. Institut für Weltwirtschaft. Bibliothek. **Regionen-katalog.** Boston, Mass., G. K. Hall, 1966. 52 v.

Lists the entries in alphabetical order according to large regional units, individual countries, geographical and economical units. All material listed under smaller regions is also entered under the country to which it belongs.

53. ——————. **Sachkatalog.** Boston, Mass., G. K. Hall, 1967. 83 v.

The subject catalog is the largest of all seven. All entries are arranged alphabetically by subject with numerous subdivisions.

54. ——————. **Standortskartei der Periodika.** Boston, Mass., G. K. Hall, 1968. 10 v.

Represents a shelflist of periodical holdings of the Library. All periodical entries in other catalogs refer to this listing. Each entry contains the complete title, changes of title or subtitle, editors, imprint, etc.

55. ——————. **Titelkatalog.** Boston, Mass., G. K. Hall, 1968. 15 v.

Lists in alphabetical order all entries known under title such as many yearbooks, periodicals, collective works, series, and anonymous writings.

56. Lifshits, I. A. **Matematiko-Ekonomicheskie Metody i Modeli;** primenenie matematicheskikh metodov i elektronnykh vychislitel'nykh mashin v tekhniko-ékonomicheskikh voprosakh. Bibliograficheskii ukazatel' (Sostavili: I. A. Lifshits i dr. Pod red. I. V. Romanovskogo i K. I. Shafranovskogo.) Leningrad, Nauka, 1964. 170 p.

Translated title: Mathematical and economic methods and models; application of mathematical methods and electronic calculating machines in solving technical and economical problems. Bibliographical guide.

57. McCulloch, John Ramsay. **The Literature of Political Economy: a Classified Catalogue of Select Publications in the Different Departments of that Science, with Historical, Critical and Biographical Notices.** London, Longman, Brown, Green, 1845. Reprinted 1938. 407 p. (Series of Reprints of Scarce Works on Political Economy, no. 5).

Divided into twenty chapters, this selective bibliography lists publications on economics under various subjects issued in the 17th, 18th and the four decades of the 19th century. Included are indexes of authors and of books.

58. Maunier, René. **Manuel Bibliographique des Sciences Sociales et Economiques.** Preface de Charles Gide. New York, B. Franklin, 1968. 228 p. (Burt Franklin: Bibliography and Reference Series, no. 207).

59. Mill, John Stuart. **Bibliography of the Published Writings of John Stuart Mill.** Edited from his Manuscripts with Corrections and Notes by Ney MacMinn, J. R. Hainds and James McNab McCrimmon. Evanston, Ill., Northwestern

University, 1945. 101 p. (Northwestern University Studies. Humanities Series, no. 12).

This is a comprehensive list of Mill's publications from 1822 to 1873, with brief annotations and in chronological arrangement. Lists letters, reviews, articles, pamphlets and books which were published during Mill's lifetime.

60. Mizuta, Hiroshi. **Adam Smith's Library; a Supplement to Bonar's Catalogue with a Checklist of the Whole Library.** Cambridge, University Press for the Royal Economic Society, 1967. 153 p.

About 480 titles are added to Bonar's catalogue by this Supplement. The second part of this volume, The Checklist, gives the authors and short titles of all the books known to have belonged to Adam Smith including both the books recorded by Bonar and all those listed in this Supplement.

61. Moscow. Publichnaia biblioteka. **Osnovy Politicheskoi Ekonomii; Rekomendatel'nyi Ukazatel' Literatury.** Moskva, Kniga, 1965. 116 p.

Translated title: Fundamentals of political economy; a reference guide to literature.

62. Mossé, Robert. et Potier, Michael de. **Bibliographie d'Economie Politique, 1945-1960; Historie des Doctrines, Statistique et Econometrie, Geographie Economique, Economie Rurale, Economie Financiers, Travail Sociologie Demographie.** Paris, Sirey, 1963. 124 p.

This is a continuation of Grandin's Bibliographie. Under 25 classes (A-Z) lists items in alphabetical order, published in French between 1945-1960. Two indexes, author and subject are included.

63. Novotny, Jan Maria. **A Library of Public Finance and Economics.** New York, Burt Franklin, 1953. 383 p. (Burt Franklin Bibliographical Series 6).

Divided into three main parts: (1) Books in all languages up to 1850, in chronological arrangement; (2) Titles from 1851 in various languages except Czech and Slovak in alphabetical order; (3) Books in Czech and Slovak from 1851 in alphabetical arrangement. Author index to part 1 is appended.

64. Organization for Economic Cooperation and Development. Library. **Catalogue des Périodiques, 1966. Catalogue of Periodicals.** Paris, 1966. 3 v.

65. Ōsaka Shōka Daigaku. Keizai Kenkyujo. **Bibliography of Economic Science.** Compiled by the Institute for Economic Research, Osaka University of Commerce. Tokyo, Maruzen, 1934-1939. 4 v.

The scope of this bibliography is limited to works in Japanese, English, German, French and Italian. Russian works have their titles translated into English or German and marked (Russ.). Listed are books, pamphlets, articles in leading periodicals, essays, and some newspaper articles on public finance. Only four volumes published: v. 1. Public Finance (1919-1933); v. 2-3. Money and Finance (1919-1934); v. 4. Commerce and Industry (1919-1936).

66. Rand Corporation. **Economics Department Publications, 1948-1962;** an author index of the open literature, with abstracts by Harriett Porch. Santa Monica, Calif., 1962. (Its Memorandum R M-2800-1).

67. Rand Corporation. **Economics Department Publications, 1959-1964:** an author index of the open literature, with abstracts by Harriett Porch. Santa Monica, Calif., 1965. 91 p. (Its Memorandum RM-2800-1 Supplement).

68. Rand Corporation. **Economics Department Publications, 1963-1966:** an author index of the open literature, with abstracts by Harriett Porch. Santa Monica, Calif., 1967. 71 p. (Its Memorandum RM-2800-2. Supplement).

69. **Revue Économique Internationale.** 1-32. Annee. Bruxelles. 1904-1940. 32 v. in 123. Monthly forming 4 v. a year. Most numbers of 1905-14 ed. have a separately paged section: Bibliographia Economica Universalis.

70. Rubel, Maximilien. **Bibliographie des Oeuvres de Karl Marx: Avec en Appendice un Répertoire des Oeuvres de Friedrich Engels.** Paris, Rivière, 1956. 272 p.

This is a comprehensive bibliography of works by Karl Marx, with an appendix listing Friedrich Engels' writings.

71. Sayre, J. Woodrow. **Paperbound Books in Economics; an Annotated Bibliography.** Rev. ed. Albany, New York State Council on Economic Education, 1965. 38 p.

Widely used in high schools. The arrangement is classified. Index of authors is included.

72. Smith, Adam. **A Catalogue of the Library of Adam Smith.** Prepared for the Royal Economic Society by James Bonar with the introd. and appendices. New York, A. M. Kelley, 1966. 218 p. (The Adam Smith Library. Reprint of Economic Classics).

This is the list of texts and papers which is believed to have belonged to Adam Smith's library with quotations showing the use made by him. The Catalogue shows Smith's preferences for literature, his favorite subjects and in which language the works were written. Items are entered in alphabetical order according to author's name, or title. Together 1,100 books and pamphlets are cataloged. Includes index. See also entry no. 60.

73. **Source Materials for Business and Economic History;** Proceedings of a Colloquium Convened at the Graduate School of Business Administration, Harvard University, October 20-22, 1966. Laurence J. Kipp, ed. Boston, Baker Library Graduate School of Business Administration, Harvard University, 1967. 154 p.

74. Warsaw. Szkola Glówna Handlowa. Biblioteka. **Katalog Biblioteki; Nauki Ekonomiczne i Handlowe.** Opracowal Andrzej Grodek. Warszawa, 1945. 941 p.

Title translated: Library catalog: economics and commerce.

DICTIONARIES AND ENCYCLOPEDIAS

75. **Dictionnaire des Sciences Economiques.** Publié sous la direction de Jean Romeuf avec la collaboration de Gilles Pasqualaggi. Pref. de Alfred Souvy. Paris, Presses universitaires de France, 1956-1958. 2 v.

An encyclopedic dictionary containing definitions of terms in economics, business and commerce with numerous diagrams. Also included are biographical sketches of famous European economists. A list of contributors is given in each volume.

76. Eichhorn, Reinhart von. **Wirtschafts-Wörterbuch.** Düsseldorf, Econ-Verlag. 1961-62. 2 v. Contents: v. 1., Englisch/Deutsch; v. 2., Deutsch/English.

This is a handbook of everyday reference of some 19,000 terms. All fields of economics, business, commerce, industry, transportation and related subjects are included. American and English usage varying in certain fields has been indicated.

77. **Ekonomicheskaia Entsiklopediia; Promyshlennost' i Stroitel' stvo.** Red. A. V. Bachurin i dr. Moskva, Sovetskaia entsiklopediia. 1962-65. 3 v. Illus.

Contains over 2,000 articles on economics, industries and construction, alphabetically arranged. Articles are signed; most include bibliographical references.

78. Gilpin, Alan. **Dictionary of Economic Terms.** London, Butterworths, 1966. 222 p.

Stresses economic conditions and practices in Great Britain: gives definitions, some figures and diagrams.

79. Hanson, John Lloyd. **A Dictionary of Economics and Commerce.** London, Macdonald & Evans, 1965. 401 p.

Most of the 4,000 entries refer to principles, theory and applied economics. Includes many cross references.

80. Horton, Byrne J. and others. **Dictionary of Modern Economics.** Washington, Public Affairs Information Press, 1948. 365 p.

Aims to assemble and coordinate reasonably correct definitions of economic terms. Includes some bibliographical references and biographies of leading economists.

81. **The McGraw-Hill Dictionary of Modern Economics; a Handbook of Terms and Organizations,** by Douglas Greenwald in collaboration with Jack McCroskey and others. New York, 1964. 697 p.

Defines 1300 frequently used modern economic terms; describes about 200 economic organizations inside and outside the U. S.; includes numerous references to sources of information. Some definitions are supplemented by charts, diagrams, and tables.

82. **Meyers Handbuch** über **die Wirtschaft.** Hrsg. von der Lexikonredaktion des Bibliographischen Instituts. Unter Leitung von G. Preuss bearb. von U. Bachert and weiteren Mitarbeitern der Fachredaktion Wirtschaft. Mannheim, Bibliographisches Institut, 1966. 1148 p.

German comprehensive handbook on economics in dictionary arrangement.

83. Nemmers, Erwin Esser and Janzen, Cornelius C. **Dictionary of Economics and Business.** Paterson, N. J., Littlefield, Adams. 1959. 326 p.

A college dictionary for students taking courses in economics, accounting, business administration and other related subjects.

84. Paenson, Isaac. **Systematic Glossary English/French/Spanish/Russian of Selected Economic and Social Terms.** New York, Macmillan, 1963. 1 v. (loose leaf).

A well indexed polyglot dictionary in a looseleaf form to keep it up-to-date. Besides definitions of economic terms, it includes brief biographical sketches of many famous economists.

85. Palgrave, Sir Robert Harry Inglis. **Palgrave's Dictionary of Political Economy,** edited by Henry Higgs. London, Macmillan, 1923-26. 3 v.

Articles signed with initials are long and authoritative, with bibliographies. Much of the information is now out of date.

86. **Russian-English Glossary of Economic and Trade Terms.** 2nd ed. New York, Telberg Book Corp., 1965. 106 leaves.

First ed. published in 1959 under title: English-Russian Glossary of Economic and Trade Terms. Includes over 2,100 Russian terms translated into English. Focuses on most used words and phrases in the Soviet economic literature.

87. Seldon, Arthur, ed. and Pennance, F. G. **Everyman's Dictionary of Economics; an Alphabetical Exposition of Economic Concepts and their Application.** London, J. M. Dent, 1965. 449 p. (Everyman's Reference Library).

88. Sellien, R. and Sellien, H., ed. **Dr. Gablers Wirtschaftslexikon.** G. Aufl. Wiesbaden, Gabler, 1965. 2 v.

One of the best German dictionary of economics, containing about 16,000 entries in alphabetical order. Some articles are signed indicating the references.

89. Sloan, Harold Stephenson and Zucher, Arnold J. **A Dictionary of Economics.** 4th ed. New York, Barnes and Noble, 1964. 371 p.

The new edition of this dictionary brings the total number of entries to more than 2,800. Includes many new statistical terms, and cross-references. All versions of definition are given when authorities differ.

90. Taylor, Philip A. S. **A New Dictionary of Economics,** New York, A. M. Kelley , 1966. 304 p.

Aimed to fill a gap that still exists in economic literature. The controversial terms are covered by various versions of definitions.

91. Tolfree, William Reay. **Notes on Economic Theory.** London, I. Pitman, 1962. 90 p.

Covers in a dictionary form such economic concepts as: production, distribution, demand and supply analysis, banking, money and foreign exchange.

92. Vaughan, F. L. and M. C. Vaughan. **Glossary of Economics, Including Soviet Terminology.** Text in English/American-French-German-Russian. New York, American Elsevier, 1967. 201 p.

Consists of: (1) an alphabetical listing of 1,669 numbered English phrases with French, German, and (in a separate section) Russian equivalents, (2) alphabetical lists in French, German, and Russian of the corresponding terms with reference to the numbered English entries; and (3) about 200 Soviet economic terms with their English, French, and German equivalents.

92a. **Wörterbuch der Ökonomie. Sozialismus.** (Hrsg. von Willi Ehlert, Heinz Joswig and Willi Luchterhand. Berlin, Dietz, 1967. 539 p.

Emphasis of this German dictionary is on Marxian economics and on socialism.

93. **Wörterbuch der Volkswirtschaft.** Hrsg. von Ludwig Elster. 4. völlig umgearb. Aufl. Jena, Fischer, 1931-33. 3 v.

This older work is a standard German encyclopedic dictionary on economics. Articles are signed and include bibliographical references. Many biographical entries.

BIOGRAPHICAL DIRECTORIES

94. American Economic Association. **Handbook of the American Economic Association. . .** New York, 1890 — Irreg.

This is a "who's who" type of directory, providing biographical information about the members including details of education, degrees, specialization, present position, rank and address.

INDEXES AND ABSTRACTS

95. Ajia Keizai Kenkyujo, Tokyo. **Selected Periodicals Index.** v. 1 — July 20, 1960 — Tokyo, Institute of Asian Economic Affairs, 1960 — Monthly.

96. American Economic Association. **Index of Economic Journals.** Homewood, Ill., Irwin, 1961-62. 5 v.

This classified index lists by author and subject articles in English from major economic periodicals published during the period of 1886-1959. Government publications are excluded.

97. **Bolletino Emerografico di Economia Internazionale;** redatto dall' Instituto di Economia Internazionale. v. 1 — 1948 — Genova, Camera di Commercio Industria Agricultura, 1948 —

Quarterly journal of economic abstracts in Italian language, international in scope. Over 700 periodicals are represented from more than 60 countries and many international organizations.

98. **Business Periodicals Index.** New York: H. W. Wilson, 1958 —

Cumulative subject index to periodicals in the field of business and related areas. Covers accounting, advertising, finance, banking, labor, insurance, taxation, and other aspects of business. Of limited use for materials in economic theory and related subjects.

99. Caffé, Federico. **Orientamenti Nella Letteratura Economica Contemporanea; Contributi Bibliografici.** Roma, Edizioni dell' Ateneo, 1953. 146 p.

Presents a collection of book reviews on economics published in various languages. Includes an index to cited authors.

100. **Documentation Economique; Revue Bibliographique Trimestrielle.** Public les Analyses Classees par Subjects des Articles Parus dans les Principales Revues Economiques, 1934-38, 1947 — Paris, Presses universitaires de France, 1947 —

This quarterly lists the abstracts of economic books and articles in 180 periodicals throughout the world. All material is arranged according to the detailed classification scheme listed on the first few pages of each issue. Indexes of subjects and authors included.

101. **Economic Abstracts;** a Semi-monthly Review of Abstracts on Economics, Finance, Trade and Industry, Management and Labor. v.1 — The Hague, M. Nijhoff, 1953 —

Contains abstracts, mostly of periodical articles, also some books and reports of government and international organizations. Covers publications in Dutch, English, French and German. Includes a subject index in each issue, and an author index for each complete volume.

102. **Journal of Economic Abstracts.** v. 1 — Jan. 1963 — Cambridge, Mass., Harvard University, 1963 —

This quarterly international journal is published under the auspices of the American Economic Association. Divided into three sections: 1) Abstract and article listing by journal, 2) by subject, and 3) authors of the abstracts. Most abstracts prepared by the author of the original article. Articles are selected from 55 contributing journals. One of the most important abstracting services for domestic material.

103. Montevideo. Centro de Documentación Cientifica, Técnica y Económica. **Indice de Trabajos Publicados en Revista de Economiá, 1947-1958;** Instituto de Teoriá, y Politica Economicas, 1954-1960; Revista de Economia Finanzas y Administracion Pública, 1958-1962. Montevideo, 1963. 115 p.

103a. Organización Sindical. Consejo Económico Sindical Nacional. **Documentacion Económica:** 1. Indice alfabétcio de materias contenidas en los publicados hasta el 31 de diciembre de 1963. 2. Indice cronológico de los documentos publicados. Madrid, 1963.

104. **Research Index.** Wallington, Surrey, Business Surveys, 1965 —

This is a semi-monthly index to about 130 British business, economic and trade periodicals. Some articles from newspapers are also included.

105. Schleiffer, Hedwig, and Crandall, Ruth. **Index to Economic History, Essays in Festschriften, 1900-1950;** with a preface by Arthur H. Cole. Cambridge, A. H. Cole; distributed by Harvard University Press, 1953. 68 p.

Lists about 520 Festschriften in alphabetical order. Included are indexes of authors and of proper names.

HANDBOOKS AND YEARBOOKS

(This is a selective listing of most typical publications in this field, including important handbooks and yearbooks in Western European languages.)

106. **Hamburger Jahrbuch für Wirtschafts- und Gesellschafts - politik.** 1 — Jahrg; 1956 — Tübingen, J. C. B. Mohr. (Veröffentlichungen der Akademie für Gemeinwirtschaft, Hamburg).

This German yearbook includes articles on economic topics, controversial interpretations of some subjects, and reports on current economic literature. Published annually, with summaries in English.

107. Hax, Karl, ed. **Handbuch der Wirtschaftswissenschaften.** Hrsg. von Karl Hax und Theodor Wessels. 2., Aufl. Köln, Westdeutscher Verlag, 1966. 2 v.

Divided into two parts: v. 1. Business administration and v. 2. Economics. Written by the specialists for college and university students. Subject indexes included in both volumes.

MONOGRAPHIC TREATISES

(This is a highly selective listing of some classical works containing additional bibliographical data.)

108. Ackley, Gardner. **Macroeconomic Theory.** New York, Macmillan, 1961. 597 p.

Treats the various theories of classical and Keynesian macroeconomics and their followers.

109. Akademiia nauk S.S.S.R. Institut ekonomiki. **A History of Russian Economic Thought: Ninth through Eighteenth Centuries,** Edited and with a foreword by John M. Letiche. Translated with collaboration of Basil Dmytryshyn and Richard Pierce. Berkeley, University of California Press, 1964. 690 p. (Publications of the Institute of Business and Economic Research, University of California).

A collective work written in form of essays by distinguished Soviet economists based on primary and secondary sources.

110. American Economic Association. **Readings in Price Theory;** Selected by a Committee of the American Economic Association. Chicago, R. D. Irwin, 1952. 568 p.

Presents a selection of articles from the economic literature of the past forty years. Emphasis is on theoretical economics. The bibliography was restricted to periodical literature, for the period of 1920 through 1949. Bibliography: p. 527-561.

110a. Baumol, William Jack. **Economic Theory and Operations Analysis.** 2nd ed. Englewood Cliffs, N. J., Prentice Hall, 1965. 606 p.

Designed as a systematic exposition of microeconomic analysis and a fruitful discussion of the many recent developments in mathematical economics.

111. Beer, Max. **Early British Economics from the XIIIth to the Middle of the XVIIIth Century.** New York, A.M. Kelley, 1967. 250 p. Reprint of the 1938 edition.

112. Bell, John Fred. **A History of Economic Thought.** 2nd ed. New York, Ronald Press, 1967. 745 p.

Designed to show the growth of economic thought from the beginnings of Western civilization to the present. "This volume brings together the most significant scholars and schools whose influence has left permanent imprint on the body of economic doctrines. Attention has been given to less well-known authors and their contributions as well as to the better known names and their contribution." (Pref.) Two indexes, name and subject, are included.

113. Bentham, Jeremy. **Jeremy Bentham's Economic Writings,** edited by W. Stark. New York, B. Franklin, 1952-1954. 3 v.

Designed as a comprehensive and critical edition of his economic writings.

114. Beutin, Ludwig. **Einführung in die Wirtschaftsgeschichte.** Köln, Böhlau, 1958. 179 p.

Discusses methodology and study of sources in the history of economics. Includes numerous bibliographical references, also indexes of names and subjects.

115. Böhm von Bawerk, Eugen. **Capital and Interest.** Translated by George D. Huncke and Hans F. Sennholz. South Holland, Ill., Libertarian Press, 1959. 3 v.

The publication of the original edition Das Kapital und Kapitalzins was a significant event in the history of economic thought. In this work the author not only expounded a complete theory of distribution but also a theory of social cooperation which exerted a profound influence on the thought of other economists. Extensive bibliography is listed in Notes at the end of each volume.

116. Boulding, Kenneth Ewart. **Economic Analysis.** 4th ed. New York, Harper, 1966.

Designed as a representative textbook stressing theoretical aspects of economics.

117. Braeuer, Walter. **Handbuch zur Geschichte der Volkswirtschaftslehre; ein Bibliographisches Nachschlagewerk.** Frankfurt am Main, Klostermann, 1952. 224 p.

International in scope this work is a bio-bibliography of the political economy from Ancient Greece (710 B.C.) to 1950.

118. Bücher, Karl. **Industrial Evolution.** Translated from the 3rd German ed. by S. Morley Wickett. New York, Holt, 1907. 393 p.

Presents the historical development of national economy from the primitive conditions to modern industrial society.

119. Cannan, Edwin. **A History of the Theories of Production and Distribution in English Political Economy from 1776-1848.** London, P. S. King, 1924. 422 p. N. Y. Kelley, 1967. (Reprints of Economic Classics.)

120. Cantillon, Richard. **Essai sur la Nature de Commerce en General;** Edited with an English Translation and Other Material by Henry Higgs. London, Macmillan for the Royal Economic Society, 1931. 394 p.

This definitive classic was written between 1730 and 1734. This edition is bilingual with an English text. Two last chapters are devoted to the author and his work.

121. Cassel, Gustav. **The Theory of Social Economy.** Transl. by Joseph McCabe. New York, Harcourt, Brace, 1924. 654 p.

Aimed "to treat the economic relations of a whole social body as far as possible irrespective of its extension, its organization, its laws of property, etc." (Pref.) Contents: 1. General survey of the social economy; 2. The pricing of the factor of production; 3. Money; 4. The theory of conjecture-movement; Index.

122. Clark, John Bates. **The Distribution of Wealth; a Theory of Wages, Interest, and Profits.** New York, Kelley & Millman, 1956. 445 p. (Reprint of Economic Classics).

"The purpose of this work is to show that the distribution of the income of society is controlled by a natural law, and that this law, if it worked without friction would give to every agent of production the amount of wealth which that agent creates." (Pref.)

123. Clark, John Bates. **The Philosophy of Wealth; Economic Principles Newly Formulated.** New York, A. M. Kelley, 1967. 236 p. (Reprint of Economic Classics) Repr. of 1887 ed.

Develops independently certain economic theories and laws which are discussed in twelve chapters of this work. Among the topics are: wealth, labor, the theory of value, the law of demand and supply, the law of distribution, wages, the ethics of trade, cooperation, non-competitive economics, the economic function of the church.

124. Cole, Arthur Harrison. **The Historical Development of Economic and Business Literature.** Boston, Baker Library, Harvard Graduate School of Business Administration, 1957. 56 p. (The Kress Library of Business and Economics. Publication no. 12).

A scholarly discussion of business and economic literature from the 16th century to the present.

125. Cole, Charles Woolsey. **Colbert and a Century of French Mercantilism.** New York, Columbia University Press, 1939. 2 v.

This is a scholarly treatise based mostly on source material in printed or manuscript form. Some rare documents are included either in full or in condensed form. Bibliography: v. 2, p. 591-620.

126. Cole, Charles Woolsey. **French Mercantilism, 1683-1700.** New York, Columbia University Press, 1943. 354 p.

A sequel to author's Colbert and a Century of French Mercantilism. Concludes the history of French Mercantilism from 1683 (the year of Colbert's death) down to 1700. Bibliography: p. 331-337.

127. Cossa, Luigi. **An Introduction to the Study of Political Economy.**
Revised by the author and translated from Italian by Louis Dyer. London,
Macmillan, 1893. 587 p.

Introduces in part one definition, characteristics, methods, etc. of
political economy. Part two deals with economic history in various countries,
discusses economic theories and schools, describes life and work of famous
economists giving numerous bibliographical citations. Two indexes of authors
and sources, and subjects are appended.

128. Dickinson, Henry Douglas. **Institutional Revenue; a Study of the
Influence of Social Institutions of the Distribution of Wealth.** New York,
Kelley, 1966. 264 p. (Reprints of Economic Classics). First published 1932.

Discusses the factor of inequality in the distribution of wealth in four
major parts: 1. Discussion of social institutions; 2. Theory of value, leading
up to 3. Theory of factor-distribution; 4. Theory of personal distribution.
Bibliography: p. 228-235.

129. Dillard, Dudley D. **The Economics of John Maynard Keynes; the Theory
of a Monetary Economy.** New York, Prentice-Hall, 1948. 364 p.

Offers an approach to a popular presentation of the economic theories
of John Maynard Keynes. Bibliography of J.M. Keynes writings, p. 336-351;
and numerous references for further reading.

130. Douglas, Paul Howard. **The Theory of Wages.** New York, Kelley, Macmillan, 1957. 639 p. (First publ. 1934).

Presents an inductive study of wage theory and attempts to determine
the basic quantitative laws of production and distribution. Divided into three
parts: (1) The development of the theory of production and the problems of
distribution, (2) An approach to the imputed productivity curves of labor and
capital, (3) The probable supply curves of labor, capital and natural resources.
Bibliography: p. 553-610.

131. Ellis, Howard Sylvester, ed. **A Survey of Contemporary Economics.**
Homewood, Ill., R. D. Irwin, for the American Economic Associations, 1948-
1952. 2 v.

Presents a collection of essays on trends in contemporary economic
thinking written by specialists in their fields. Each essay has its author and
two critics; in vol. 2. two comments accompany every article. Extensive
references in the form of footnotes are included. Names and subject indexes
are added at end of each volume.

132. Fisher, Irving. **The Nature of Capital and Income.** New York, Macmillan, 1906, 427 p. (Reprint of Economic Classics).

Aimed to find a bridge between theories of abstract economics and
practical business transactions. The nature of income is thoroughly explained.

133. Fisher, Irving. **The Theory of Interest as Determined by Impatience to Spend Income and Opportunity to Invest it.** New York, Kelley & Millman, 1954. 566 p. illus. (Reprints of economic classics).

Revision of author's The Rate of Interest which was published in 1907, with additions of new material. Bibliography: p. 543-550.

134. Gide, Charles, and Rist, C. **History of Economic Doctrines from the Time of the Physiocrats to the Present Day.** Authorized translation by R. Richards. 2nd English ed. London, Harrap, 1960. 800 p.

Divided into 6 parts: (1) The Founders, (2) The Antagonists, (3) Liberalism, (4) Dissenters, (5) Reconstruction of Doctrines, (6) Predominance of Production. This classical work has been translated into many languages.

135. Gide, Charles. **Political Economy.** Authorized translation from the 3rd ed. (1913) of the "Cours d'Economie Politique". Boston, Heath, n.d., 762 p.

This is a translation of the well known standard university textbook on economics, known and popular not only in France but also in other countries.

136. Gossen, Hermann Heinrich. **Entwicklung der Gesetze des Menschlichen Verkehrs, und der daraus Fliessenden Regeln für Menschliche Handeln.** Neue Ausg. Berlin, R. L. Prager, 1889. 277 p.

Postulates the principle of diminishing marginal utility.

137. Gray, Sir Alexander. **The Socialist Tradition, Moses to Lenin.** London, Longmans, Green, 1947. 523 p.

Presents outstanding figures in the development of socialist thought who played an important role in contributing to economic theories.

138. Gruchy, Allan Garfield. **Modern Economic Thought; the American Contribution.** New York. Prentice Hall, 1947. 670 p.

This is the study of distinctive American contribution to modern economic thought. Six outstanding American economists have been chosen to indicate how those contributions fit into the framework of a twentieth-century version of economic science. (Thorstein Veblen, John R. Commons, Wesley C. Mitchell, John M. Clark, Rexford G. Tugwell, and Gardiner C. Means) Bibliography: p. 631-655.

139. Haberler, Gottfried. **Prosperity and Depression, a Theoretical Analysis of Cyclical Movements.** New York, rev. and enl. ed. Cambridge, Harvard University Press, 1958. 520 p.

Presents an analysis of the existing theories of business cycles, and a discussion of the nature and possible causes of economic fluctuations.

140. Hansen, Alvin Harvey. **Business Cycles and National Income.** Expanded ed. with a revised bibliography by Richard V. Clemence. New York, Norton, 1964. 721 p.

Divided into five parts: (1) The nature of business cycles; this part presents the historical development of fluctuations in the United States; (2) The theory of income and employment; emphasis is on theories of Wicksell, Aftalion and Keynes; (3) Business-cycle theory (historical development) (4) Business cycles and public policy; (5) Prosperity and recession since the Second World War. Bibliography: p. 692-710.

141. Hansen, Alvin Harvey. **A Guide to Keynes.** New York, McGraw Hill. 1953. 237 p. (Economics Handbook Series).

Aims to help student in understanding the difficult chapters in the general theory of employment, interest and money by John M. Keynes.

142. Harris, Seymour Edwin, ed. **The New Economics: Keynes' Influence on Theory and Public Policy.** London, D. Dobson, 1948. 686 p.

Bibliography of Keynes' writings: p. 663-686.

142a. Hayck, Friedrich August von. **The Pure Theory of Capital.** Chicago, University of Chicago Press, 1941. 454 p.

Aimed to find the answer to the problem of the cause of industrial fluctuations. Bibliography: p. 441-449.

143. Heilbroner, Robert L. **The Making of Economic Society.** Englewood Cliffs, N. J., Prentice-Hall, 1962. 241 p.

Presents some of the basic concepts of economic theory and history. Contents: 1. The economic problem; 2. The pre-market economy; 3. The emergence of the market society; 4. The industrial revolution; 5. The impact of industrial technology; 6. The evolution of guided capitalism; 7. The drift of modern economic history; 8. The making of economic society.

144. Heimann, Eduard. **History of Economic Doctrines; an Introduction to Economic Theory.** London, Oxford University Press, 1945. 203 p.

This is a critical survey of the entire field of economic theory from the dawn of civilization to the present.

145. Hume, David. **Writings on Economics.** Edited and introduced by Eugene Rotwein. Madison, University of Wisconsin Press. 1955. 224 p.

Hume's economic writings comprise a relatively small portion of his works. This collection contains nine of author's twelve essays from his Political Discourses first published in 1752 and some passages from his letters to A. Smith, Montesquieu, Turgod and Oswald. In the introductory part the editor presents an analytical study of Hume's economic thoughts.

146. Hutchison, Terence Wilmot. **Review of Economic Doctrines, 1870-1929.** Oxford, Clarendon Press, 1953. 456 p.

Divided into three parts: 1. The architects of equilibrium economics and their main critics (in 17 chapters). 2. From 'Static' to 'Dynamic' analysis (Chap. 18-31). and 3. The economics of instability and disturbance (Chap. 22-25). Bibliography: p. 432-437.

147. Johnson Edgar Augustus Jerome. **Predecessors of Adam Smith; the Growth of British Economic Thought.** New York, Prentice Hall, 1937. 426 p. (Reprint of Economic Classics).

Reviews voluminous British economic literature before Adam Smith.

148. Kaldor, Nicholas. **Essays on Economic Policy.** London, Duckworth, 1964. 2 v.

The papers collected in these two volumes discuss the application of economic theories to issues of practical economic policy. Contents: 1. Policies for full employment; 2. The control of inflation; 3. The problem of tax reform; 4. Policies for international stability; 5. Country studies.

149. Keynes, John Maynard. **The General Theory of Employment, Interest and Money.** London, Macmillan, 1936. 403 p.

150. Koopmans, Tjalling Charles. **Three Essays on the State of Economic Science.** New York, McGraw-Hill, 1957. 231 p.

Discusses some recent developments in economic theory, emphasizing author's concern about development and the use of mathematical and statistical concepts and tools in economics.

151. Kuznets, Simon Smith. **Modern Economic Growth: Rate, Structure, and Spread.** New Haven, Yale University Press, 1966. 502 p. (Studies in Comparative Economics, 7).

Presents a comparative study of the economic growth of nations throughout the history, and particularly in the last two centuries. Bibliography: p. 511-520.

152. Lewis, William Arthur. **The Theory of Economic Growth.** Homewood, Ill., Irwin, 1955. 453 p.

Describes the factors determining economic growth: Contents: 1. Introduction; 2. The will to economize; 3. Economic institutions; 4. Knowledge; 5. Capital; 6. Population and resources; 7. Government.

153. List, Friedrich. **National System of Political Economy.** Transl. from the German by G. A. Matile. Including notes of the French translation by Henri Richelet; with a preliminary essay and notes by Stephen Colwell. Philadelphia, Lippincott, 1856. 61, 497 p.

154. List, Friedrich. **Schriften, Reden, Briefe.** Hrsg. von Erwin, V. Beckerath et al. Berlin, Hobbing, 1932-35. 12v.

This multivolume work contains all writings of the famous German economist. List's bibliography is placed in volume 9 (p. 265-416). Volume 10 contains Indexes of subjects, geographical names, corrections, and alphabetical contents.

155. Little, Ian Malcolm David. **A Critique of Welfare Economics.** 2nd ed. Oxford, Clarendon Press, 1957. 302 p.

Presents an exposition, criticism and appreciation of the theory of welfare economics. Neither methodology nor new theories or theorems are stated.

156. Lundberg, Erik. **Studies in the Theory of Economic Expansion.** London, P. S. King, 1937. 265 p. Reprinted by Kelley and Millman, New York, 1955.

The aim of this study is to investigate the conditions of a determinate sequence in time of economic changes. Bibliography: p. 262-265.

157. Malthus, Thomas Robert. **Principles of Political Economy, Considered with a View to Their Practical Application.** 2nd ed. 1836. With an introd. by Morton Paglin. New York, A. M. Kelley, 1964. 446 p. (Reprint of Economic Classics).

To increase an effective demand during slack periods, author proposed public works and investment on private luxury. He criticized thrift as a virtue with limits, and argued that the principles of saving, pushed to excess, would destroy the motive of production. To maximize wealth a nation must balance "the power to produce and the will to consume." With those theories Malthus became the forerunner of "Keynesian economics."

158. Marget, Arthur W. **The Theory of Prices; a re-examination of the Central Problems of Monetary Theory.** New York, A. M. Kelley, 1966. 1938-42. 2 v. (Reprints of Economic Classics).

Besides being a formal treatise on price theory, this volume is a polemical tract about John Maynard Keynes' writings, particularly his General Theory of Employment, Interest and Money. The second volume deals with the theory of the effect of money upon output, the theory of savings and investment, and some more polemics with Mr. Keynes.

159. Marshall, Alfred. **Principles of Economics.** 9th variorum ed. With annotations by C. W. Guillebaud. 1961. 2 v.

Regarded as the standard classic of modern economics. Its treatment of the theory of value, price, and distribution is done in such a comprehensive and thorough way that it laid the foundation of neo-classical economics. Volume 1 of this edition is a reprint of the 8th ed., 1920. Volume 2 consists of the commentaries and notes related to the text and changes in the text of various editions, of new reprinted material which was not part of 8th ed., of new comprehensive index to the Principles, and of some of Marshall's articles related to the Principles.

160. Marshall, Howard Drake. **The Great Economists; a History of Economic Thought.** New York, Pitman, 1967. 397 p.

Attempts to expose in simple and clear language the theories of famous economists explaining historical background. Bibliography: p. 377-383.

161. Marx, Karl, **Capital: a Critique of Political Economy.** Ed. by Frederic Engles, New York, International Publishers, 1967. 3 v.

Intended to show the economic laws that govern modern society. Only first volume was completed and published by the author himself in 1867. Two other volumes were published by Engels from the voluminous notes and manuscripts left by Marx; volume two issued in 1885, and volume three in 1895.

162. Menger, Karl. **Principles of Economics.** First general part, translated and edited by James Dingwall and Bert F. Hoselitz. With an introd. by Frank H. Knight. Glencoe, Ill., Free Press, 1950. 328 p.

A great work in economics by the founder of the "Austrian School" and the pioneer of the modern theory of utility. This volume was written as the first of four planned volumes of the "Principles". First published in 1871.

163. Mill, James. **Selected Economic Writings.** Edited and with an introduction by Donald Winch, Chicago, University of Chicago Press, 1966. 452 p.

Reprinted text of Mill's extracts is divided into four parts: Early economic writings; James Mill and David Ricardo; J. Mill on scope and method and J. Mill and India. A biographical sketch of Mill is included.

164. Mill, John Stuart. **The Collected Works.** Edited by J. I. P. Robson. Toronto, University of Toronto Press, 1963.

Includes author's philosophical, political, and economic writings. His Principles of political economy, published in 1848 was for more than a generation very influential text in economic thinking. In this work the author provides a detailed explanation of the principles which have to guide government in its control of a nation's economy.

165. Mitchell, Wesley Clair. **Types of Economic Theory; From Mercantilism to Institutionalism.** Edited with introduction by Joseph Dorfman. New York, A. M. Kelley, 1967. (Reprints of Economic Classics).

166. Nef, John Ulric. **War and Human Progress; an Essay on the Rise of Industrial Civilization.** Cambridge, Mass., Harvard University Press, 1950. 464p.

Contents: part 1. The new warfare and the genesis of industrialism, 1494-1640. Part 2. Limited warfare and humane civilization, 1640-1740.

Part 3. Industrialism and total war 1740-1950.

167. Ozga, S. Andrew. **Expectations in Economic Theory.** Chicago, Aldine Pub. Co., 1965, 303 p.

This study is an outgrowth of lecture notes for a graduate course on risk, uncertainty, and expectations given at the London School of Economics in 1962-63. It deals with the analysis of expectations as an important element in economic theory.

168. Pareto, Vilfredo. **Cours d'Economie Politique Professé à l'universite de Lausanne.** Lausanne, F. Rouge; Paris, Pichon, 1896-97. 2 v.

Aimed to provide an outline of economics this treatise consists of two main parts: one deals with principles of political economy, another is concerned with applied economics. The text is extensively supported with statistical data.

169. Petty, Sir William. **The Economic Writings of Sir William Petty. Together with the Observations upon the Bills of Mortality,** more probably by Captain John Grount. Ed. by Charles Henry Hull. New York, A.M. Kelley, 1963-64. 2 v. (Reprint of Economic classics).

The author is a known 17th century English economist and the political arithmetician who could be regarded as a first econometrician. He was ahead of his time in his analytical skill, with his clear schematic views of the economy. Bibliography including Sir William Petty's writings: v. 2, p. 633-672.

170. Pigou, Arthur Cecil. **Income: an Introduction to Economics.** London, Macmillan, 1960. 119 p.

Based on author's seven lectures to engineering students in Cambridge 1945, this book provides an outline sketch of an important part of economics.

171. Pigou, Arthur Cecil. **Income Revisited,** Being a Sequel to Income: and Introduction to Economics. London, Macmillan, 1955. 86 p.

172. Quesnay, Francois. **Ouevres Économiques et Philosophiques de F. Quesney.** Ed. by August Oncken. Frankfurt, J. Baer, 1888. 814 p. Reprinted 1965.

The author, a French economist of the 18th century, is the founder of the economic system known as the physiocratic system. His most famous work is Tableau Economique (1758) which is regarded as an ancestor of modern tables of national income and expenditure. Bibliography of Quesnay's works: p. 809-814.

173. Rae, John. **Life of Adam Smith. With an Introduction: Guide to John Rae's Life of Adam Smith,** by Jacob Viner. New York, A.M. Kelley, 1965. 145, 449 p. (Reprints of Economic Classics).

An indispensable reading for the study of 18th century economic thought. Includes a brief bibliography of Adam Smith's publications.

174. Recktenwald, Horst Claus, ed. **Lebensbilder Grosser Nationalökonomen;**
Einführung in die Geschichte der Politischen Ökonomie. Köln, Kiepenheuer
& Witsch, 1965. 666 p.

Describes life and work of many great economists, beginning with
Francois Quesnay (1694-1774) and ending with J. M. Keynes (1851-1926)
and W. Eucken (1891-1950). Bibl. references included in "Anmerkungen"
p. 587-649.

175. Ricardo, David. **Principles of Political Economy and Taxation.** Edited,
with intro. essay, notes and appendices by E.C.K. Gonner. London, G. Bell,
1919. 455 p.

Author's principal work in economics which was first published in 1817.
In this book the theories of value, rent, wages, and taxation are exposed and
examined. His theory of value made a considerable influence on Karl Marx's
political and economic teachings. Bibliography: p. 439-446.

176. Ricardo, David. **The Works and Correspondence of David Ricardo.**
Edited by Piero Sraffa and M. H. Dobb. Cambridge, England, University
Press, 1953-55. 10 v.

Contents: 1. Principles of political economy and taxation. 2. Notes on
Malthus. 3.-4. Pamphlets and papers. 5. Speeches and evidence. 6.-9. Letters.
10. Biographical miscellany. Notes on Malthus and letters of Malthus to
Ricardo are first published in this edition. Bibliography: v. 10, p. 355-402.

177. Rodbertus, Johann Karl. **Soziale Briefe an von Kirchmann.** Berlin,
Gerhardi, 1850.

This work has been translated by Julia Franklin as Overproduction and
Crises (2nd ed. London 1908). Author was a well known German social
reformer and economist of the nineteenth century.

178. Roll, Erich. **A History of Economic Thought.** 2nd ed. rev. and enl.
London, Faber and Faber, 1945. 535 p.

179. Roscher, Wilhelm George Friedrich. **System der Volkswirtschaft;** Ein
Hand- und Lesebuch für Geschäftsmänner und Studierende. Stuttgart, J.G.
Cottäsche Buchhandlung, 1894-1903. 5 v. in 6.

Author's fundamental treatise is comprised of 5 volumes: 1. Grundlagen
der Nationalökonomie; 2. Nationalökonomik des Ackerbaues und der
verwandten Urproductionen; 3. Nationalokönomik des Handels- und
Gewerbfleisses (2 pts.); 4. System der Finanzwissenschaft; 5. System der
Armenpflege und Armenpolitik.

180. Samuelson, Paul A. **The Collected Scientific Papers.** Edited by Joseph E. Stiglitz. Cambridge., Mass., M.I.T. Press, 1965. 2 v.

This collection of the author's 129 articles on economic theory is divided into five parts: 1. Problems in pure theory; 2. Topics in mathematical economics; 3. Trade, welfare and fiscal policy; 4. Economics and public policy; 5. General economic essays, works in economic history, and some comments on methodology.

181. Samuelson, Paul A. **Foundations of Economic Analysis.** Cambridge, Mass., Harvard University Press, 1947. 447 p. (Harvard Economic Studies, v. 80).

Aimed to prove the existence of meaningful theorems in diverse field of economic affairs. Essentially mathematical tools are used to support validity of economic theories. He received the Nobel Prize in Economics in 1970.

182. Say, Jean Baptiste. **A Treatise on Political Economy; or The Production, Distribution and Consumption of Wealth.** New York, A. M. Kelley, 1964. 488 p. (Reprints of Economic Classics) First American ed. 1821.

Translation of "Traite D'Economie Politique" first published in 1803, which has been translated into many other languages and adapted as an university textbook.

183. Schultz, Henry. **The Theory and Measurement of Demand.** Chicago, University of Chicago Press, 1938. (Reprint 1958) 817 p.

Based on many statistical sources, graphical and mathematical analysis, the author's aim was to derive the concrete statistical demand functions of sixteen agricultural commodities, to make comparison of elasticities of those functions, to develop a theory of demand for completing and competing products, and to test this theory. Bibliography: p. 777-803.

184. Schumpeter, Joseph Alois. **Business Cycles; a Theoretical Historical, and Statistical Analysis of the Capitalist Process.** Abridged with an introd. by Rendigs Fels. New York, McGraw-Hill, 1967. 461 p.

Contents: (2) Equilibrium and the theoretical norm of economic quantities, (3) How the economic system generates evolution. (4) The contours of economic evolution. (5) Time series and their normal. (6-7) Historical outlines. (8) 1919-1929. (9) The world crisis and after. The importance of this work lies in its ideas, and that it can stimulate a new research in this branch of economics.

185. Schumpeter, Joseph Alois. **History of Economic Analysis;** edited from manuscript by Elizabeth Boody Schumpeter, New York, Oxford University Press, 1954. 1260 p.

Describes the development of scientific analysis in economics from ancient Greece to the present times, taking under consideration social and political history and philosophy. Includes an author and subject index.

186. Schumpeter, Joseph Alois. **The Theory of Economic Development; an Inquiry into Profits, Capital, Credit, Interest and the Business Cycle.** Transl. from the German by Redvers Opie. Cambridge, Harvard University Press, 1949. 255 p. (Harvard Economic Studies, v. 46).

German title "Theorie der wirtschaftlichen Entwicklung" was first published in 1911. Contents: (1) The circular flow of economic life as conditioned by given circumstances, (2) The fundamental phenomenon of economic development, (3) Credit and capital, (4) Entrepreneurial profit, (5) Interest on capital, (6) Business cycle.

187. Schumpeter, Joseph Alois. **Ten Great Economists, from Marx to Keynes.** London, Allen & Unwin, 1952. 305 p.

Includes: 1. K. Marx, 2. M. E. L. Walras, 3. C. Menger, 4. A. Marshall, 5. V. Pareto, 6. E. V. Bohm-Bawerk, 7. F. W. Taussig, 8. I. Fischer, 9. W. C. Mitchell, 10. J. M. Keynes. Additionally appendix includes three more: 1. G. F. Knapp, 2. F. von Wieser and 3. L. von Bortkiewicz.

188. **Scrittori Classici Italiani di Economia Politica.** Milano, G. G. Destefanis, 1803-16. 50 v.

This is a multivolume work of Italian economic writers from the ancient to modern times. Most of the biographical sketches are written by the editor Pietro Custodi.

189. Silverman, Herbert Albert. **Substance of Economics for the Students and the General Reader.** 10th ed. Pitman, 1937. 341 p.

The approach in this textbook is a combination of a descriptive survey of the economic system with an elementary account of the governing principles presented in clear and a concise manner. Bibliography: p. 327-331.

190. Simonde de Sismondi, Jean Charles Leonard, **Nouveaux Principes d' Economie Politique; our De La Richesse dans ses Rapports avec la Population,** Paris, Chez Delaunay, 1819. 2 v.

In this work observing the economic crisis in England during his trip (1818-19) the author delivers a devastating criticism of "Laisses faire", the basic system upon which the classical school of economists has been founded. He showed that general crises are not only possible but inevitable in a free capitalist economy where rich becomes richer and a poor becomes poorer.

191. Smith, Adam. **An Inquiry into the Nature and Causes of the Wealth of Nations.** Edited with an introd., notes, margins, summary and an enl. index by Edwin Cannan, with an introd, by Max Lerner. New York, Modern Library, 1937. 976 p. (The Modern Library of the World's Best Books)

The publishing of The Wealth of Nations in 1776 started a new period in the development of economic thought. Smith's doctrine has revolutionized contemporary European society. The text of present edition is a republication of the fifth, the last before author's death. Included are two indexes: subject and authorities.

192. Sombart, Werner, **The Quintessence of Capitalism; a Study of the History and Psychology of the Modern Business Man.** Translated and edited by M. Epstein, New York, Fertig, 1967. 400 p.

Translation of "Der Moderne Kapitalismus, historish-systematische Darstellung des Gesamteuropäischen Wirtschaftslebens von seinen Anfängen bis zur Gegenwart." Bibl. references included in "Notes" p. 363-392.

193. Spann, Othmar. **The History of Economics.** Trans. from the 19th German ed. by Eden and Cedar Paul. New York, Norton 1930. 328 p.

Discusses the basic problems of economics in the changing light of historical evolution, presenting brief formulation and critique of the more important economic theories.

194. Spengler, Joseph John and Allen, William R. eds. **Essays in Economic Thought: Aristotle to Marshall.** Chicago, Rand McNally, 1960. 800 p. illus.

Outlines the historical development of economic theories from the ancient Greeks to neo-classical economics of Alfred Marshall. Included are two detailed indexes: names and subjects.

195. Spiegel, Henry William, ed. **The Development of Economic Thought;** Great Economists in Perspective. New York, J. Wiley, 1952. 811 p.

Presents a collection of outstanding essays by a number of great economists. It is international in scope and represents multiplicity of points of view from Aristotle and Plato through the classical school to the most recent, giving the reader a first-hand view of the development of economic thought as seen through the eyes of the important writers.

196. Steuart Denham, Sir James. **An Inquiry into the Principles of Political Economy.** Edited and with an introduction by Andrew S. Skinner. Chicago, University of Chicago Press, 1966. 2 v.

The author, a well known Scottish economist of the 18th century, attempts to present economic theories from the point of view of late mercantilism. His theories have found more recognition in Germany than in his native Great Britain. Bibliography: p. 744-46.

197. Stigler, George Joseph. **Production and Distribution Theories: the Formative Period.** New York, Macmillan, 1941. 392 p.

Intended to fill in part of an important gap in the economic literature: the development of the modern theory of production and distribution. The period covered is from 1870-1895.

198. Stigler, George Joseph. **The Theory of Price.** New York, Macmillan, 1966. 355 p.

Emphasis is on the close relationship between theory and practical experience.

199. Stonier, Alfred William, and Hague, Douglas C. **A Textbook of Economic Theory.** 3rd ed. London, Longman. 1964. 574 p.

Designed for students with no previous knowledge of economic theory, although some parts could be of value to more advanced students. The text is divided into two major parts: (1) Price theory, and (2) Employment theory. General index is included.

200. Taussig, Frank William. **Principles of Economics,** 4th ed. New York, Macmillan, 1945-46. 1939. 2 v.

One of the older texts on this subject presented in an excellent literary style.

201. Turgot, Anne R. J. **Oeuvres de Turgot et Documents le Concernant; Avec Biographie et Notes.** Paris, Felix Alcan, 1913-23. 5 v.

This is the complete works of a famous French economist of eighteenth century who advocated economic reforms in France to forestall revolution. The collection contains: t. 1 Turgot etudiant et magistrat, t. 2-3. Turgot Intendant de Limages (1761-1774), t. 4-5. Turgot ministre (1774-1781). Indexes of geographical and personal names are included.

202. Veblen, Thorstein. **The Theory of the Leisure Class, and Economic Study of Institutions.** London, Allen, Unwin, 1957. 404 p.

Two main topics are analyzed: "Conspicuous consumption" and "Conspicuous waste", the symbols of the "Leisure class".

203. Vickrey, William Spencer. **Metastatics and Macroeconomics.** New York, Harcourt, Brace & World, 1964. 314 p.

This volume is a sequel to author's Microstatics. Bibliography: p. 281-304.

204. Vickrey, William Spencer. **Microstatics.** New York, Harcourt, Brace World, 1964. 406 p.

Presents an exposition of the basic structures of current economic theory. The emphasis is on the logical structure of the different theoretical tools. Bibliography: p. 369-395.

205. Wagner, Donald Owen. **Social Reformers: Adam Smith to John Dewey.** With a foreword by Carlton J. H. Hayes. New York, Macmillan, 1934. 749 p.

Presents the wide gallery of famous personalities of the 18th and 19th centuries to the present. Some were outstanding economists, the others political personalities or social philosophers. General index is included.

206. Walras, Leon. **Elements of Pure Economics; or the Theory of Social Wealth.** Transl. by William Jaffe. London, Allen & Unwin, 1954. 620 p.

Translation of "Eléments d'économie politique pure." A very

influential classic, utilizing simple mathematics which inspired such famous men as Vilfredo Pareto, Irving Fisher, E. Barone, Knut Wicksell, Joseph Schumpeter and other economists. Pure economics is the theory of price determination under an assumption of perfectly free competition; it is a mathematical theory. Includes a subject and an author indexes.

207. Weber, Max. **General Economic History.** Translated by Frank H. Knight. Glencoe, Ill., Free Press, 1927. 401 p.

The significance of this work lies in the penetrating analysis of economic life in the period of the preparation for, and development of modern capitalism. Bibliography included in "Notes" p. 371-381.

208. Whittaker, Edmund. **A History of Economic Ideas.** New York, Longmans, Green, 1940. 766 p.

The organization of this study is topical instead of being chronological, treating basic economic concepts rather than schools of thought. A considerable attention has been devoted to the contributions of American writers.

209. Wicksell, Knut. **Lectures on Political Economy.** Trans. from the Swedish by F. Classen and edited with an introd. by Lionel Robbins. London, Routledge, 1934-35. 2 v.

This work of the outstanding Swedish economist deals with such topics as: the theories of value, of production and distribution, with capital accumulation, the conception and functions of money, currency, the velocity of circulation of money; banking and credit, and the exchange value of money.

210. Wicksteed, Philip Henry. **The Common Sense of Political Economy and Selected Papers and Reviews on Economic Theory.** Edited with introd. by Lionel Robbins. Rev. and enl. ed. London, Routledge & K. Paul, 1957. 2 v.

Divided into three parts: 1. Systematic and constructive exposition of the marginal analysis; 2. Excursive and critical studies of more technical problems of analysis; 3. Analytical and practical problems: housing, unemployment, redistribution of wealth, taxation, land nationalization.

211. Wieser, Friedrich, Freiherr von. **Natural Value.** Edited with a preface and analysis by William Smart; the transl. by Christian A. Malloch. New York, A. M. Kelley, 1956. 243 p.

Contents: (1) The elementary theory of value. (2) Exchange value and natural value. (3) The natural imputation of the return from production. (4) The natural value of land, capital, and labour. (5) The natural cost value of products, (6) Value in the economy of the state.

212. Wieser, Friedrich, Freiherr von. **Social Economics.** Translated by A. Ford Hinrichs, with a preface by Wesley Clair Mitchell. New York, A. M. Kelley, 1967. 470 p. (Reprints of Economic Classics).

"Theorie der Gesellschaftlichen Wirtschaft," published in 1914. The original Wieser's treatise is the first systematic study of economic theory produced by the Austrian School. Includes an index.

CHAPTER TWO

ECONOMIC CONDITIONS IN VARIOUS COUNTRIES
(Economic Development - Underdeveloped Areas)

This chapter covers the economic conditions in a number of countries or georgraphical regions. The coverage is rather selective, nevertheless, certain countries, e.g., the Soviet Union, because of its political importance, are represented with materials in their native languages. First part of this chapter consists of general reference sources, e.g., guides, bibliographies, dictionaries, yearbooks, etc. that have a more universal coverage. The second part provides listings of material in alphabetical arrangement by country or geographical region.

GUIDES TO ECONOMIC HISTORY

213. American Historical Association. **Guide to Historical Literature.** Board of editors: George Frederick Howe and others, New York, Macmillan, 1961. 962 p.

Extensively covers economic history and conditions of the United States and other countries. Arrangement is by large subject and country groups. Entries are accompanied with brief annotations. Included is a detailed general index.

214. Harvard University. Graduate School of Business Administration. **Resources for the Study of Economic History; a Preliminary Guide to Pre-Twentieth Century Printed Material in Collections Located in Certain American and British Libraries.** Compiled by Dorothea D. Reeves, introd. by A.H. Cole, pref. by D. T. Clark. Boston, Baker Library, 1961. 62 p.

Bibliographies (Current)

215. **Bibliographie über Entwicklungsländer.** Bearb. von der Forschungsstelle der Friedrich-Ebert Stiftung in Zusammenarbeit mit dem Institut für Selbsthilfe und Sozialforschung. Hannover, Verlag für Literatur und Zeitgeschehen, 1961 — v. 1 —

Transl: Bibliography on developing countries.

216. International Association for Research in Income and Wealth. **Bibliography on Income and Wealth.** v. 1 — 1937-47 — Cambridge, England. Bowers and Bowers.

Presents a cooperative effort of scholars from many countries and from various organizations of the world. Published annually in the form of mimeographed reports which are cumulated into multiannual issues. Annotations

are in English, French, or Spanish. The Soviet material is not included.
Contains: 1. General; 2. Discussion of concepts; 3. International comparisons
of national estimates; 4. Estimates and analyses by countries.

217. Polski Instytut Spraw Miedzynarodowych. Warsaw. Zaklad Informacji
Naukowej i Dokumentacji. **Zeszyty Bibliograficzne. Seria II: Sytuacja
gospodarcza i spoleczna panstw imperialistycznych.** r. 1 —   1964 —
Warszawa.

    Title translated: Bibliographic issues. Series 2: Economic and social
conditions in imperialist countries. This Polish bibliography covers: U. S.,
Great Britain, France and West Germany.

BIBLIOGRAPHIES (RETROSPECTIVE)

218. Ahmad, Jaleel. **Natural Resources in Low Income Countries; an
Analytical Survey of Socio-economic Research.** Pittsburgh, University of
Pittsburgh Press. 1960. 118 p.

    This annotated bibliography covers, as comprehensively as possible,
works dealing with socio-economic aspects of resource development in the
underdeveloped countries of the world. The area is restricted to countries
and regions in Asia (except Japan), Africa, Latin America and Southern
Europe. The survey is limited to published and unpublished research between
the years 1948 through 1959. The basic text contains a review of over five
hundred studies: A geographic index is included.

219. Antwerp. Institut Universitaire des Territoires d'Outremer. **Bibliografie
over het derde Wereldblok: Coöperatie, Ekonomische Ontwikkelingsplannen.**
Recueil Bibliographique Tiers-monde; Cooperation, Plan de Development
Economique. Developing Countries Bibliographic Compendium; Cooperation,
Economic Development Planning. Antwerpeu, 1964. 157 p.

    Includes about one thousand items drawn from Belgian, Dutch, English,
French, German, Italian, Spanish, etc. publications. The material is arranged
according to international decimal classification system. Author index and
the list of organizations interested in developing countries are added.

220. Anstruy, Jacques. **La Scandale du Developpement. Commentaires par
G. Leduc et L. J. Lebret; Bibliographie Analytique et Critiq̇ue par Guy Caire.**
Paris, M. Riviere, 1965. 535 p. (Bilons de la connaissance economique).

    Divided into three parts: (1) Nature of development, (2) Logic of
development, and (3) Finality of development. More than a third of this
book is dedicated to bibliography.

221. Bremer Ausschuss für Wirtschaftsforschung. **Dokumente und Berichte
über Entwicklungs pläne; Ein Bibliographischer Nachweis.** 3 voll. neu bearb.
Ausg. Bremen, 1965. 157 1.

    Emphasis is on economic planning for development. The material is divided in sections according to large geographic areas, and subdivided by country. The main sources are government documents, reports, memoranda, and other official publications.

222. Brussels, Université libre. Centre d'économie regionale. **Bibliographie Internationale d'Economie Regionale.** Bruxelles Universite libre de Bruxelles, Institut de sociologie, 1964. 757 p.

An international bibliography of regional economics covers ten European countries (Belgium, France, Gt. Brit., Germany, Italy, Netherlands, Poland, Russia, Spain, Yugoslavia) with short sections of Asia, Australia and New Zealand). Intended to be kept up-to-date periodically.

223. **Danckwortt, Helga. Entwicklungshilfe, Entwicklungsländer; ein Verzeichnis von Publikationen in der Bundesrepublik Deutschland und Westberlin, 1950-59.** zusmmengestellt von Helga und Dieter Danckwortt im Auftrage der Carl Duisberg-Gesellschaft mit Forderung durch das Land Nordrhein-Westfalen. Köln, 1960. 471 p.

Economic assistance and underdeveloped countries, a list of publications in the Federal Republic Germany and West Berlin in 1950-59.

224. Delilez, Jean Pierre. **LaPlanification dans les Pays d'Économie Capitaliste.** Preface de Charles Bettelheim. . . Paris, La Haye, Mouton, 1968. 272 p. (Confluence; etas des recherches en sciences sociales, v. 14).

225. Goris, Hendrika. **List of National Development Plans.** 2nd ed. Washington, International Bank for Reconstruction and Development, Development Services Dept., 1968. 129 1.

226. Hald, Marjorie W. **A Selected Bibliography on Economic Development and Foreign Aid.** Santa Monica, Calif., Rand Corp., 1957. 93 p. (Rand Corporation Research Memorandum).

Contains fifteen hundred items on economic development in English arranged among eight main headings, subdivided into countries or topics. Entries follow in alphabetical order. Most publications are issued between 1950 through 1957. Selected country index is added.

227. Hazlewood, Arthur. **The Economics of Development; an Annotated List of Books and Articles Published 1958-1962.** London. Published for the Oxford University, Institute of Commonwealth Studies, by Oxford University Press, 1964. 104 p. (Oxford University, Institute of Commonwealth Studies Reading Lists.)

This bibliography is a sequel to the author's "Economics of Underdeveloped Areas," published in 1959. Included are: indexes of authors and editors, and of places.

228. Hazelwood, Arthur. **The Economics of Underdeveloped Areas. An Annotated Reading List of Books, Articles and Official Publications.** 2nd enl. ed. London, Oxford University Press, 1959. 156 p. (Oxford University Institute of Commonwealth Studies Reading List).

A valuable bibliography in English language containing books, articles, and government documents published between 1930 and 1958. Includes an index of authors.

229. Kabir, A. K. M. **Social Change and Nation Building in the Developing Areas;** a Selected Annotated Bibliography, by A. K. M. Kabir. Dacca, National Institute of Public Administration, 1965. 79 p.

230. Katz, Saul M. and McGowan, Frank. **A Selected List of U. S. Readings on Development, Prepared for the United Nations Conferences on the Application of Science and Technology for the Benefit of the Less Developed Areas.** Washington, Agency for International Development; U. S. Government Print. Office, 1963. 363 p.

This work represents an important sample of current U. S. publications in science and technology, which could be useful to the developing nations. A wide range of subjects related to development has been covered to illustrate how science and technology can be applied for human welfare. 1195 books, pamphlets, and periodical articles published in the U. S. are included. Name index.

231. **Literatur über Entwicklungsländer.** Hannover, Verlag für Literatur und Zeitgeschehen, 1961-65. 2 v. and 2 supplements.

Covers literature on developing countries from 1950 to 1960 in German, English, French and Russian.

232. Organization for Economic Cooperation and Development. **Catalogue of Publications, 1966.** Paris, 1966. 84 p.

Covers such subjects as: economics, international trade, statistics, development, agriculture, food, fisheries, energy, industry, and manpower.

233. Organization for Economic Cooperation and Development. Library. **Planification Économique. Economic Planning.** Paris, 1964. 57 p. (Its Bibliographie speciale analytique, 3).

234. Organization for Economic Cooperation and Development. Library. **Politique Régionale.** Paris, 1966 — (Its Bibliographie speciale analytique, 8).

Introductory material in French and English; annotations in French or English.

235. Regional Economic Development Institute. **A Bibliography of Resource Materials in the Field of Regional Economic Development.** Prepared for the U. S. Dept. of Commerce. Washington, U. S. Govt. Print Off., 1966. 99 p.

236. ReQua, Eloise, and Statham, Jane. **The Developing Nations: a Guide to Information Sources** Concerning their Economic, Political, Technical and Social Problems. Foreword by George I. Blanksten. Detroit, Gale Research Co., 1965. 339 p. (Management Information Guide 5).

Lists books, government documents, publications of international organizations, periodical articles and reports. The entries are annotated and arranged according to major subject fields and geographic regions. Most of the included material belongs to the period of 1950-1965. This is one of the most extensive bibliographies in this field.

237. Shaukat, Ali and Jones, Garth N. **Planning, Development and Change; and Annotated Bibliography on Development and Administration.** Lahore, Dept. of Public Administration, University of the Panjab, 1966. 217 p. (Punjab, Pakistan (Province) University Lahore, Dept. of Public Administration. Public Administration Series 1).

238. Spitz, Alan A. **Development Administration; an Annotated Bibliography.** Compiled by Alan A. Spitz and Edward W. Weidner. Honolulu, East-West Center Press, 1963. 116 p.

A selective bibliography of 340 items, mostly periodical articles and reports arranged alphabetically by author under five main headings. Includes a general index.

239. Stanford Research Institute. International Development Center. **Human Resources and Economic Growth;** an international annotated bibliography on the role of education and training in economic development. Edited by Alexander-Fruitschi M. Crites. Menlo Park, Calif., 1963. 398 p.

240. Stobbe, Hanna. **Methodisch-Theoretisches Schrifttum zur Wirtschaftlichen Entwicklung in Entwicklungsländern und Schrifttum zur Entwicklungs- politik.** Bearb. von Hanna Stobbe und Viktor v. Crousaz. Kiel, 1965. 474 p. (Kieler Schrifttumskunde zur Wirtschaft und Gesellschaft, 9).

Literature on development economics and politics in underdeveloped areas.

241. United Nations, Dag Hammarskjold Library. **Economic and Social Development Plans:** Centrally-Planned Economies, Developed Market Economies. New York, United Nations, 1966. 59 p. (Its Bibliographical Series, no. 11).

242. United Nations. Economic Commission for Europe. **Studies and other Publications** issued. . . for Europe, 1947-1966. New York, 1967. 81 p.

Covers such topics as: economic problems, agriculture, energy, housing, industry, statistics, timber, trade, transport, and water problems.

243. U. S. Dept. of State. Division of Library and Reference Services. **Point Four, Near East and Africa. A Selected Bibliography of Studies on Economically Underdeveloped Countries.** Washington, Government Printing Office. Repr. Greenwood Press, 1969. 136 p.

244. U. S. Dept. of Commerce. Office of Technical Services. **Book Reviews: Literature Recommendations.** Washington, Dept. of State, Agency for International Development, Communications Resources Division, 1962. 170 p.

245. U. S. Dept. of State. Office of Intelligence Research and Analysis. **Economic Problems of Underdeveloped Areas:** External Research, a Listing of Recent Studies. Washington, External Research Staff, Office of Intelligence Research, Dept. of State, 1956. 59 p.

246. U. S. International Cooperation Administration. Office of Industrial Resources. **Industrialization and Economic Development, Literature Recommendations.** Washington, 1960. 29 p.

247. U. S. National Science Foundation. Office of Special Studies. **A Selected Bibliography of Research and Development and its Impact on the Economy.** Washington, 1958. 21 p.
    Contains a list of selected books, pamphlets and articles related to scientific research and economic development.

248. Viet, Jean. **Assistance to Under-developed Countries; an Annotated Bibliography.** L'assistance aux pays sous-developpes; bibliographie commentee. Paris, UNESCO, 1957. 83 p. (Reports and Papers in the Social Sciences Rapports et Documents de Sciences Sociales, no. 8. United Nations Educational, Scientific and Cultural organization, Document).

249. Viet, Jean. **International Cooperation and Programmes of Economic and Social Development, an Annotated Bibliography. Cooperation Internationale et Programmes de Developpement Economique et Social. Bibliographie Commentee.** Paris, UNESCO, 1962. 107 p. (Reports and papers in the social sciences, no. 15).
    To some extent, this selected work is a continuation of "Assistance to Underdeveloped Countries," an annotated bibliography published in 1957. It covers books, pamphlets, documents, and articles on economic and social development of new countries, with an author index at the end.

250. Washington, D. C. Economic Development Institute. **Selected Readings and Source Materials on Economic Developments;** a list of books, articles and reports recommended as reading material for the ninth General course of the Economic Development Institute, 1963/64. Washington, International Bank for Reconstruction and Development, 1964. 92 p.

251. Wolf, Charles and Sufrin, Sidney C. **Capital Formation & Foreign Investment in Underdeveloped Areas;** an Analysis of Research Needs and Program Possibilities Prepared from a Study Supported by the Ford Foundations. Syracuse, N. Y., Syracuse University Press, 1955. 134 p.

Analyzes current literature and research dealing with this topic. Emphasis is on the Near East, South, and Southeast Asia.

DICTIONARIES & ENCYCLOPEDIAS

252. Besters, Hans, ed. **Entwicklungspolitik. Handbuch und Lexikon.** Im Auftrag von Bernhard Hanssler und Hans Hermann Walz. Hrsg. von Hans Besters und Ernst E. Boesch. Stuttgart, Kreuz-Verlag; Mainz, Matthias-Grunewald-Verlag, 1966. 14 leaves, 1770 columns.

This is a handbook and an encyclopedic dictionary of economic policy in underdeveloped areas.

253. Scharf, Traute. **Dictionary of Development Economics.** New York, American Elsevier, 1969. 225 p.

In English, French and German, this dictionary contains 3112 entries, presenting the terminology of development, growth and planning at all stages and with all its implications within the soci-economic framework. It includes some terms relating to the basic concepts of socio-economic development as well as those which are distinctive to the field. The dictionary is arranged by subject — rather than alphabetically — in 12 chapters, in order to facilitate an interdisciplinary approach and groups together terms which are associated either by usage or meaning.

DIRECTORIES AND HANDBOOKS

254. Conway, Hobart McKinley. **Area Development Organizations.** Atlanta, Conway Research, 1966. 331 p.

255. Organization for Economic Cooperation and Development. Development Centre. **Catalogue of Social and Economic Development Institutes and Programmes: Training.** Paris, 1968. 355 p.

Provides information on training facilities in the field of social and economic development in the various countries in the world. The arrangement is alphabetical by country, listing applicable institutions with personnel, programme and activities.

256. ——————. **Catalogue of Social and Economic Development Institutes and Programmes: Research.** Paris, 1968.

Having a similar title and arrangement as previous one this directory lists the research institutions in the field of social and economic development. Also includes, an analytical index of research projects undertaken by institutes.

257. United Nations. Dept. of Economic Affairs. **Directory of Economic and Statistical Projects:** a classified list of work completed, in progress or planned by United Nations and specialized agencies. Lake Success, 1948. 130 p.

258. United Nations. Economic Commission for Europe. **List of Institutions in the Field of Applied Economics in E.C.E. Countries** (scientific research institutes, universities and faculties of economics) Geneva, United Nations, 1966. 107 p.

Lists ca. 700 institutions in 28 countries, giving name of school, faculty, university, etc. Includes Communist block countries, Turkey, Gt. Brit. and the U. S.

259. Willmington, S. Clay, and Sievers, Gale. **Complete Handbook on the Foreign Aid Policy of the United States;** a Complete Manual and Reference for High School Debaters and Others Interested in the Subject. Skokie, Ill., National Textbook Corp. 1966, 239 p.

858 abstracts of books, pamphlets, articles on foreign aid are listed, most of them recently published. Included is "Who's who in foreign aid," and bibliography: p. 229-239.

GENERAL SURVEYS

260. American University, Washington, D. C. Foreign Area Studies. **Area Handbook. . .** series for various countries. Washington, U. S. Govt. Printing Off., 1963 —

Surveys historical backgrounds, cultural and socio-political life, and economic conditions of many countries of the world. Each volume deals with one country only. Excellent bibliographies are included.

261. Bauer, Peter Tamas, and Yamey, B. S. **Economics of Underdeveloped Countries.** London, Nisbet, 1957. 271 p. (The Cambridge Economic Handbooks).

The purpose of this study is to illuminate certain features of the economy of the underdeveloped parts of the world. Also discussed is the role of government in promoting economic development. Includes an index.

262. Commonwealth Economic Committee. **Commonwealth Development and Financing.** London, H.M.S.O., 1961 — no. 1 —

(1) Canda, 1961, (2) Federation of Rhodesia and Nyasaland, 1961, (3) Pakistan, 1961, (4) New Zealand, 1963, (5) Nigeria, 1963, (6) Australia, 1963, (7) India, 1963, (8) Jamaica, 1964, (9) Uganda, 1966, (10) Malta, 1966, (11) Kenya, 1967.

263. **Current Economic Indicators:** a Quarterly Statistical Review of Developments in the World Economy, v. 1 — 1960 — New York, U. N. Economic and Social Council.

Surveys the world economic situtation at the present pointing out the short-term outlook; indicates any changes which may affect the future of economic activity. The statistical material is divided into three parts: 1. The world economy; 2. The under-developed areas; 3. Selected industrial countries, such as: Canada, France, Germany (Western), Great Britain, Japan and the U. S.

264. **Economic Almanac;** a Handbook of Useful Facts about Business, Labor and Government in the United States and other Areas. New York, National Industrial Conference Board, 1940 — Annual.

Designed as a useful information source on economic and business statistics, alphabetically arranged by subject, with an index. Includes statistics about Canada and some other countries. Gives sources of data.

265. **Ékonomika Kapitalisticheskikh Stran.** 1956 — Moskva, Izd-vo Sotsiial'no-ekon. Lit-ry. Annual. Title varies.

Transl.: Economy of capitalist countries.

266. **Images Économiques du Monde.** 1956 — Paris, Société d'edition d'enseignement supérieur. Annual.

Covers economic conditions throughout the world with statistical data and brief explanatory texts. Includes a detailed index and separate maps with charts.

267. International Bank for Reconstruction and Development. **The Economic Development of Ceylon;** Report. . . Baltimore, Published for International Bank for Reconstruction and Development by the Johns Hopkins Press, 1953. 829 p.

268. —————. **The Economic Development of Iraq;** Report of a Mission. Baltimore. Johns Hopkins Press, 1952. 463 p.

269. —————. **The Economic Development of Jamaica;** Report of a Mission. . . Baltimore, Published for the International Bank for Reconstruction and Development by the Johns Hopkins Press, 1952. 288 p.

270. —————. **The Economic Development of Jordan;** Report of a Mission. . . at the Request of the Government of Jordan. Baltimore, Published for the International Bank for Reconstruction and Development by the Johns Hopkins Press, 1957. 488 p.

271. —————. **The Economic Development of Kenya;** Report . . . Baltimore, Johns Hopkins Press, 1963. 380 p.

272. International Bank for Reconstruction and Development. **The Economic Development of Kuwait;** Report. . . Baltimore, Published for the International Bank for Reconstruction and Development by the Johns Hopkins Press, 1965. 194 p.

273. _____. **The Economic Development of Libya;** Report . . . Baltimore, Published for the International Bank for Reconstruction and Development by Johns Hopkins Press, 1960. 524 p.

274. _____. **The Economic Development of Malaya;** Report . . . Baltimore, Johns Hopkins Press, 1955. 707 p.

275. _____. **The Economic Development of Mexico.** Report of the Combined Mexican Working Party. Baltimore, Johns Hopkins Press, 1953. 392 p.

276. _____. **The Economic Development of Morocco;** Report . . . Baltimore, Johns Hopkins Press, 1966. 356 p.

277. _____. **The Economic Development of Nicaragua;** Report . . . of a Mission. . . Baltimore, Published by the International Bank for Reconstruction and Development by the Government of Nicaragua, 1952. 108 p.

278. _____. **The Economic Development of Nigeria;** Report . . . Baltimore, Johns Hopkins Press, 1961. 686 p.

279. _____. **The Economic Development of Spain;** Report of a Mission. . . Baltimore, Johns Hopkins Press, 1963. 416 p.

280. _____. **The Economic Development of Syria;** Report of a mission, Baltimore, Johns Hopkins Press, 1956. 486 p.

281. _____. **The Economic Development of Tanganyika;** Report . . . Baltimore, Published for the International Bank for Reconstruction and Development by Johns Hopkins Press, 1961. 548 p.

282. _____. **The Economic Development of Thailand;** Report of a Mission. . . Baltimore, Johns Hopkins Press, 1959. 301 p.

283. _____. **The Economic Development of the Territory of Papua and New Guinea;** a Report of a Mission Organized . . . at Request of the Government of the Commonwealth of Australia. Baltimore, Johns Hopkins Press, 1965. 488 p.

284. _____. **The Economic Development of Uganda;** Report . . . Baltimore, Johns Hopkins Press, 1962. 475 p.

285. International Bank for Reconstruction and Development. **The Economic Development of Venezuela;** Report of a Mission. . . Baltimore, Johns Hopkins Press, 1961. 494 p.

Surveys all phases of economic activity with special considerations to the development potentialities of each country in the following fields: agriculture, forestry, manufacture, mining, power, transportation, foreign and domestic trade. Also discusses such problems as: education, vocational training, health and cultural development. Textual parts are supplemented by tables, charts, diagrams, maps and plans. Reference sources are given.

286. International Conference on Input-Output Techniques, Geneva. **Structural Interdependence and Economic Development;** Preceedings. Edited by Tibor Barna, in collaboration with William I. Abraham and Zoltan Kenessey. London, Macmillan, 1963. 365 p.

Bibliographical references at end of most of the chapters. Contains papers presented at the Third International Input-Output Conference held in September 1961 in Geneva. Divided into four parts: 1. Models of economic development; 2. Regional models; 3. Input-Output techniques and national planning; 4. Problems of estimation and statistics.

287. **The International Yearbook and Statesmen's Who's Who.** London, Burke's Peerage. 1953 — Annual.

Gives information on the economic and political structure of each country in the world, followed by biographies of most important persons in each country. The material is divided into three parts. Part 1. International organizations; part 2. States of the World in alphabetical order; part 3. Biographical section and general index.

288. Keenleyside, Hugh Llewellyn. **International Aid: a Summary With Special Reference to the Programmes of the United Nations.** Toronto, McClelland & Stewart, 1966. 343 p.

This is a valuable source of information on international economic and technical aid written by the U. N.'s director general of technical assistance for eight years. The material is divided into four parts: 1. Review of current U.N. aid programs; 2. A brief historical account; 3. Description of the financial and procedural operations involved; 4. Suggestions for the refinement of the programs of the future. Index is included.

289. Lewis, William Arthur. **Economic Survey, 1919-1939.** London, G. Allen and Unwin, 1960. 221 p.

Reviews in condensed form the economic conditions in the world during the period between both world wars. This work should be regarded as a starting point in the study of that period. The included references and bibliographies are indicating where to look for more detailed knowledge about this topic. List of cited authors and an index are included.

290. Mulhall, Michael George. **Progress of the World in Arts, Agriculture, Commerce, Manufactures, Instruction, Railways, and Public Wealth Since the Beginning of the Nineteenth Century.** London, E. Stanford, 1880. 569 p.

Presents a survey of the economic conditions of the world in the first three quarters of the nineteenth century using numerous statistical data.

291. New York Times. **World Economic Review and Forecast.** 1965 — New York, Grosset and Dunlap. Annual.

Contains articles on national economies, finances, industries, technology and transportation, money, arts, communications, fashions, etc. In appendix are listed: chronology of major financial events of the previous year, international trade fairs for the running year, and the tables of significant economic indicators.

292. Organization for Economic Cooperation and Development. **Economic Surveys.** Paris, 1953. Annual.

The 1965-66 series includes 22 countries: 17 of Western Europe, and Iceland, Canada, Japan, Turkey and U.S.A.

293. Organization for Economic Cooperation and Development. **Main Economic Indicators.** March 1962 — Paris OECD. Monthly. Supersedes part 1 of the Organization's General Statistics. Title also in French; Principaux Indicateurs Economiques.

Intended as a guide to recent economic developments and as a basic source of international statistical data. The material has been divided into three parts: (1) indicators by subject, (2) indicators by country, and (3) foreign trade indicators. Most of the material is presented in a tabular form; many diagrams are also included.

294. **Overseas Survey.** 1951 — London, Barclays Bank, D.C.O. Annual.

A survey of trade and economic conditions in the territories in which the Barclay Bank is represented. Forty five countries were included in the 1967 edition. Supplemented by a monthly Overseas Review.

295. Studenski, Paul. **The Income of Nations; Theory, Measurement and Analysis, Past and Present; a Study in Applied Economics and Statistics.** New York, New York University Press, 1958. 554 p.

Surveys and discusses the income of nations in a global development. The material has been divided into four parts: 1. History, 2. Theory and Methodology, 3. Estimates for Selected Countries, and 4. Developments in sixty six other countries. Included are: a statistical appendix with explanations, summary table, notes, and an index. Bibliography references included in "Notes" p. 513-544.

296. United Nations. Dept. of Economic and Social Affairs. **World Economic Survey.** no. 1 — 1945/47 — New York, Published for the United Nations by Columbia University Press. 1948 — Annual.

Part I deals with the economic growth in the post-war decade, and Part II presents the current economic development. Draws a data from government, intergovermental, or United Nations sources.

297. United Nations. Statistical Office. **Statistics of National Income and Expenditures.** no. 1-10. New York, 1952-57. Semi-annual. (Statistical papers, Series 4).

New issues supersede previous ones by carrying the series back to 1938. Estimates of the country's national accounts are given in the tabular form under name of each country. The broad topics of national income and expenditures have been divided into 8 subjects. Sources of the estimates for each country are cited.

298. U. S. Dept. of State. External Research Division. **Research on Underdevelopment;** assessment and inventory of research on economic, social, and political problems of underdeveloped areas. Draft. Washington, 1960. 1 v. (Its External Research Report E. R. 30).

299. U. S. Agency for International Development. Statistics and Reports Division. **U. S. Overseas Loans and Grants and Assistance from International Organizations:** Obligations and Loan Authorizations. 1945/59 — Washington. Annual.

300. U. S. Library of Congress, Legislative Reference Service. **Trends in Economic Growth: Comparison of the Western Powers and the Soviet Bloc.** A study prepared for the Joint Committee on the Economic Report. Washington, U. S. Govt. Print Off., 1955. 339 p.

301. **Weltwirtschaft.** Bd. 1 — Jahrg. 1950 — Kiel, Institut für Weltwirtschaft an der Universität Kiel. Semi-annual.

Reviews economic conditions in the various countries of the world.

302. Wolf, Charles, Jr. **Foreign Aid: Theory and Practice in Southern Asia.** Princeton, Princeton University Press, 1960. 442 p.

Appraises the foreign aid record of the United States in the South and Southeast Asia, pointing out the most important question: how to improve the allotment of foreign aid in a region, once the total amount to be allocated has been decided? Mathematical formulas are used to help in solving some economic problems.

ECONOMIC DEVELOPMENT IN VARIOUS COUNTRIES

Africa

303. African Bibliographic Center. **A Select Bibliographical Listing on Technical Assistance in Africa.** 1961-62— Washington. (Its Special Bibliographic Series).

Designed to present a relatively current listing of materials recently published. Emphasis is placed on English language publications. The Russian titles are transliterated and translated. The entries are alphabetically arranged by subject. An author index is included.

304. London, University, School of Oriental and African Studies. **A Cumulation of Selected and Annotated Bibliography of Economic Literature on the Arabic-Speaking Countries of the Middle East, 1938-1960.** Boston, G. K. Hall, 1967. 358 p.

Lists books, articles, reports, documents in English, French, and Arabic, arranged by region and country, sub-arranged by subject. Approximately 9,600 entries have been collected. Annual supplements are added.

305. Landskron, William A. **Official Serial Publications Relating to Economic Development in Africa South of the Sahara; a Preliminary List of English-language Publications.** Cambridge, Mass., Center for International Studies, Massachuset Institute of Technology, 1961. 43 p.

Lists serial publications in country arrangement. No information as to beginning date of publication is given.

306. Scientific Council for Africa South of the Sahara. **Inventory of Economic Studies Concerning Africa South of the Sahara; an Annotated Reading List of Books, Articles and Official Publications.** Ed. Peter Ady. London Commission for Technical Cooperation in Africa South of the Sahara, 1960. 301 p. (Its Publication, no. 30. Joint project, no. 4).

Arrangement is by geographical area and then by subject. Listed are books, periodical articles and documents beginning from 1945.

Asia

307. Ajia Keizai Kenkyujo. Tokyo. **Documentary Materials in Asian Countries:** Report of a Survey by a Study Group of the Institute of Asian Economic Affairs. Tokyo, Institute of Asian Economic Affairs, 1963. 198 p.

This translation of Japanese original reviews, publications and research reports issued by various government agencies and universities for the following Asian countries: Burma, Ceylon, Cambodia, India, Indonesia, Laos, Malaya, Pakistan, Philippines, Singapore, South Vietnam and Thailand. Listed publications are in English and in the native languages.

308. Benko, E. de, and Krishnan, V. N. **Research Sources for South Asian Studies in Economic Development;** a select list of serial publications. East Lansing, Mich., Michigan State University, 1966. 97 p. (Asian Studies Center. Occasional paper no. 4).

309. **Far Eastern Economic Review. . .** a Yearbook. Hong King, 1960 — Annual.

A most valuable source of economic information on countries and regions of East Asia excluding Asiatic Russia. Mainland China is also included. Main topics are: food and population, regional cooperation, banking and finance, trade and air, business and regional surveys, and statistics. Supplemented by the weekly Far Eastern Economic Review, 1946 —

310. **Southern Asia Social Science Bibliography, no. 1** — 1952 — Calcutta, Research Centre on the Social Implications of Industrialization in Southern Asia, 1954 — Annual. Title varies, Formed by merger of: South Asia Social Science Abstracts and South Asia Social Science Bibliography.

Covers such fields of social sciences as: sociology, social anthropology, political science and economics, which is the largest section. Lists books, pamphlets and periodical articles published in English; for Vietnam in French. Indexes of authors, subjects, and a list of periodicals are included.

311. United Nations. Economic Commission for Asia and the Far East. **Guide to Asian Economic Statistics.** Bangkok, 1957. 272 p.

Items arranged by subject. Includes a list of main publications of international agencies which. . . contain economic statistics for ECAFE countries.

Australia

312. Australia. Government. **The Australian Economy.** Canberra, Government Printer, 1956 — Annual.

Surveys the Australian economic conditions in a given year in comparison to previous years using numerous tables and illustrative material.

313. **Australian Public Affairs Information Service. A Subject Index to Current Literature (APAIS)** no. 1 — July 1945 — Monthly, with annual cumulations (since 1955 —).

Prepared as a subject guide to material on Australian political, economic and socio-cultural affairs; it indexes relevant articles in a wide range of periodicals in Australia and overseas. At the end of each issue is an author index.

314. Palmer, George R. **A Guide to Australian Economic Statistics.** Rev. ed. Melbourne, Macmillan, 1966. 324 p.

Canada

315. Bank of Canada, Ottawa. **Statistical Summary.** Jan. 1937 — Ottawa. Monthly.

An excellent summary of economic conditions in Canada. . . . Supplements have been published annually since 1954. Each volume brings together the data for several years.

316. **Bibliography of Current Publications on Canadian Economics, 1935-1952.** Toronto, University of Toronto Press, 2 v. Published in the Canadian Journal of Economics and Political Science. (Discontinued in 1952).

Items are entered in alphabetical order by subject. Included are government documents as well as a decennial index.

317. **Contribution to Canadian Economics.** Toronto, University of Toronto Press, 1928-34. 7 v. Superseded by Canadian Journal of Economics and Political Science.

Besides scholarly papers on economics, each issue contains a special section entitled, "A bibliography of current publications on Canadian economics."

318. Easterbrook, William Thomas, Watkins, M. H., eds. **Approaches to Canadian Economic History; a Selection of Essays.** Toronto, McClelland and Stewart, 1967. 292 p. (Carleton Library, no. 31).

Includes such topics as: economic factors in Canadian history, land policy and agriculture, banking and capital formation, the state and economic life. Bibliography: p. 259-292.

319. Innis, Harold Adams. **Selected Documents in Canadian Economic History, 1497-1783.** Toronto, University of Toronto Press, 1929. 581 p.

"The scope of this volume is limited to the period prior to 1783" (Pref.) Contents: pt. 1. The fishing industry and pt. 2. The fur trade. A select bibliography on Canadian economic history for the period after 1783: p. 579-581.

China

320. Chen, Nai-Ruen. **Chinese Economic Statistics; a Handbook for Mainland China.** Chicago, Aldine, 1966. 539 p.

Covers all aspects of economy in Communist China from 1949 to 1959. Bibl. 499-514.

321. **The Economy of Mainland China, 1949-1963; a Bibliography of Materials in English.** Berkeley, Calif., Committee on the Economy of China, Social Science Research Council, 1963. 297 p.

Part one lists references to primary sources (Chinese official documents, reports, announcements, etc.) semi-official and non-official publications such as articles and reports in newspapers. Part two covers materials published outside China. Includes translations of Communist Chinese materials.

322. Li, Cho-Min. **Economic Development of Communist China; an Appraisal of the First Five Years of Industrialization.** Berkeley, University of California Press, 1959. 284 p. (California, University Institute of Business and Economic Research Publications).

Presents an analysis of China's economy from 1952 to 1957 based on original sources in the Chinese language. Surveyed are such topics as industry, agriculture, national product, capital formation, finances, foreign trade, population. Many tables are attached. Bibliography: p. 261-273.

323. Sun, E-tu (Zen) and De Francis, John. **Bibliography on Chinese Social History; a Selected and Critical List of Chinese Periodical Sources.** New Haven, Institute of Far Eastern Languages, Yale University, 1952. 150 p.

324. Yüan, T'ung-li. **Economic and Social Development of Modern China; a Bibliographical Guide.** New Haven, Human Relations Files, 1956. 87 p. (Behavior Science Bibliographies).

The purpose of this compilation is to serve as a practical guide to publications on China's economy. Only essential titles listed in American libraries, limited to monographs and pamphlets in English, French, and German, from 1900 to 1955, are included.

Denmark

325. Denmark. Ministry of Foreign Affairs. **Economic Survey of Denmark.** 19 — Copenhagen, Schultz Farlag. Annual.

Surveys Danish economy in a given year, stressing development of agriculture, and reviews the prospects of economic growth.

Eastern Europe

326. Bodnar, Artur. **Gospodarka Europejskich Krajow Socjalistycznych;** zarys rozwoju w latach 1950-1975. Warszawa, Ksiazka i wiedza 1962. 390 p.

The economy of the European socialist countries; an outline of development in the years 1950-1975. Presents a comprehensive survey of the East European economies based on a wide variety of sources, not easily available in western countries.

Europe

327. Brussels. Université libre. Centre d'économie régionale. **Bibliographie Internationale d'Économie Régionale.** Bruxelles Université libre de Bruxelles, Institut de sociologie, 1964. 757 p.

An international bibliography of regional economics covers ten European countries (Belgium, France, Gt. Brit., Germany, Italy, Netherlands, Poland, Russia, Spain, Yugoslavia) with short sections on Asia, Australia and New Zealand.

328. Bullock, Alan Louis Charles and Taylor, A. J. P. **Select List of Books on European History, 1815-1914.** Edited for the Oxford Recent History Group, 2nd ed. Oxford, Clarendon Press, 1957. 79 p.

Limited to secondary works (books) in English and in the major West-European languages on history and economic history of Europe. The material is generally arranged by country in alphabetical order. No index is included.

329. **The Cambridge Economic History of Europe from the Decline of the Roman Empire.** Edited by J. H. Claphan and others. Cambridge, Cambridge University Press, 1942 –

This multivolume work of high scholarship, the product of study and research of many authorities and specialists, should be regarded as a major contribution to economic history. Very detailed bibliography sections follow the textual part in each volume. Indexes are included.

330. European Cultural Centre. **The European Bibliography.** Editors: Hjalmar Pehrsson and Hanna Wulf. Leyden, A. W. Sijthoff, 1965. 472 p.

Divided into nine chapters this selective and annotated bibliography lists books and some very important pamphlets in European history, arts, education, politics, law, general description, etc. Chapter 8: p. 327-421 is dedicated to Europe's economics. The greater part of the books listed have been published between 1945 and the end of 1963. Some fundamental works published before 1939 have been included. All notes have been written in English and French. However, notes in the original language of the book have been added in case of works written in German, Dutch, Italian and Spanish. Includes an index.

331. Knowles, Lilian Charlotte Anne **Economic Development in the Nineteenth Century: France, Germany, Russia and the United States.** London, G. Routledge, 1932. 368 p. (Studies in Economics and Political Science, no. 109).

Companion volume to the author's "The Industrial and Commercial Revolutions in Great Britain During the Nineteenth Century" (1921). The purpose "in writing this book has been to sketch the economic development of a hitherto neglected and yet most important century" (Pref.) Index is included.

332. Organization for European Economic Cooperation. Library. **Aide Américaine a l'Europe, 1947-1956:** bibliographie sélectionnée, documents officiels. . . **American Aid to Europe, 1947-1956;** selected bibliography, official United States documents on economic, financial and military aid, catalogued at the Library. Paris, 1956. 66 p.

333. Tarr, Raissa. **European Recovery Program (Marshall Plan). Programme de Relèvement Européen.** Paris, Organization for Economic Co-operation and Development, 1967. 99 p. (Bibliographie Spéciale Analytique. Special Annotated Bibliography, 14).

334. Twentieth Century Fund. **Europe's Needs and Resources, Trends and Prospects in Eighteen Countries.** by J. Frederic Dewhurst and others. New York, 1961. 1198 p.

This companion volume to America's Needs and Resources ' offers comprehensive statistics for 18 European countries excluding the Communist block area.

335. United Nations. Economic Commission for Europe. **Economic Survey of Europe.** 1947 — Geneva. Annual. Title varies: 1947, A survey of the economic situation. . . . 1952, Economic survey of Europe since the war.

Designed as a series of annual surveys of current economic conditions in Europe, including Eastern Europe. Includes numerous statistical tables and figures.

336. Wild, J. E. **The European Common Market and European Free Trade Association.** 3rd rev. ed. London, Library Association, 1962. 62 p. (Special subject list no. 35).

Lists books, pamphlets, reports, periodical articles, bibliographies, and reading material. Some entries are annotated. Name and subject indexes.

337. Wittkowski, Adolf. **Schrifttum zum Marschallplan und zur Wirtschaftlichen Integration Europas.** Im Auftrage und unter Mitwirkung des Bundesministeriums für den Marschallplan. Bad Godesberg, Bundesministerium für den Marschallplan, 1953. 382 p.

Title translated: The literature to Marshall plan and to economical integration of Europe.

Finland

338. Finland. Ministry of Finance. Division for Economic Affairs. **Economic Survey.** Helsinki, Akateeminen Kirkakauppa, 1948 — Annual.

Editions are in Finnish, Swedish and English.

France

339. Chambre de Commerce et d'Industrie, Paris, Biblioteque. **Bibliographie: Études et Articles Selectionés.** Paris, 1931 — Monthly. Title varies: 1931-49, Bibliographie d'Ouvrages et d'Articles Sélectionnés.

Covers various phases of economics, law, finances, business, commerce and industry.

340. Clough, Shepard Bancroft. **France: a History of National Economics, 1789-1939.** New York, C. Scribner, 1939. 498 p.

341. Cornut, Paul **Répartition de la Fortune Privée en France: par Departement et Nature de Biens au Cours de la Premiere Moitie du XX Siecle.** Pref. de F. Trevoux. Paris. A. Colin, 1963. 656 p.

Designed as an important survey of the size and distribution of wealth in France by departments (administrative unit of country division like a district or province) during the first half of the twentieth century, emphasizing the period of 1949-1953.

Germany

342. Born, Karl Erich, ed. **Moderne Deutsche Wirtschaftsgeschichte.** Köln. Kiepenheuer und Witsch, 1966. 535 p. (Neue Wissenschaftliche Bibliothek).

Presents a survey of the research problems related to the German economic history of industrial development in 19th and 20th century. The new research methods into German economic history are discussed. Included are indexes of persons and of institutions.

343. Brook, Warner Frederick. **Social and Economic History of Germany, 1888-1938;** a Comparative Study, with a foreword by J. F. Rees. New York, Russell & Russell, 1962. 291 p.

Divided into four chapters: 1. Elements and faces of the period; 2. The era of William II; 3. The Weimar Reich; 4. The Third Reich.

344. Piettré, Andre. **Economic Allemande Contemporaine; Allemagne Occidentale; 1945-52.** Préf. d'André Siegfried. Paris, M. T. Genin, 1952. 672 p.

345. Stolper, Gustav. **German Economy, 1870 to the Present.** by Gustav Stolper, Karl Hauser, and Knut Borchardt. Transl. by Toni Stolper. New York, Harcourt, Brace & World, 1967. 353 p.

Translation of Deutsche Wirtschaft seit 1870. This is a valuable edition of Stolper's original work "Deutsche Wirtschaft 1870-1940, which has been revised and enlarged and has been carried down to the present (1966). Index. Bibliography: p. 331-338.

Germany (Democratic Republic)

345a. Germany (Democratic Republic, 1949 —   )   Zentralinstitut für Bibliothekswesen. **Bibliographie zur Theorie und Praxis der Sozialis- tischen Wirtschaft.** (Bearb. von einem Kollektiv der Berliner Stadtbibliothek unter Leitung von Erich Kurschner) Leipzig, Verlag für Buch- und Biblio- thekswesen, 1955. 104 p.

Title translated: Bibliography on theory and practice of socialist economy.

Germany (Federal Republic)

346. Deutsche Bundesbank. **Report.** Frankfurt am Main, 1949— Annual.

A. Economic trends and policy of the Bundesbank; B. Annual statement using statistical tables. Supplemented by Monthly report of the Bundesbank.

347. Wallich, Henry Christopher. **Mainsprings of the German Revival.** New Haven, Yale University Press, 1955. 401 p. (Yale Studies in Economics, v. 5) Bibliography: p. 388-393.

348. **Wirtschaft und Statistik.** Bonn, Statistisches Bundesamt. Monthly.

Presents articles on economics, economic development and indicators, graphs, price index and numerous statistical tables, statistical cumulations, etc.

Great Britain

349. Akademiia nauk S.S.S.R. Fundamental'naia biblioteka obshchestvennykh nauk. **Natsionalizatsiia i Problemy Natsionalizirovanykh Otraslei v Velikobritanii v Poslevoennyi Period;** bibliograficheskii ukazatel'knig i zhurnal'nykh statei za 1946-1963 g.g. Moskva, 1964. 137 p.

Title transl: Nationalization and problems of nationalized branches in Great Britain during and after the World War II period: Bibliographical listing of books and periodical articles, 1946-1963.

350. Anderson, Adam. **An Historical and Chronological Deduction of the Origin of Commerce, from the Earliest Accounts.** Containing a History of the Great Commercial Interests of the British Empire. Without introd. An 18th century guidebook for economic policy, by Joseph Dorfrman. New York, A. M. Kelley, 1967. 4 v. (Reprint of Economic Classics). Reprinted from 1788-1801 ed.

Arranged chronologically: vol. 1. covers the period from 2300 B.C. to 1500 A. D.; vol. 2. 1501 to 1700; vol. 3. 1701- to 1762; vol. 4. was compiled by Combe and covers the period 1763 to 1788. This set is an important work in economic history.

351. Ashley, Sir William James. **Introduction to English Economic History and Theory.** New York, A. M. Kelley, 1966. 2 v. in 1. (Reprints of Economic Classics).

Bibliographical references in "Notes" at end of each volume. Divided into two parts: 1. The Middle Ages; 2. The end of the Middle Ages. Index is included at the end of each part.

352. **Bibliography of British History.** Issued under the direction of the American Historical Association and the Royal Historical Society of Great Britain. Oxford,

Clarendon Press, 1928-59. 3 v.

Covers also economic history of Great Britain. Particularly important for economists are volumes: Tudor period, 1485-1603, ed. by Conyers Read. 2nd ed. 1959 and The eighteenth century, 1714-1789, ed. by Stanley Pargellis and D. J. Medley, 1951.

353. **British Commonwealth Year Book.** 1st. — 1952 — London, Newman Neame, etc. Annual. Title varies: 1952, Commonwealth co-operation. 1953/54 - 1959/60, The Empire and Commonwealth year book.

354. Carter, Charles Frederick and Roy, A. D. **British Economic Statistics; a Report.** Cambridge, Eng., University Press, 1954. 188 p. (National Institute of Economic and Social Research. Economic and Social Studies, 14).

355. Clapham, Sir John Harold. **An Economic History of Modern Britain.** Cambridge, Cambridge University Press, 1959. 3 v.

Contents: v. 1. The early railway age, 1820-1850. v. 2. Free trade and steel, 1850-1886. v. 3. Machines and national rivalries (1887-1914) with an epilogue (1914-1929). Index is added at the end of each volume. Bibliographical footnotes.

356. Devons, Ely. **An Introduction to British Economic Statistics.** Cambridge, Eng., University Press, 1956. 254 p.

357. **Dun & Bradstreet's Guide to Key British Enterprises.** 1961 — London.

A standard reference source for the subject.

358. The Economist (London). **The Businessman's Guide to Britain, 1956;** compiled by the Economist Intelligence Unit. London, Chatto & Windus, 1956. 155 p.

359. Great Britain. Central Office of Information. **Britain: an Official Handbook.** London, H.M. Stationery Office. 1946 — Annual from 1954 —

Gives summaries of institutions and life in Great Britain. Covers the national economy, industry, transport, finances, labor, trade, social welfare, politics, arts, etc. Includes detailed index.

360. Great Britain. Ministry of Labour. **Statistics on Incomes, Prices, Employment & Production.** Bulletin no. 1 — April 1962 — London, H. M. Stationery Office.

Covers data for the United Kingdom except Northern Ireland.

361. Hall, Hubert, ed. **A Select Bibliography for the Study, Sources and Literature of English Mediaeval Economic History.** Compiled by a Seminar of the London School of Economics under the supervision of Hubert Hall. London, King, 1914. 350 p. (Studies in Economics and Political Science.

Series of Bibliographies, 41). Another issue is reprint: New York, B. Franklin, 1960.

Contents: 1. Introductory (Numerous bibliographical sources). 2. The sources of medieval economic history, 3. Modern works.

362. Hamilton, Henry. **History of the Homeland, the Story of the British Background.** London, G. Allen and Unwin, 1947. 597 p. (Primers for the Age of Plenty, no. 4).

Offers a very well organized list of references at the end of the textual part. Bibliography: p. 565-579.

363. Hanson, Laurence William. **Contemporary Printed Sources for British and Irish Economic History, 1701-1750.** Cambridge, University Press, 1963. 978 p.

364. Knowles, Lillian Charlotte Anne (Tomm). **Economic Development of the British Overseas Empire.** London, Routledge, 1924 — v. (Studies in Economics and Political Science, no. 76).

Contents: v. 1. The Empire as a whole; the British tropics; v. 2. Comparative view of Dominion problems: Canada; v. 3. Economic history of Australasia and South Africa. Indexes are included. Bibliography: v. 2, p. 589-599.

365. Knowles, Lilian Charlotte Anne (Tomm). **The Industrial and Commercial Revolutions in Great Britain During the Nineteenth Century.** 4th rev. ed. London, Routledge, 1926. 416 p. (London School of Economics. Studies in Economics and Political Science, no. 61.)

Brings out the causes which led to the introduction of machinery which made Great Britain the industrial power of the nineteenth century world. Stressed is the role of mechanical transport in the world position of the United Kingdom. A general index is included. Bibliography: p. 393-403.

366. Lewes, F. M. M. **Statistics of the British Economy.** London, Allen & Unwin, 1967. 200 p.

Covers: labor, production, distribution, transport, companies, finance, overseas trade, and national accounting. Bibliography at the end of each chapter.

367. Mantoux, Paul Joseph. **The Industrial Revolution in the Eighteenth Century:** an Outline of the Beginning of the Modern Factory System in England. Rev. ed. Translated from the French by M. Vernon. London, J. Cape, 1928. Reprinted 1961 —

This is a translation of a French classic in economic history. Bibliography: p. 491-518.

368. Power, Eileen Edna. **Industrial Revolution, 1750-1850; a Select Bibliography.** Compiled for the Economic History Society. London, Economic History Society, 1927. 30 p. (Economic History Society. Bibliographies, no. 1).

369. Pugh, Ralph Bernard. **The Records of the Colonial and Dominion Offices.** London, H.M. Stationery Off., 1964. 118p. (Public Record Office Handbooks, no. 3).

Describes the systems of administration of the Commonwealth of Nations matters, examines the records established in the 17th century until 1947. Includes an annotated list of the records.

370. Society of Investment Analysts. **A Bibliography for Investment and Economic Analysis.** London, 1965. 104p.

Provides source material on economic conditions of Great Britain according to special classification scheme.

371. Williams, Judith Blow. **A Guide to the Printed Materials for English Social and Economic History, 1750-1850.** New York, Columbia University Press, 1926. 2 v. (Records of Civilization: Sources and Studies).

An annotated and selective bibliography of books, pamphlets, periodicals related to social and economic conditions in Great Britain during the Industrial Revolution. The material is divided into two large parts: (1) works of general reference, and (2) works regarding special subjects, with an index of authors and a guide to subjects at the end.

India

372. Anstey, Vera (Powell) **Economic Development of India,** 4th ed. London, Longmans, Green, 1957.   677 p.

Presents "a synthetic impartial view of the recent development, present position, and main problems of Indian economic life" (Pref.) Included are maps, statistical tables and an index. Bibliography: p. 639-656.

373. India. Dept. of Economic Affairs. **India Pocket Book of Economic Information,** 19 — New Delhi, 19 —

A valuable reference handbook on economic conditions in India, with statistical tables, figures, maps, and bibliographical sources.

374. India. Government. **Economic Survey. . .** New Delhi; Govt. of India Press, Annual.

In two parts: part 1 contains a general survey of economic development in the preceding year; part 2 gives more detailed analysis in various sectors of the national economy. Includes many tables and diagrams.

Indonesia

375. Hicks, George L. and McNicoll, Geoffrey. **The Indonesian Economy, 1950-1965; a Bibliography.** New Haven, Southeast Studies, Yale University, 1967. 248 p. (Yale University, Southeast Asia Studies. Bibliography Series, no. 9)

An annotated bibliography of publications on the postwar Indonesian economy written in English and Indonesian languages. It includes books, pamphlets, periodicals, serial articles, annuals, government documents, and reports, divided into 27 subject groups. Author and subject indexes, as well as a list of serials are appended.

Iran

376. Organization for Economic Cooperation and Development. Development Centre. **Bibliographie sur l'Iran.** Bibliography on Iran. Paris, 1965. 305 p.

Italy

377. Banco di Roma. **Review of the Economic Conditions in Italy.** Rome, 1947 — v. 1 —

Includes lengthy statistical section, and few book reviews.

378. Clough, Shepard Bancroft. **The Economic History of Modern Italy.** New York, Columbia University Press, 1963. 458 p.

Presents an economic history of Italy for the last one hundred years, illustrated with facts and figures. Therories are avoided. Main aspects of this work are Italy's agriculture, banking, population and labor. Includes a general index. Bibliographical references included in "Notes" p. 385-422.

379. Cossa, Luigi. **Saggi Bibliografici di Economia Politica.** Pref. di Luigi Saggi. Bologna, A. Forni, 1963. 452 p. (Bibliografie e opere classiche di economia politics, no. 1).

Japan

380. **Economic Survey of Japan.** Tokyo, Japanese Government Publications Service Center, 1969. 237 p.

Published annually it presents the conditions of the Japanese economy and the problems confronting it. Numerous statistical tables, charts, and diagrams accompany articles, reports, and briefs. A special section with basic data for charts and tables in the text is appended.

381. **Japan Science Review: Economic Sciences.** no. 1 — 1953 — Tokyo, Japan Union of Associations of Economic Sciences. Annual.

Covers two kinds of bibliographies; one which lists publications issued in postwar Japan in Western languages, and the other which includes publications in Japanese only.

382. **Japanese Economic Statistics, Bulletin no. 1 —** Tokyo, Economic Planning Agency, Japanese Government, 19 — Monthly.

In two parts: 1. Indicators, 2. Supplementary statistics. Covers: production and business, prices, foreign trade, finance, labor and wages, household economy, pre-war base indexes, national income and accounting, industrial production, transportation, etc.

383. **Keizagaku Bunken Kiho. Quarterly Bibliography of Economics.** Compiled by Keizai Shiryo Kyogikai (Association for Documentation in Economics) Tokyo, Yuhikaku, 1956 — v. 1, no. 1 — Quarterly.

The most valuable current Japanese bibliography which includes periodical articles in Japanese, Chinese and Russian (only up to 1960), English, French and German.

384. Komiya, Ryutaro, comp. **A Bibliography of Studies in English on the Japanese Economy.** Tokyo, University of Tokyo Press, 1966. 52 p. (Tokyo Daigaku. Nihon Keizai Kenkyusho. Research materials series, no. 3).

The aim of this bibliography is to survey articles, books, and pamphlets published in English on the Japanese Economy. Government publications and unpublished Ph.D. theses have been excluded. Most of the material is of the last two decades.

385. **The Oriental Economist's Japan Economic Yearbook.** Tokyo, Oriental Economist, 1954 — Biennial (irregular).

A comprehensive economic yearbook in the English language devoted exclusively to the study and analysis of Japan's economic, financial, and industrial development. Contents: Chronology for the covered year, economic transitions, industries, statistics, list of companies, and index to company list.

386. Remer, Charles Frederick, and Kawai, Saburo. **Japanese Economics: a Guide to Japanese Reference and Research Materials.** Ann Arbor, University of Michigan Press, 1956. 91 p. (University of Michigan. Center for Japanese Studies. Bibliographical Series, no. 5).

Presents an annotated bibliography on Japanese economic reference literature.

387. Rosovsky, Henry, comp. **Quantitative Japanese Economic History; an Annotated Bibliography and a Survey of U. S. Holdings.** Compiled by Henry Rosovsky in association with Harry Nishio and Konosuke Odaka. Published by the Center for Japanese Studies of the Institute of International Studies, and the Institute of Business and Economic Research, University of California

(Berkeley) 1961. 173 p.

Restricted to sources in the Japanese language published since 1868 to the present. Includes a detailed table of contents and indexes of authors and tables.

Latin America

388. Bayitch, S. A. **Latin America: A Bibliographical Guide to Economy, History, Law, Politics and Society.** Coral Gables, Florida, University of Miami Press, 1961. 335 p. (University of Miami School of Law, International legal studies.)

Contains: 1. Introduction; 2. General information on Latin America; 3. Fundamentals and backgrounds; 4. Guide, by subjects; 5. Guide, by countries. Subject index with country-subdivision.

389. Bayitch, S. A. **Latin America and the Caribbean: a Bibliographical Guide to Works in English.** Coral Gables, University of Florida Press; Dobbs Ferry, N. Y., Oceana Publications, 1967. 943 p.

A valuable list emphasizing economic, political and legal aspects.

390. Committee on Latin America. **Latin American Economic & Social Serials.** With a pref. by Sir John Walker and a note on periodical indexes by A. J. Walford and Peter Hoare. Hamden, Conn., Published on behalf of COLA by Archon Books, 1969. 189 p.

391. Harvard University. Bureau for Economic Research in Latin America. **The Economic Literature of Latin America; a Tentative Bibliography.** Cambridge, Mass., Harvard University Press, 1935-1964.

The objective of this bibliography is to serve as a working tool for students interested in the economic affairs of Latin America. Included are monographs, pamphlets, periodical articles, and a few government publications. Classification is by area and country, which are further subdivided into topics. Includes an index.

392. Inter-American Statistical Institute. **Boletin Estadistico,** Washington, 1965 — Monthly.

Provides monthly economic statistics for Latin America countries. Each issue covers one topic only.

393. Rosario, Argentine Republic (Santa Fe) Universidad Nacional de Litoral. **Desarrollo Economico, Mercado Comun y Alianza para el Progreso; Bibliografia Actualizada.** 2 ed. Rosario, 1963. 265 p.

394. Sable, Martin H. **A Guide to Latin American Studies.** Los Angeles, Latin American Center, University of California, 1967. 2 v. (783 p.)

Presents an annotated list of books, pamphlets, serials, and periodical articles on Latin America. The entries are arranged by subject emphasizing economic conditions, banking, commerce, international financial and technical assistance, and statistics.

395. Sable, Martin H. **Master Directory for Latin America,** containing ten directories covering organizations, associations, and institutions in the fields of agriculture, business industry-finance, communications, education-research, government, international cooperation, labor-cooperatives, publishing and religion, and professional, social and social service organizations and associations. Los Angeles, Latin American Center, University of California, 1965. 438 p. (Latin American Center, University of California, Los Angeles. Reference series, no. 21).

396. Sable, Martin H. **Periodicals for Latin American Economic Development, Trade and Finance;** an Annotated Bibliography. Los Angeles, Latin American Center, University of California, 1965. 72 p. (California University, University of Los Angeles. Latin American Center. Reference Series, no. 3).

This is a selected and annotated list of English and foreign language periodicals published mainly in the United States, in Latin America and in some West European countries, covering economics and related fields.

397. Sauter, Hermann. **Wirtshaft und Entwicklung Lateinamerikas; Ausgewählte, Neuere Literatur.** Hamburg, Institut für Iberoamerika-Kunde, 1967-68. 3 v. (Reihe "Bibliographie und Documentation", Heft, 11).

Economy and development of Latin America; selected new literature.

398. United Nations. Economic Commission for Latin America. **Economic Survey of Latin America.** New York, 1949 — Annual.

Presents agricultural, economic, business and trade development in Latin America, giving numerous tables, figures and sources cited.

399. United Nations. Economic Commission for Latin America. **Economic Bulletin for Latin America, 1956 —**

Supplements and updates the annual Economic Survey.

400. Wilhelms, C., and Almeida Sedas, J. G. de comp. **Quellenverzeichnis zur Wirtschaftsstatistik Iberoamerikas.** Hamburg. Institut fur Iberoamerika-Kunde, 1966. 199 p.

Lists sources for Latin America study, mainly the official statistical publications and bank reports, supplying names and addresses of statistical bureaus and institutes.

401. Wish, John R. **Economic Development in Latin America, an Annotated Bibliography.** New York, Praeger, 1965. 144 p. (Praeger Special Studies in International Economics and Development).

Contains current publications (books, pamphlets, articles, documents) on Latin America's economy. Included material has been divided into six groups: 1. Orientation, 2. Economic development, 3. Marketing, 4. Agriculture, 5. Communications, and 6. Methodology.

Middle East

402. **A Selected and Annotated Bibliography of Economic Literature on the Arabic-Speaking Countries of the Middle East, 1938 - 1952.** Beirut, American Univ. of Beirut, Economic Research Institute, 1954. 199 p. Annual supplements. 1955 —

Lists books, pamphlets, periodical articles and reports in English, French and Arabic. Material is arranged by country. Includes an author index.

403. United Nations. Dept. of Economic and Social Affairs. **Economic Developments in the Middle East. . .** New York, 1955 — Biennial.

Supplement to the "World Economic Survey." Surveys such topics as agriculture, industry, petroleum, imports and exports and statistical appendix. Supersedes Economic Developments in the Middle East, 1945 to 1954. N. Y., United Nations, 1955. 236 p.

New Zealand

404. Carey, Richard H., and Holmes, Frank W. **A Preliminary Bibliography of New Zealand Economics and Economic History.** Wellington, Victoria University of Wellington, 1967. clviii, 4p.

Incorporates works listed in A Bibliography of New Zealand Economics and Economic History, by B.G. Hardie, 1953; includes the relevant work done between 1952 and 1965.

405. Condliffe, John Bell. **New Zealand in the Making**; a Study of Economic and Social Development. 2nd rev. ed. London, Allen & Unwin, 1959. 316p.

Describes the economic development of the Dominion prior to 1935; however, some economic questions, such as the economic status of the Maoris, the exploration of the native forests and phormium industry have been carried down to 1956. An index is included. Notes and references p. 285-307.

406. New Zealand. Government. **Economic Review,** 1966. Wellington, Government Printer, 1966 —

Published annually. Surveys the national economy in the past year indicating the trends for the future.

Norway

407. Norway. Statistisk Sentralbyra. **Norges Økonomi Etter Krigen.** . . Oslo, 1965. 437 p.

Surveys in twelve chapters the Norwegian post-war economy, 1946-63, with summaries in English.

407a. Norway, Statistisk Sentralbyra. **Okonomisk Utsyn over Aret.** . . Oslo, 19 — Annual.

Contains two main parts: world economic conditions, and Norway economy. Summary is given in English.

Pakistan

408. Siddiqui, Akhtar H. **The Economy of Pakistan; a Selected Bibliography, 1947-1962.** Karachi, Institute of Development Economics, 1963. 162 p. (Institute of Development Economics, Karachi Special Publications.)

Includes more than 4,200 items (books, pamphlets, government documents, periodicals, articles, reports, and papers on Pakistan's economy). The arrangement is by subject according to a special classification scheme devised by the International Committee for Social Sciences Documentation, Paris. Detailed subject and author indexes, also list of periodicals are added at end of the book.

409. Pakistan. Ministry of Finance. Economic Adviser. **Pakistan Economic Survey.** . . Karachi, Manager of Publications. Annual.

Contains numerous statistical tables, graphs, bibliographical footnotes, and summary of main findings.

Peru

410. Organization for Economic Cooperation and Development. Development Centre. **Bibliographie sur la Perou. Bibliography on Peru.** Paris, 1965. 211 p.

Poland

411. **Rocznik Bibliograficzny Polskich Wydawnictw Ekonomicznych;** t. 1 — 1945/46 — Warszawa, Nakl. Centralnego Urzedu Planowania. Annual.

Title translated: Bibliographical yearbook of Polish economic publications.

412. Warsaw. Szkola Glówna Planowania i Statystyki: Biblioteka. **Bibliografia Publikacji Poracownikow Naukowych Szkoly Glównej Planowania i Statystyki w Okresie xx-lecia PRL.** Warszawa, 1965. 2 v.

This is a collection of bibliographies of about three hundred Polish economists living and teaching in Poland's capital Warsaw in the last two decades after the war. The general arrangement is alphabetical by name, and chronological under name. Includes books, pamphlets, articles and reports.

Portugal

413. **Bibliografia Sobre a Economia Portuguesa.** v. 1 — 1948/49 — Lisboa, Instituto Nacional de Estatistica. Annual, (Publicacoes do Centro de Estudos Economicos).

Russia (The Soviet Union)

414. Akademiia nauk S.S.S.R. Fundamental'naia biblioteka obshchestvennykh nauk. **Marksistsko-Leninskaia Politicheskaia Economiia; Bibliograficheskii Ukazatel'.** Moskva, 1956 —

Transl.: Marxist and Leninist political economy; a bibliographical guide.

415. Akademiia nauk S.S.S.R. Fundamental'naia biblioteka obshchestvennykh nauk. **Narodnoe Khoziaistvo S.S.S.R.** Osnovnye fondy promeshlennosti i ikh izpol'zovanie. Ukazatel' sovetskoi literatury, 1945-1964. (Sostaviteli: T.P. Andrushchenko, E.B. Margolina; otv. redaktor E.V. Bazhanova) Moskva, Nauka, 1966. 161p.

Title translated: The capital investment in the national economy. The basic funds of industry and their use; a guide to Soviet literature, 1945-1964.

416. _____. **Narodnoe Khoziaistvo S.S.S.R. v 1917-1920 gg. Bibliograficheskii ukazatel Knizhnoi i zhurnalnoi literatury na Russkom iazyke, 1917-1963 gg.** Moskva, 1967. 618p.

Title translated: The National Economy of the Soviet Union during the Years 1917-1920. Bibliographical guide to monographic and periodical literature published in Russian in 1917-1963. This is the first comprehensive Soviet retrospective bibliography in economics, with a total of 9311 entries, most of them annotated. Future volumes are planned.

417. Akademiia nauk S.S.S.R. Fundamental'naia biblioteka obshchestvennykh nauk. **Razvitie Mirovoi Sotsiialisticheskoi Sistemy Khoziaistva; Ekonomicheskoe Sotrudnitchestvo Evropeiskikh Sotsialisticheskikh Stran-Uchastnits SEV;** bibliografiia. Knigi i stat'i 1957-1962 gg. (Otvetstv. red. E.M. Kan) Moskva, 1964. 167p.

Title translated: The Growth of the World Socialist System of Economy; economic cooperation among the European socialist countries-members of SEV (Council of Economic Assistance). Bibliography. Books and articles 1957-1962.

418. Akademiia nauk S.S.S.R. Fundamental'naia biblioteka obshchestvennykh nauk. **Tsenoobrazovanie v Narodnom Khoziaistve S.S.S.R.** Tsenoobrazuiushchie Faktory. Bibliograficheskii ukazatel' knizhnoi i zhurnal'noi sovetskoi literatury . . za 1960-1964 gg. (Sostavitel' T.P. Bogatyreva) Moskva, 1966. 227p.

Designed as a bibliographical guide to Soviet literature (books and periodical articles including "Pravda" and "Ekonomicheskaia gazeta") on prices in the Soviet economy during the period of 1960-1964.

419. Alampier, P. M. **Ekonomicheskoe Raionovanie S.S.S.R.** Moskva, Ekomizdat, 1959-63. 2v.

This is another systematic and annotated list of literature on economic regions in the Soviet Union published between 1918-1963. Includes 450 entries.

420. Borisova, N. V. and others. **Bibliograficheskii Spravochnik Opublikovannykh Nauchnykh Rabot Professorsko-Prepodavatel' skogo Kollektiva Moskovskogo Ekonomiko- Statisticheskogo Instituta.** Moskva, 1962. 91 p.

This is a bibliographical listing of publications written by the professors and instructors of the Economic-Statistical Institute in Moscow. The period covered is from 1920 to June 1962.

421. _____. **Bibliograficheskii Spravochnik Pechatnikh Rabot Prepodavatelei i Vospitannikov Moskovskogo Ekonomiko-Statisticheskogo Instituta.** Moskva, 1957. 63 p.

Transl.: Bibliographical listing of published works written by teachers and instructors of the Moscow Economic-Statistical Institute.

421a. **Bibliografiia po Voprosam Politicheskoi ekonomii (1917-1966)** Pod obshchei redaktsiei N. A. Tsagolova. Moskva, Izd-vo Moskovskogo universiteta, 1969. 551 p.

"First attempt to systematize literature on political economy published in the U.S.S.R. in Russian language for the period from 1917 to 1966" (Pref.). This work represents the most comprehensive bibliography on economics in Russian. Includes an index of persons.

422. Chernevskii, P. O. comp. **Ukazatel' Materialov dlia Istorii Torgovli, Promyshlennosti i Finansov v Predelakh Rossiiskoi Imperii ot Drevneishikh Vremen do Kontsa XVIII Stoletiia.** St. Petersburg, 1883.

Transl.: A guide to the materials in history of trade, industry and finance published in the Russian Empire from the earliest time to the end of the 18th century. This is a partially annotated guide to selective bibliography of books and periodical articles on history of Russian economic development.

423. **Ekonomicheskaia Nauka i Khoziaistvennaia Praktika; Ekonomicheskii Ezhegodnik.** Moskva, Ekonomika, 1965 —

Translated title: Economics—Theory and practice; Economic Yearbook. Presents in textual and tabular forms, economic conditions in the Soviet Union and the Soviet Bloc countries supplying statistical data of the past, the present and the plans for future development. A special bibliographical chapter lists the most recent literature on economics in these countries.

424. **Ékonomicheskaia Zhizn' S.S.S.R.: Khronika Sobitii i Faktov, 1917-1965.** Izd. 2., dop. Glav. redaktor S. G. Strumilin. Red. kollegiia: G. V. Aleksenko

Moskva, Sov. entsiklopediia, 1967. 2 v.

Title translated: Economic life of the U.S.S.R.; chronicle of events and facts, 1917-1965.

425. Ékonomika i Planirovanie Sovetskoi Kooperativnoi Torgovli. Izd. 2., perer. i dop. Moskva, Ekonomika, 1967. 414 p.

Title translated: Economics and planning of Soviet cooperative commerce.

426. Ékonomika Sotsiialisticheskikh Stran v Tsifrakh; kratkii statisticheskii sbornik. 1960 — Moskva, Izd-vo sotsiial'noekon. lit-ry. Annual. Title varies: 1960-61: Ekonomika stran sotsiialisticheskogo lageria v tsifrakh.

Transl.: Economy of socialist countries in numbers; a short statistical survey.

427. Georgievskii, P. I. Ukazatel' Russkoi Ekonomicheskoi Literatury s Prilozheniem Spiska Statei Nekotorykh Inostrannykh Zhurnalov. St. Petersburg. 1903-05. 2 v.

Transl. A guide to Russian economic literature with supplementary listings of articles in some foreign periodicals. Presents a well arranged bibliography of books, pamphlets and periodical articles published between 1878-1902. About 3,000 entries are included. This work supplements N. Novikov's Bibliograficheskii Ukazatel'.

428. Grierson, Philip. Books on Soviet Russia, 1917-42; a Bibliography and a Guide to Reading. London, Methuen, 1943. 354 p.

A bibliography of books and pamphlets on post-revolutionary Russia that have been published in Great Britain covering the twenty-five years period between 1917-1942. Contents: 1. Introduction; 2. The Revolution and the civil war; 3. The Soviet State; 4. The economic life of the Soviet Union; 5. Culture and social life; Appendixes and an Index.

429. Holzman, Franklyn D. ed. Readings on the Soviet Economy. Chicago, Rand McNally, 1962. 763 p. (Rand McNally Economic Series).

This collection of forty-one articles and excerpts from books on Soviet economy covers the following major subject fields: 1. Statistics and measurement, 2. The price system, 3. Aspects of the Soviet industrialization model, 4. Economic growth, 5. Planning, 6. Enterprise and organizations of industry, 7. Agricultural organization and policies, 8. Finance, 9. The consumer and worker, 10. Foreign trade. Bibliography: p. 747-763.

430. Horecky, Paul L. ed. Russia and the Soviet Union: a Bibliographic Guide to Western Language Publications. Chicago, Univ. of Chicago Press, 1965. 473 p.

Lists 1,966 numbered entries by 31 contributors in nine chapters: 1. General references; 2. General and descriptive works; 3. Land; 4. The people;

5. The nations; 6. History; 7. The state; 8. The economic and social structure; 9. The intellectual and cultural life. Includes an author and title index.

431. Karataev, S. L. **Bibliografiia Finansov, Promyshlennosti i Torgovli so Vremen Petra Velikogo po Nastoiashchee Vremia, s 1714 po 1879 g. Vkliuchitel'no.** St. Petersburg, 1880.

Transl.: Bibliography of finance, industry and trade from the time of Peter the Great to the present. Planned to be published in three volumes; only volume one has been issued. Contains over 6,000 entries of economic literature covering the period from 1714 to 1879. This work includes also historical survey of Russian economic literature for the period covered, and author and translators index.

432. Koltun, M. I. Ékonomischeskoe Raionirovanie Sovetskogo Soiuza i Dorevoliutsionnoi Rossii. (Istoriia i teoriia voprosa). Bibliograficheskii ukazatel'. Red. V. V. Klevenskaia. Moskva, Gos, b-ka S.S.S.R., 1959. 44 p.

Title translated: Economic regions of the Soviet Union and Prerevolutionary Russia; a bibliographical listing. Contains books, pamphlets and articles published from 1727 to 1958. Includes more than 400 entries of which part is annotated. A name index is added.

433. Moscow. Gosudarstvennaia publichnaia biblioteka. **Velikaia Programma Stroitel'stva Kommunizma; Ukazatel' Literatury.** Moskva, Izd-vo Vses. Knizhnoi palaty, 1962. 79 p.

Transl.: The great program of building of communism; listing of literature.

434. Moscow, Publichnaia biblioteka. **Chto Chitat' po Politicheskoi Ekonomii;** Rekomendatel'nyi ukazatel' literatury (Sostavitel' G. K. Donskaia. Red. M. N. Iakovleva). Moskva, 1959-60. 2 v. (Biblioteka Samoobrazovaniia).

Transl.: What to read in political economy; a reference guide of literature.

435. Moscow. Publichnaia biblioteka. Otdel Spravochno-bibliograficheskoi i inofrmatsionnoi raboty. **Ekonomika S. S. S. R. Annotirovannyi Perechen' Otechestvennykh Bibliografii, Opublikovannykh, v 1917-1964 gg.** Sostavitel' V. E. Sivolgin. Moskva, Kniga, 1965. 158 p.

Title translated: The economy of the U.S.S.R., an annotated guide to Russian bibliographies published during 1917-1964. The arrangement of this very comprehensive bibliography of bibliographies is based on special classification prepared by Moscow Public Library. Author and title index is included.

436. **Narodnoe Khoziaĭstvo S.S.S.R. . . . . Statisticheskiĭ Ezhegodnik.** Moskva, Statistika, 1956 — Annual.

Presents a comprehensive yearly survey of various aspects of the Soviet life. All material is arranged under numerous main headings. Retrospective figures go back to 1940. Includes explanatory notes and an index.

437. **Novaia Sovetskaia Ékonomicheskaia Literatura.** 1934 — Moskva, Akademiia nauk S.S.S.R. Fundamental'naia biblioteka obshchestvennykh nauk, 1934 —

Transl.: The new Soviet economic literature. Title varies. Contains books, pamphlets, periodical articles, reports and papers on economics and Soviet economic conditions, in Russian and other languages of the Soviet Union.: Includes also reviews and translations from foreign languages. Sometimes brief annotations are used. All aspects of economic life of the U.S.S.R. are well covered.

438. Novikov, N. "Bibliograficheskii Ukazatel' Knig i Statei po Politicheskoi Ekonomii na Russkom Iazyke, s 1801 po 1898 g." (In Konrad, I. **Ocherk Osnov Politicheskoi Ekonomii.** Moscow. 1898).

Transl.: Bibliographical guide to books and periodical articles in political economy issued in Russian language. Published as an addition to Russian translation of the "work by I. Konrad," Ocherk osnov politicheskoi ekonomii," this bibliography lists books published in the period of 1880 to 1898 and periodical articles published between 1801 and 1898.

439. Panchenko, E. N. and Boiko, N. P. **Ukazatel' Rabot, Opublikovannykh Nauchnymi Sotrudnikami Instituta Ekonomiki; Akademii Nauk U.S.S.R. Posle XX S"ezda K.P.S.S. (1956-1964).** Kiev, Akademiia nauk U.S.S.R., Inst. ekonomiki, 1964. 287 p.

This is a bibliographical listing of publications on economics written by the collaborators of Economic Institute of the Academy of Sciences of the Ukrainian Soviet Socialist Republic and issued during the period of 1956-1964. 1300 items are listed. Updated every three or four years.

440. Pokrovskii, Ivan Fedorovich. **Propaganda Literatury po Voprosam Konkretnoi Ekonomiki;** Leningrad, Publichnaia biblioteka im. M. E. Saltykova-Shchedrina, 1960. 233 p.

Transl.: Propaganda of the literature on applied economics.

441. Schwartz, Harry. **The Soviet Economy; a Selected Bibliography of Materials in English.** Syracuse, Syracuse University Press, 1949. 93 p.

Contains monographs, pamphlets, periodical articles and reports on Soviet economy in English, also includes translations of some valuable material published originally in Russian. Index of authors is added.

442. U. S. Congress. Joint Economic Committee. **Dimensions of Soviet Economic Power; Studies.** Washington, U. S. Govt. Print. Off., 1962. 744 p.

"A selected bibliography of recent Soviet monographs": p. 671-688. Designed as a survey study of all sectors of Soviet economic life, it covers data for various years between 1914 and 1960. Includes statistics on population, agriculture, culture and education as well as all other branches of national economy.

443. U. S. Congress. Joint Economic Committee. **Annual Economic Indicators for the U.S.S.R.: Materials.** Washington, U. S. Govt. Print Off., 1964. 218 p.

"Designed primarily to bring up to date the basic quantitative data contained in the compendium 'Dimensions of Soviet Economic Power' which the Joint Economic Committee published in December 1962."

444. _____. **Current Economic Indicators for the U.S.S.R.: Materials.** Washington, U. S. Govt. Print Off., 1965. 220 p.

This is a successor to the previous two reports (above) bringing up-to-date the basic statistical data.

445. U. S. Library of Congress. Legislative Reference Service. **Soviet Economic Growth: a Comparison with the United States;** a Study Prepared for the Subcommittee on Foreign Economic Policy of the Joint Economic Committee, Washington, 1957. 149 p.

445a. **Ves' S.S.S.R.; Ekonomicheskii, Finansovyi, Politicheskii i Administrativnyi Spravochnik.** Moskva. Gosizdat, 1926. 1269 p.

Contains over 1,000 books and periodical publications issued during the period of 1917-1925. Transl.: All U.S.S.R.; Economical, financial, political, and administrative guide.

446. Vol'f. R. A. **Itogi Pervogo 10-letiia Sotsiialisticheskogo Stroitel'stva, S.S.S.R. (1917-1927 gg);** sistimaticheskii ukazatel' knig i zhurnal'nykh statei, vyshedshikh v sviazi s 10-letiem Oktiabr'skoi revoluitsii. Moskva, Gos. tsentr. kn. palata R.S.F.S.R., 1931. 133 p.

Title translated: Summary of the first decade of the Socialist regime in the U.S.S.R. (1917-1927): a systematic listing of books and periodical articles. Contains more than 2,000 entries including about 900 items on economics. An author index is added.

447. Wynar, Bohdan S. "Current Russian Bibliographies in Economics". **Western Business Review.** 6: 41-48, May, 1962.

This is a comprehensive article attempting "to present a picture of the Soviet system for bibliographical listings in the field of Economics".

448. Wynar, Bohdan S. "Pre-Soviet Bibliographies on Economics". **The Library Quarterly,** 36: 258-269, July, 1963.

This article surveys Russian bibliographies on economics in the Pre-revolutionary period supplying data about publication of economic books and indicating deficiencies of those bibliographies.

South Africa

449. Andrews, H. T., and others, ed. **South Africa in the "Sixties"; a Socio-Economic Survey.** Cape Town, South Africa Foundation, 1965. 233 p.

In two parts: pt. A, South Africa — land of opportunity; pt. B, The influence of South African race problems on economic development. Includes an Appendix: A blueprint for the development. . ., and an Analytical index.

450. Houghton, D. H. **The South African Economy.** Cape Town, Oxford University Press, 1964. 261 p.

Presents country's economic development, supplying maps, statistical tables, figures, and many references. Bibliography: p. 246-54.

Spain

451. Banco Espanol de Credito. **Anuario del Mercado Espanol.** Madrid. Annual.

Gives a comprehensive analysis of the Spanish economy.

452. Barcelona. Cámara Oficial de Comercio y Navagación. Boblióteca. **Catàlogo dela Bibliòteca por Orden Alfabetico de Autores.** Barcelon, Tip. La Académica de Herederos de Serra y Russell, 1946. 546 p.

Sweden

453. Konjunkturinstitutet, Stockholm. **The Swedish Economy.** Stockholm, 19 —

A valuable source of information about the Swedish economy in English. Includes numerous tables, graphs, notes and sources.

Switzerland

454. Swiss Credit Bank. **The Swiss Economy in . . .** Zurich. Annual.

Contents: 1. General survey; 2. Financial developments; 3. Industry reports. Includes: economic indicators, Swiss stock and cover prices, with many tables, and graphs.

United States
(Historical Works Containing Bibliographical Listings)

455. Allen, Frederick L. **The Big Change: America Transforms Itself, 1900-1950.** New York, Harper, 1952. 308 p.

Describes the major changes in American life during the first half of the twentieth century. Contents: part 1. The old order; Part 2. The momentum of change; Part 3. the New America. An index is added. Includes bibliographical references in Appendix: p. 295-298.

456. Bruchey, Stuart. **The Roots of American Economic Growth, 1607-1861; an Essay in Social Causation.** New York, Harper and Row, 1964. 234 p.

The author applies a broad approach to this study making implications to political science, sociology, social psychology, etc. Bibliography: p. 217-230.

457. Dorfman, Joseph. **The Economic Mind in American Civilization.** New York, Viking, 1946-49. 5 v.

Divides the history of economic thinking in the U. S. into two great periods: pre- and post Civil War. All the economic activity in the first period were directed toward expansion of foreign trade. The post Civil War era brought to the old the new economic problems, such as elimination of depressions, stabilizing employment, inequality of wealth, monopolies, growth of organized labor, the role of government in nations economic activity. Discusses the role of American economists in solving the economic problems of the country. Bibliographical notes at end of each volume.

458. Fine, Sidney. **Laissez Faire and the General Welfare State; a Study of Conflict in American Thought 1865-1901.** Ann Arbor, University of Michigan Press. 1957 1956. 468 p. (Michigan University Publications. History and Political Science, v. 22).

The author's interpretation of the term "Laissez faire" is "to embrace the arguments of those who accepted, government as a necessity but nevertheless wished to see its functions reduced to the narrowest possible limits." (Preface). Bibliography: p. 403-445.

459. Hughes, Jonathan. **The Vital Few; American Economic Progress and Its Protagonists.** Boston, Houghton Mifflin, 1965. 504 p.

Describes men and forces which combined have built the American economy. This book is a history and an economics; the personal history of such men as: William Penn, Brigham Young, Eli Whitney, Thomas Edison, Andrew Carnegie, Henry Ford, E. H. Harriman and J. P. Morgan.

460. Harris, Seymour Edwin ed. **American Economic History.** New York, McGraw-Hill, 1961. 560 p.

Twenty economists present their views of American economic history discussing such topics as the role of ideas on American economic history, issues of policy, population, employment, national resources, labor, transportation, industrial relations, agriculture, and regional economic conditions. Includes an index.

461. Janeway, Eliot. **The Economics of Crisis: War, Politics and the Dollar.** New York, Weybright and Talley, 1968. 317 p.

Brings together both the politics and economics of crisis pointing out the problems facing the United States. Aimed to study the economic and financial effects of past crises. "It considers the functioning of the economy and the processes of finance in terms of the operations of politics — and vice versa." (Pref.) Bibliography: p. 303-311.

462. Krooss, Herman Edward. **American Economic Development; the Progress of a Business Civilization.** 2nd ed. Englewood Cliffs, N. J., Prentice-Hall, 1966. 498 p.

Traces American economic development in topical instead of in chronological arrangement. Index is included. Bibliographical references at end of most chapters.

463. Kuznets, Simon Smith. **National Income and its Composition, 1919-1938.** by S. S. Kuznets, assisted by Lillian Epstein and Elizabeth Jenks. New York, National Bureau of Economic Research, 1941. (Reprint 1965). 929 p.

Assesses the annual estimates of national income for the United States since the end of World War I to the end of 1938. The material has been divided into five parts in which the following topics are discussed: 1. Concepts: classifications, and procedures, 2. Changes in national income; 1919-1933, 3. Characteristics of the estimates, 4. Basic data, sources and methods, 5. Supplementary data. Over two hundred tables are included and analyzed. Comprehensive and a tabular indexes are added.

464. Leontief, Wassily W. **The Structure of American Economy, 1919-1939; an Empirical Application of Equilibrium Analysis.** New York, Oxford University Press, 1951. 264 p.

The economic theory of general equilibrium (general interdependence) is applied to an experimental study of inter-relations among various sections of national economy disclosed through covariations of prices, investments, outputs, and incomes. Appendices I-III contain mathematical formulas applied in text and statistical tables. Included is a general index. Bibliographical references: p. 223-244.

465. Michigan. University. Survey Research Center. **Income and Welfare in the United States;** a Study by James N. Morgan and others with the assistance of Norma Meyers and Barbara Baldwin. New York, McGraw Hill, 1962. 531 p.

Combines demographic, economic, sociological and psychological factors to give a thorough explanation of what determines the economic position of the family.

466. Reagan, Michael D. **The Managed Economy.** New York, Oxford University Press, 1963. 288 p.

Deals with the system of political economic relationships in the United States. Contents: 1. Property, power and American Political thought; 2. The public role of the private corporation; 3. Government: the visible hand; 4. The political economy of the future; Index. Bibliography: p. 269-279.

467. Wright, Chester. **Economic History of the United States.** 2nd ed. New York, McGraw-Hill, 1949. 941 p.

The struggle of the American people to achieve a high standard of living is the central and unifying idea of this study. Author analyses the causes chiefly responsible for the results obtained by the American nation in solving its fundamental economic problems. Includes a detailed general index. Bibliography: p. 911-926.

(Reference Materials)

468. Associated University Bureaus of Business and Economic Research. **Index of Publications, 1950-1956.** Eugene, Ore., 1957. Supplements.

Divided into two sections: Publications arranged by institution and by subject.

469. Bogue, Donald Joseph and Beale, Calvin L. **Economic Areas of the United States.** New York, The Free Press of Glencoe, 1961. 1162 p. (Studies in Population Distribution no. 15).

Designed as a comprehensive description of the system of area classification for the United States; explains the general system of area classification and assesses in detail each area unit.

470. Bourque, Philip J., and Hansen, Gerald. **An Inventory of Regional Input-Output Studies in the United States.** Seattle, Graduate School of Business Administration, University of Washington, 1967. 21 p. (Graduate School of Business Administration, University of Washington. Occasional paper 17).

471. Cole, Arthur Harrison. **Measures of Business Change; Baker Library Index,** with the assistance of Virginia Jenness and Grace V. Lindfords. Chicago, Irwin, 1952. 444 p.

This annotated bibliography is divided into two main parts; (1) National measure of change, which covers index numbers of business commodity prices, construction costs, employment and finance; (2) Regional and local measures, covering various regions and places of the U. S. In all 449 entries are listed. Included are: list of indexes in order of presentation, reference list of basic sources and a general index.

472. Dusenberry, J. S. and others, eds. **The Brookings Quarterly Econometric Model of the United States.** New York, Rand McNally, 1965. 776 p.

Offers the explanation of variation of G.N.P. and its components in the U.S. Empirical data cover income determination, agriculture, industry, foreign trade and other aspects of American economy.

473. **Economic Indicators.** May 1948 — Washington, U.S. Council of Economic Advisers. Monthly. Prepared for the Joint Economic Committee by the Council of Economic Advisers.

Contents: Total output, income, and spending; Employment, unemployment and wages; Production and business activity; Prices; Money, credit, and security markets; Federal finance. All presentations are in tabular and graphical forms.

474. **Handbook of Basic Economic Statistics;** a Manual of Basic Economic Data on Industry, Commerce, Labor and Agriculture in the United States. 1947 — Washington, Economic Statistics Bureau of Washington, D. C. Monthly, quarterly, and annually.

Covers all major branches of U. S. economy. Tables are arranged under following headings; national product and income, employment and earnings of labor, production, profits and working capital, prices, general business indicators, social security operations, federal operations, etc. Subject index is included.

475. Haren, Claude Clarence and Glasgow, Robert B. **Median Family Income and Related Data, by Counties.** Including Rural Farm Income. Washington, Resource Development Economics Division, Economic Research Service, U. S. Dept. of Agriculture, 1964. 137 p. (U. S. Dept. of Agriculture. Statistical Bulletin, no. 339).

Table 1 presents data for every U. S. county giving comparison between 1959 median incomes and 1949. Table II lists counties according to 1959 income data.

476. Harvard University. Graduate School of Business Administration. **Resources for the Study of Economic History; a Preliminary Guide to Pre-Twentieth Century Printed Material in Collections Located in Certain American and British Libraries.** Compiled by Dorothea D. Reeves. Introd. by Arthur H. Cole, prefaced by Donald T. Clark. Boston, Baker Library, 1961. 62 p. (The Kress Library of Business and Economics. Publication, no. 16).

Lists over thirty libraries which have strong collections in economic and business history.

477. Hasse, Adelaid Rosalie. **Index of Economic Material in Documents of the States of the United States.** Washington, Carnegie Institution, 1907-

1922. 13 v. in 16.

Lists government material on American economic history covering 13 states. The arrangement is alphabetical by topic, and chronological within the group. Includes many cross-references.

478. Hawaii. Industrial Research Advisory Council. **Abstracts: Agricultural, Industrial and Economic Research, Territory of Hawaii, 1930-1952.** Honolulu, 1953. 893 p.

Lists abstracts on Hawaii agricultural, economic and industrial conditions during the period of 1930-1952.

479. **Historical Statistics of the United States; Colonial Times to 1957.** Washington, U. S. Govt. Print Office, 1960.

Supplement for the years 1950-1962, published 1965. Aimed to bring together historical series of wide general interest and to inform the user where additional data can be found. All of the broad subject areas are covered.

480. Larson, Henrietta Melia. **Guide to Business History: Materials for the Study of American Business History and Suggestions for their Use.** Cambridge, Harvard University Press, 1948. 1181 p. (Harvard Studies in Business History, v. 12).

Contains 4904 annotated items related to history of American business, biographies of businessmen, history of individual business and individual firms, research and reference materials. An index is included. A very important study guide.

481. Miller, Herman Phillip. **Trends in the Income of Families and Persons in the United States, 1947 to 1960.** Washington, U. S. Dept. of Commerce Bureau of the Census, U. S. Govt. Print Office, 1963. 349 p. (U. S. Bureau of the Census. Technical Paper no. 8).

Presents statistical data and analysis of changes in income of families and persons in the United States for the period of 1947 to 1960.

482. National Planning Association. Center for Economic Projections. **National Economic Projection Series.** 1959 — Washington. Annual. Title varies: 1959 — National Economic Projections.

483. **Resources for the Future. Resources in America's Future.** Patterns of Requirements and Availabilities, 1960-2000, by Hans H. Landsberg. Published for the Resources for the Future by the Johns Hopkins Press, 1963. 1017 p.

Surveys the projection of demand and supply of United States natural resources to the year 2000, giving statistical data of numerous subjects for the year 1950, 1960 with projections for 1980 and the last year of this century.

484. Twentieth Century Fund. **America's Needs and Resources:** a New Survey, by J. Frederic Dewhurst and associates. New York, 1955. 1145 p.

A cooperative effort of many authorities and specialists in their field to survey the entire economy of the United States.

485. U. S. Bureau of Labor Statistics. **Economic Forces in the United States, in Facts and Figures:** Its People, its Labor Force, its Economy. Washington, U. S. Govt. Print Off., 1963 —

Designed as an information guide for foreigners to basic facts of the United States, its people, economy, life and civilization.

486. U. S. Office of Business Economics. **Survey of Current Business.** Washington, 1921 — Monthly.

"Business Statistics"; a weekly supplement to the Survey.

487. U. S. Office of Business Economics. **U. S. Income and Output; a Supplement to the Survey of Current Business.** Washington, 1958. 241 p.

Provides detailed data on gross national product and national income including components for 1929-1957.

488. U. S. President. **Economic Report of the President to the Congress.** 1st — January, 1947 — Washington, Govt. Print Office, Annual, Title varies slightly.

Reports on all phases of economic activity of the nation in the previous year, giving statistical data about employment, national finances, income production, welfare, etc. Numerous tables and charts are included in Appendices.

West Indies

489. **Caribbean Economic Almanac, 1964-66.** 2nd ed. . Port of Spain, Economic and Business Research Information and Advisory Service, 1964. 270 p. Biennial.

"Designed to give manufacturers and businessmen basic data needed to make full use of Caribbean markets and to provide research students with reliable material."

490. Jamaica. Central Planning Unit. **Economic Survey, Jamaica, 1966.** Kingston, 1967. 109 p.

Brings a wealth of information on economic activity, including agriculture, mining, tourist trade, etc.

CHAPTER THREE

PRIVATE AND PUBLIC FINANCE

(Banking, Currency and Money; Insurance; Investments;
Stock Markets; Taxation)

BIBLIOGRAPHIES (CURRENT)

491. **Business and Technology Sources.** Cleveland, Business and Technology
Dept. Cleveland Public Library. 1930 —

Bulletin of the Business Information and Science and Technology
Departments, Cleveland Public Library. Under various headings are listed
titles recently published in the United States and Canada. The last issue of
the Bulletin contains a list of the annual annotated selection of some of the
outstanding business books of the year.

492. Canadian Tax Foundation. **Index of Canadian Tax Foundation.** Publications to December 31, 1964. Toronto, 1965. 107 p. Supplement 1965 —

Lists under four general subject classifications: public finance, consumption
taxes, death duties and income taxes, all publications of this institution to
December 1964, and then by supplements.

493. Health Insurance Institute, New York. **A List of Current Health
Insurance Books.** 1951 — New York. Annual. Title varies: 1951-1961,
"List of Worthwhile Health Insurance Books."

This annotated bibliography has a wide coverage including list of
periodicals, organizations and services.

494. Insurance Information Institute. **Basic Insurance Books, Casualty, Fire,
Marine Surety.** 195 — New York. Annual.

Lists books and pamphlets with brief annotations, also includes
periodicals.

495. Tax Foundation, New York, Library. **The Library Bulletin.** 19 — New
York. Monthly.

496. **Tax Institute Bookshelf.** no. 1/2 — July 1944 — New York, N. Y.,
Tax Institute. Irregular.

Presents a current bibliography of books, pamphlets, documents and
articles on taxation.

BIBLIOGRAPHIES (RETROSPECTIVE)

497. American Bankers Association. Dept. of Automation and Market
Research. **A Banker's Bibliography on Market Research.** New York, 1963.
53 p.

498. American Finance Conference. **A Bibliography of Reference Materials on Consumer Installment Credit,** Chicago, 1956. 30 p. (Its Special Bulletin no. 65).

499. Belgium. Ministère des affaires économiques. Bibliotheque. **Bibliographie: i Livres, Brochures, Documents, Articles de Revues Traitant de:** richesse nationale, revenue national, comptabilité nationale, budget national catalogués a la Bibliotheque centrale du Ministere des affairs économiques (Fonds Quetelet) à la date du 15 mai 1954. Bruxelles, 1954. 113 p.

500. Brewington, Ann and Knisely, Verona B. **The Social Concept of Money: a Bibliography.** Chicago, The University of Chicago Press, 1935. 107 p. (Materials for the Study of Business).

This is a classified and annotated bibliography with an author index primarily aimed to aid teachers and students in their study of this topic. The included material is arranged alphabetically under various headings which are subdivided into sections such as books, pamphlets and bulletins, articles, and courses of study.

501. Burgess, Norman. **How to Find Out About Banking and Investment.** Oxford, Pergamon Press, 1969. 300 p. (The Commonwealth an international library. Libraries and technical information division).

502. Dievoet, Émile van. **Catalogus van de Internationale Verzekerings-bibliotheek te Leuven.** Catalogue de la bibliothèque internationale des assurances de Louvain. Leuven, Assurantie van de Belgische Boerenbond, 1954. 447 p.

This is a bibliographic catalog of international insurance.

503. Donaldson, Gordon and Stubbs, Carolyn, comps. **Corporate and Business Finance, a Classified Bibliography of Recent Literature.** Boston, Baker Library, Graduate School of Business Administration. Harvard University, 1964. 85 p. (Baker Library, Graduate School of Business Administration, Harvard University. Reference List, no. 22).

504. Ferguson, Elizabeth, ed. and others. **Sources of Insurance Statistics.** New York, Special Libraries Association, 1965. 191 p.

Presents a useful tool in locating statistical data on insurance.

505. Harvard University. International Program in Taxation. **Bibliography on Taxation in Underdeveloped Countries.** Cambridge, Law School of Harvard University, 1962. 75 p.

Lists about 2,100 entries on taxation related to under-developed areas. Arrangement is alphabetical by regions and countries.

506. Insurance Society of New York. Library. **Life Insurance Catalog.** Boston, G. K. Hall, 1960. 352 p.

This is a subject catalog of the Library of the Insurance Society of New York established in 1901.

507. International Committee for the Study of the History of Banking and Credit. **History of the Principal Public Banks. Accompanied by Extensive Bibliographies of the History of Banking and Credit in Eleven European Countries.** Collected by J. G. Van Dillen, London, F. Cass, 1964. 480 p. First published 1934.

Contributions are in French, German, English, and Italian. Part 1 contains 11 articles about history of banks and banking in: Belgium, Denmark, England, France, Germany, Italy, the Netherlands, Poland, Russia, Spain and Sweden. Part 2 lists bibliographies related to banking in some most important countries of Europe, covering various periods of 16th to 19th centuries. Bibliography: p. 353-480.

508. International Labor Office. Library. **Cooperation.** Rev. ed. Geneva, 1964. 102 p. (Its Bibliographical Contributions, no. 23. Contributions Bibliographiques, no. 23). First published in 1958 under title: Bibliography on cooperation.

Divided into four parts: part 1. has arrangement by country, part 2. lists entries by subject, part 3. presents publications of the International Labor Office, part 4. consists of author and country indexes.

509. International Social Security Association. Documentation Service. **Bibliographie Universelle de Sécurité Sociale. World Bibliography of Social Security, 1960-1963.** Genève, 1964. 134 p. (Its Documentation series, no. 2).

510. _____. **Liste Universelle des Périodiques de la Sécurité Sociale. World List of Social Security Periodicals.** 2nd ed. Genève, Secretariat general, Association internationale de la securite sociale, 1966. 59 p. (Its Documentation series, no. 3).

Text in English, French, German and Spanish.

511. Kincaid, Elbert Alvis. **Carter Glass Papers;** selective inventory of 423 boxes Alderman Library of the University of Virginia, with special reference to material concerning the Federal Reserve System. Charlottesville, Va., 1954. 614 leaves.

512. _____. **Inventory of the Carter Glass Papers at the University of Virginia.** Prepared for the Committee on the History of the Federal Reserve System and the Brookings Institution. Washington, 1958. 135 p.

513. Knox, Vera H. **Public Finance: Information Sources.** Detroit, Gale Research Co., 1964. 142 p. (Management Information Guide, 3).

This is an annotated guide for students and professionals working in the field of public finance and taxation. Most of the material listed covers the period of the 1960's, however older studies are included when they are considered basic in importance. Two indexes: author and subject are included. The chapter Public finance covers all major countries of the world.

514. Mateu y Llopis, Filipe. **Bibliografia de la Historia Monetaria de Espana,** con Suplementos Referentes 2 los paises con ella màs Relacionados. Madrid, Fabrica Nacional de Moneda y Timbre, 1958. 410 p.

Bibliography of Spain's monetary history.

515. Masui, Mitsuzo, ed. **A Bibliography of Finance.** Kobe. The International Finance Seminar in the Kobe University of Commerce, 1935. 1614, 116 p.

Contents: British books and articles; Ouvrages francaises; Deutsche Literatur; American books and articles; Author index. Listed are books and articles from 15th century to 1933, arranged by country.

516. Organization for Economic Cooperation and Development. Library. **Bibliographie Spéciale Analytique. Inflation.** Paris, 1965. 84 p.

This is an annotated bibliography of monographs and serial articles on inflation and anti-inflationary measures, with country subdivision.

517. Organization for Economic Cooperation and Development. Library. **Inflation.** Paris, 1965. 84 p.

Introductory material in French and English; annotations in French or English.

518. Schweizerische Nationalbank. Volkswirtschaftliche und Statistische Abteilung. **Schweizerische Bibliographie über Geld, Währung und Notenbank-wesen.** Zürich, 1957. 141 p. (Its Mitteilungen, 40. Heft). Title and text also in French and Italian.

Designed as an annotated bibliography of books, pamphlets and articles related to Swiss currency, monetary and bank policy, money and capital market, international payments, etc. Includes an index of authors.

519. Shoup, Carl Sumner. **Bibliography in Public Finance for Graduate Students.** New York, Columbia University, 1960. 89 p.

520. Sichtermann, S. **Schrifttum des Bank- und Kreditwesens von 1920 bis 1960, nach Stichworten Geordnet.** Frankfurt am Main, 1963-64. 305 p.

Issued by the Zeitschrift für das gesamte Kreditwesen, contains about 30,000 items with subject arrangement.

521. Society of Investment Analysts. **A Bibliography for Investment and Economic Analysis.** London, 1965. 105 p.

Presents an annotated list of British and international publications on investment analysis in systematical arrangement.

522. Special Libraries Association. Committee on Insurance Library Manual. **The Creation and Development of an Insurance Library.** 3rd rev. ed. Editors: Angelica Blomshield and Elizabeth Ferguson. New York, Special Libraries Association, 1949. 51 p.

523. Stobbe, Hanna. **Einkommensverteilung als Theoretisches und Statistisches Problem.** Kiel, 1964. 203 p. (Kieler Schriftumskunden zur Wirtschaft und Gesellschaft, 7).

This bibliography of income distribution is a companion volume to author's Volkswirtschaftliche Gesamtrechnung. The work is divided into two parts: 1. Subjects, and 2. Countries which are further subdivided into topics and the name of country respectively. The entries are listed in chronological order beginning in the 1880's, ending with the first years of the 1960's. Indexes of periodicals, personal names, corporations and government agencies are included.

524. _____. **Volkswirtschaftliche Gesamtrechnung.** Kiel, 1960. 260 p. (Kieler Schrifttumskunden zur Wirtschaft und Gesellschaft, Bd. 1).

Transl.: National Accountancy.

525. U. S. Board of Governors of the Federal Reserve System. Library. **Selected Bibliography on Monetary Policy and Management of the Public Debt. 1947-1960.** Washington, 1961. 15 p.

Designed as a selective list of books, pamphlets, government reports, hearings, symposia and periodical articles on monetary policy and public debt.

526. Westerfield, Ray Best. **Selected Bibliography of Money, Credit, Banking and Business Finance.** Cambridge, Mass., Bankers Pub. Co., 1940. 136 p.

A very useful retrospective bibliography. Lists monographs, dictionaries and encyclopedias, directories, manuals, periodicals, reports of various financial institutions, statistical publications, and services. All material is arranged by the subject; author index is included.

527. Whitney, Howard S. **Bibliography on Cooperatives and Social and Economic Development;** prepared by Howard S. Whitney and Hassan A. Ronaghy, with the assistance of Adloe L. Larson, Wayne H. Weidemann and Mary Jean McGrath, in cooperation with the International Cooperative Development Service of the Agency for International Development. Madison International Cooperative Training Center, University Extension Division, University of Wisconsin, 1964. 79 p.

528. International Social Security Association. Documentation Service. **Social Security Abstracts.** v. 1 — 1965 — Geneva, 1965 — Quarterly.

Provides abstracts of selected entries from the World Bibliography of Social Security.

DICTIONARIES AND ENCYCLOPEDIAS

529. Clark, Donald Thomas, and Gottfried, Bert A. **Dictionary of Business and Finance.** New York, Crowell, 1957. 409 p.

The dictionary covers such fields as: accounting, advertising, banking, credit, finance, government, import, investments, labor, law, real estate, statistics, stocks, warehousing, etc. Appendix with information in tabular form is added.

530. Davids, Lewis E. **Dictionary of Insurance.** Paterson, N. J., Littlefield, 1959. 217 p. (The New Littlefield College Outlines, 62).

Defines many terms and phrases in the insurance field for the layman, for insurance worker and for student.

531. Doris, Lillian, ed. **Corporate Treasurer's and Controller's Encyclopedia.** Prepared with the Cooperation of the Editorial staff of Prentice-Hall, Inc. Englewood Cliffs, N. J., Prentice-Hall, 1958. 4 v. (1336 p.).

Covers various phases treasurer's and controller's activities and duties by long articles providing facts, information and suggestions.

532. **Elsevier's Banking Dictionary in Six Languages: English-American, French, Italian, Spanish, Dutch and German.** Compiled and arranged on an English alphabetical base by Julio Ricci. Amsterdam, New York, Elsevier Pub. Co., 1966. 302 p.

Based on banking terminology currently in use, contains 2,041 items in an alphabetical arrangement. Includes: French, Italian, Spanish, Dutch, and German indexes.

533. **Enzyklopädisches Lexikon für das Geld, Bank— und Börsenwesen.** 3. Aufl., redigiert und erg. von Erich Achterberg und Karl Lanz. Frankfurt am Main, F. Knapp, 1967-68. 2 v. 1894 p.

Encyclopedic dictionary of money, banking and stock marketing, prepared by one hundred and fifty specialists from Germany and abroad. Bibliographical references are included.

534. Gallagher, Vincent Leo and Heath, Gerald R. **Insurance Words and their Meanings;** a Glossary of Fire and Casualty Insurance Terms. 5th ed. Indianapolis, Ind., Rough Notes Co., 1961. 111 p.

535. Gaynor, Frank. **International Business Dictionary in Five Languages: English, German, French, Spanish and Italian.** New York, Philosophical Library, 1946. 452 p.

In addition to the vocabulary of business terms in five languages, this work includes such topics as: geographic names, nationalities, monetary units, weights and measurements, German, French, Spanish and Italian Cross-indexes.

536. Gunston, C. A. and Corner, C. M. **Deutsch-englisches Glossarium Finanzieller und Wirtschaftlicher Fachausdrücke.** S. Aufl. Frankfurt am Main, Knapp, 1967. 1122 p.

An important German-English Glossary of financial and economic terms stressing their precise application. The 5th ed. is a reprint of the 4th (1962) ed. with a 160 page added supplement.

537. Horn, Stefan F. **Glossary of Financial Terms in English, American, French, Spanish, German.** Amsterdam, Elsevier, 1965. 271 p.

The entries are alphabetically arranged. Under each term in English are given explanations in French, Spanish and German. Indexes in French, Spanish, and German are appended.

538. Müller, Gerhard, and Löffelholz, Josef. **Bank-Lexikon; Handwörterbuch für das Bank und das Sparkassenwesen.** 6. neubearb, und erw. Aufl. Wiesbaden, Betriebswirtschaftlicher Verlag Dr. Th. Gabler, 1969. 2004 p.

This is a standard German handbook for banking terms.

539. Munn, Glenn Gaywayne. **Encyclopedia of Banking and Finance.** Ed. by F. L. Garcia. 6 ed. Boston Bankers Pub. Co., 1962. 788 p.

Thousands of terms are listed in the fields of banking, commerce, economics, finance, law, money, etc. Bibliographical references are given. Entries are arranged in alphabetical sequence, and numerous cross-references are provided.

540. **Polk's Bankers Encyclopedia.** Detroit, Polk's Bankers Encyclopedia Co., 1896 — Semiannual.

Supplies a comprehensive directory of all American banks, giving information on bank statements, staff, attorneys, security dealers, etc. No information is given about earnings, dividends, or stocks.

541. **Polk's Bankers Encyclopedia (Purple Book) Foreign Section.** Alphabetical list of banks and bankers throughout the world (except the United States, U. S. Possessions and Canada). Sept. 1925 — Sept. 1930. Detroit, Polk's Bankers Encyclopedia Co., 1930 — Annual.

Similar in arrangement and coverage to the work listed above.

542. Prentice-Hall, Inc. **Encyclopedic Dictionary of Business Finance.** Englewood Cliffs, N. J., 1960. 658 p. Illus.

Aimed to provide easy to understand explanations; to present comprehensive treatment of most important terms in each subject field; to include how-to-do material when the word entails financial practice; to illustrate with figures and forms the practical application of certain financial principles.

543. Das Spezial-Archiv der Deutschen Wirtschaft. **Das Banken-Ortslexikon für den Zahlungsverkehr;** eine Übersicht Sämtlicher Kreditinstitute in der Bundesrepublik Deutschland, Gross-Berlin sowie den grösseren Orten der Ostzone. Bearb. von H. Mildner und W. Köhler. Heppenheim, Hoppenstedt, 1950. 1204 p.

Title translated: The Dictionary of bank location for financial transactions; a survey of all credit institutions in the Federal Republic of Germany, Great Berlin, and larger towns in the East Germany.

544. Standard and Poor's Corporation. **Stock Market Encyclopedia.** 6th ed. New York, 1965. 1 v.

545. Steneberg, Wilhelm. **Handwörterbuch des Finanzwesens in Deutscher und Englischer Sprache; Wörterbuch des Geld-Bank- und Börsenwesens sowie Verwandter Fachgruppen, unter Gleichzeitiger Berücksichtigung Amerikanischer und Englischer Verhältnisse.** 2. durchges. Aufl. Berlin, Siemens, 1947. 2 v. (Siemens' Wissenschaftliche Fachwörterbücher. Bd. 1).

Contents: v. 1. English-German. v. 2. German-English. This is the slightly revised ed. of Handwörterbuch compiled in 1933 by Karl T. Langguth.

546. Thomson, William. **Dictionary of Banking.** 11th ed. London, Pitman, 1965. 641 p.

The aim of this dictionary is to provide information upon any subject connected with banking. The book is furnished with many cross-references, and at the end of each leading subject lists bibliographies related to that subject.

547. Wyckoff, Peter. **Dictionary of Stock Market Terms.** Englewood Cliffs, N. J., Prentice-Hall, 1964. 301 p.

DIRECTORIES

548. **The Bankers' Almanac and Year Book.** Containing a Complete Banking Directory of the United Kingdom and the British Colonies, the Principal Banks of the World and a Banker's Guide to the Principal Insurance Offices. London, Groombridge, 1844 — Title varies: 1919/20 - The Bankers' Almanac and Year Book.

Brings a wealth of information on banks and banking throughout the world giving addresses, capital holdings, etc. The arrangement is by country with emphasis on British banks.

549. Collins, George W. **Stock Exchange: International Directory.** Washington, 1965. 101 p.

Presents a geographical listing, giving brief general and historical description, address, etc. . . of each institution.

550. Deutsche Bundesbank. **Verzeichnis der Kreditinstitute and ihrer Verbände sowie der Treuhander für Kreditinstitute im Bundesgebiet einschl. Berlin (West).** Frankfurt am Main, 1960. 203 p.

Directory of West German banks and credit instituions including West Berlin.

551. **Directory of Business and Financial Services.** 1st — 1924 — New York, Special Libraries Association. Irregular.

Title varies: Handbook of Commercial Information Services, etc. The sixth edition of this annotated Directory provides a selected list of business, economic and financial publications printed periodically with regular supplements. The included publications are often distinguished by the looseleaf format. Excluded are periodicals which could be found in standard reference sources, bank and brokerage letters, clipping services, market surveys, regional studies and government publications. Items are arranged under the name and address of the publisher. Two indexes of publishers, services and authors, and subjects are added.

552. Dun & Bradstreet, Inc. **Million Dollar Directory.** 1959 — New York. Annual.

Lists about 29,000 companies with a net worth of $1 million or over in alphabetical, geographical and product sections. Also includes a list (alphabetical) of top executives, their company affiliations, and positions.

553. **Investment Information and Advice: a Handbook and Directory.** Rochester, N. Y., 1962 — Title varies: - 1962, Directory of Investment Advisory Services.

Presents a most useful guide to investment services. The included material is divided under nine headings, giving the address and cost of the service followed by a description of the kind of service supplied.

554. Lanz, Karl. **Banken der Welt; Kurzmonographien in Deutscher und Englischer Sprache. Banks of the World; Brief Monographs in German and English.** Frankfurt am Main, F. Knapp, 1963. 456 p.

555. **Rand McNally International Bankers Directory. The Bankers Blue Book.** International directory of banks and bankers. July 1876 — Chicago, Rand McNally. Semiannually. Title varies: Rand McNally Bankers Directory, etc.; Subtitle varies also.

Includes also the bank statements for all American and Canadian banks.

556. Reimann, Guenter and Wigglesworth, Edwin F. **International Guide to Foreign Commercial Financing.** New York, International Reports, Inc., 1961. 2 v.

557. Special Libraries Association. New York Chapter. **1951 Union List of Economic and Financial Services.** New York, Financial Group. New York Chapter Special Libraries Association, 1952. 50 p.

558. **Who's Who in Banking; the Directory of the Banking Profession.** New York, Business Press, 1966 —

Lists brief biographical sketches of bankers (mostly from commercial banks) in the U. S., Puerto Rico, and the Virgin Islands.

559. **Who's Who in Insurance.** 1948 — New York, Underwriter Print. and Pub. Co., Annual.

A section of Insurance Almanac; formerly issued in Insurance Almanac.

560. **World Wide Chamber of Commerce Directory.** 1965 — Loveland, Colo., Johnson Pub. Co., Annual.

Supersedes Chamber of Commerce Directory of the United States, including Alaska and Hawaii.

HANDBOOKS

561. Auburn, H. W. **Comparative Banking in Australia, Austria, Belgium, Canada, Denmark, Finland, France, Germany, Greece, Hong Kong, India, Israel, Italy, Japan, Lebanon, Netherlands, Norway, Portugal, Spain, Sweden, Switzerland, Turkey, United Kingdom, U.S.A., the U.S.S.R.** 3rd ed. Dunstable, Waterlow, 1966. 218 p.

This collection of studies on banking in various countries should be very useful for students and businessmen who require a knowledge of the main banking institutions in foreign countries.

562. Badger, Ralph E. **The Complete Guide to Investment Analysis.** With the collaboration of Paul B. Coffman and members of the staff of Standard Research Consultants, Inc. New York, McGraw-Hill, 1967. 504 p.

Develops a working technique for analysis of the value determining factors of a stock market. The work is written in a clear, concise and readable style. Such topics are covered as investment motivations, investment programs, market forecasting, accounting techniques, types of securities, pension funds, etc. An index is included.

563. Cox, Edwin Burk, ed. **Basic Tables in Business and Economics.** New York, McGraw-Hill, 1967. 399 p.

Presents the most useful data for business and economics. Contains: general information; tables covering basic logarithm, interest and annuity, statistics, mortality, immigration, labor force, employment, productivity and earnings; business and finance, consumption, insurance, government finance and international business.

564. Doris, Lillian, ed. **Business Finance Handbook.** Englewood Cliffs, N. J., Prentice-Hall, 1957. 919 p.

565. Doris, Lillian. **Corporate Treasurer's and Controller's Handbook.** New York, Prentice Hall, 1950. 1277 p. illus.

566. Dun and Bradstreet, Inc. **Reference Book** v. 1 — 1859 — New York.
This is a useful credit guide book for the United States.

567. **Financial Handbook.** 1st - New York, Ronald Press, 1925 —
This is a reference source on corporation finance, banking and money. It includes corporate stock, bonds, international transactions, credit and other topics of interest for every businessman.

568. Friedberg, Robert. **Paper Money of the United States; a Complete Illustrated Guide with Variations;** Large size notes, fractional currency, small size notes, encased postage stamps from the first year of paper money, 1861 to the present. 5th ed. Additions and revisions by Jack Friedberg. New York, Coin and Currency Institute, 1964. 306 p.
A useful reference work containing pictures of various types of bank notes, treasury notes, Federal Reserve notes, silver certificates, etc. Each picture contains information as to date of issue, the bank, signatures and collectors value.

569. Gerloff, Wilhelm, and Neumark, Fritz, eds. **Handbuch der Finanzwissenschaft.** 2. völlig neubearb. Aufl. Tübingen, Mohr, 1952-58. 3 v.
Contains scholarly articles on public finance. Volume 1 is concerned with the study of public finance in relationship to other disciplines. Volume 2 concentrates on public credit, corporations and taxation. Volume 3 surveys public finances in various major countries of the world.

570. Janberg, Hans, ed. **Finanzierungs — Handbuch.** Wiesbaden, Betriebswirtschaftlicher Verlag T. Gabler, 1964. 742 p.

571. **Moody's Municipal & Government Manual. American and Foreign.** New York, 1955 —
Supersedes Moody's Manual of Investments, American and Foreign. Government securities.

572. Moore, Justin Hartley. **Handbook of Financial Mathematics.** New York, Prentice Hall, 1929. 1216 p.

This handbook covers the topics of general and financial operations from the mathematical standpoint. Many mathematical formulas are presented in such a way that they can be used with the greatest speed and accuracy. Numerous tables, answers to problems, a list of symbols are included. The detailed index is added.

573. Tax Foundation, New York. **Facts and Figures on Government Finance,** 1964-1965. 13th ed. Englewood Cliffs, N. J., Prentice-Hall, 1965. 275 p.

Included data on federal, state, and local taxes, revenues, expenditures, and debt, cover the period from 1909 to 1962.

574. **World Monetary Reform: Plans and Issues.** Edited by H. G. Grubel. London, Oxford University Press, 1964. 446 p.

Presents a useful information handbook on international liquidity.

REPORTS & YEARBOOKS

575. **Bank for International Settlements.** Annual Report. 1st — 1930/31 — Basel. Report year ends March 31.

Extremely valuable annual survey of economic conditions in various parts of the world, emphasising monetary sectors, with many tables and figures.

576. **Beerman's Financial Yearbook of Europe.** 1st — Jan. 1965 — London, R. Beerman. Annual.

The 1968 ed. has 1500 pages and covers various sectors of business, finance and industry in Western Europe. The main body of the yearbook contains information and data on some 800 major firms under six headings: 1. Finance, 2. Services, 3. Light industry, 4. Engineering, 5. Building, and 6. Metals and minerals.

577. **Best's Insurance Reports.** 1st — 1899/1900 — New York, A. M. Best. Annual.

578. **Insurance Almanac: Who, What, When and Where in Insurance,** an annual of insurance facts. v. 1 — 1912 — New York, Underwriter Print. and Pub. Co. Annual. Title varies.

A useful source of information in insurance including directories.

579. **Inter-American Development Bank. Activities.** 1961/64 — Washington, D. C.

Supplies information data by year, country and industry.

580. **International Credit Union Yearbook.** 1954 — Madison, Wis., Credit Union National Association. Title varies: 1954-62, Credit Union Yearbook.

581. International Monetary Fund. **Annual Report on Exchange Restrictions.** Washington, 1950 — Annual.

Consists of two parts: one general and the other has country subdivision covering their imports, exports, balance of payments, exchanges, etc.

582. **International Reports on Finance and Currencies.** New York, International Reports, Inc., 19 — Weekly.

583. **Moody's Bank & Finance Manual:** Bank, Insurance and Finance Companies, Investment Trusts, Real Estate. American and Foreign. 195 — New York, Moody's Investors Service, Annual.

Supersedes Moody's Manual of Investments: American and Foreign. Bank, insurance companies, investment trust, real estate finance and credit companies.

584. **Pick's Currency Yearbook.** New York, Pick Pub. Co., 1955 — Annual.

Description of currencies arranged by country in alphabetical order. Includes also a select bibliography, directory of central banks and an index. Supplemented by the monthly "Pick's World Currency Report," 1945 —

585. **Savings Banks Fact Book.** 1956 — New York, Savings Banks Trust Co. Annual.

586. **Spectator Insurance Year Book.** v. 1 — 1874 — Philadelphia, Spectator Co. Annual.

Formerly: Insurance year book. Issued in parts such as, fire, casualty, marine, etc. Life insurance, 1951/52 —

587. **Stock Exchange Year Book.** 1 — 1875 — London, New York, Cassell, Petter & Galpin, etc. Annual. Title varies slightly.

A careful digest of information relating to the origin, history and present position of each of the public securities and joint stock companies known to the markets of the United Kingdom.

STATISTICS

588. **Federal Reserve Chart Book on Financial and Business Statistics.** 1 — June 1947 — Washington, U. S. Board of Governors of the Federal Reserve System. Monthly.

589. **Federal Reserve Chart Book on Financial and Business Statistics. Historical Supplement.** Washington, U. S. Board of Governors of the Federal Reserve System. Annual.

Brings a wealth of statistical information with emphasis on finance.

590. France. Ministere de l'économie et des finances. **Statistiques et Etudes Financières.** Paris, Imprimerie Nationale, 1949 — Monthly.

Presents survey articles with numerous tables and graphs. A monthly Supplément (1949 —) is devoted to a single topic.

591. **International Financial Statistics.** 1948 — Washington, International Monetary Fund. Monthly.

Member countries are listed in alphabetical order giving statistical information regarding such financial matters as: exchange rate, international liquidity, banks and banking, money, international transactions, interest, price, production, etc. This is a very important source of financial information.

592. International Monetary Fund. Statistics Bureau. **Direction of Trade.** 1958/62 — Washington. Annual.

"A Supplement to International Financial Statistics." Vols. for 1958/ 62 — issued with the International Bank for Reconstruction and Development.

593. Organization for Economic Cooperation and Development. **Geographical Distribution of Financial Flows to Less Developed Countries (disbursement)** 1960-1964. Paris. O.E.C.D., 1966. 179 p.

594. Organization for Economic Cooperation and Development. **Statistics of National Accounts, 1950-1961.** Paris, 1964. 282 p.

Covers all O.E.C.D. member countries giving comparative data on growth rate, G.N.P. and government expenditures. Includes documentation for the country statistics with adjustments.

595. Organization for European Economic Cooperation. **Statistics of National Product and Expenditure.** no. 1 — 1952 — Paris.

Consists of statistics of national product and expenditure for O.E.E.C. countries, the United States and Canada giving comparisons and combined estimates for countries included.

596. Reserve Bank of India. **Banking and Monetary Statistics in India.** Bombay, 1954. 1005 p. Supplement, 1964. 2 v. in 1.

597. Standard and Poor's Corporation. **Trade and Securities Statistics; Security Price Index Record.** New York, 1962. 202 p.

Contains indexes of employment, prices, business activity in various lines, stock price indexes for industries, Prices, production and inventories of commodities.

598. United Nations. Statistical Office. **Yearbook of National Accounts Statistics.** Annuaire de Statistiques des Comptabilites Nationales. 1957 – New York.

Supersedes its Statistics of national income and expenditure.

599. U. S. Board of Governors of the Federal Reserve System. **Federal Reserve Bulletin.** 1 – 1915 – Washington, U. S. Govt. Print Off.

Contains current statistical data on business and finance in the U. S. and in the world, giving the principal sources of statistics. Included are also articles on banking, currency and similar subjects.

600. U. S. Bureau of the Budget. **The Budget of the United States Government for the Fiscal Year Ending June 30, 19–,** Budget message of the President and Summary budget statements. Washington, U. S. Govt. Print Off., 1922 – Annual.

Contains the budgetary messages of the Presidents, tables of receipts and expenditures, description of government programs including specifications, series of analyses and historical tables. This is a very important document for the study of federal finance.

601. U. S. Bureau of the Census. **City Finances.** 1932 – Washington, Annual.

Title varies: 1932-39, Financial Statistics of Cities Having Population of over 100,000. 1939-4 , Financial Statistics of Cities; Vols for 1946 – each in three parts: 1. Summary of city government finances; 2. Compendium of city government finances; 3. Large-city finances. Provides useful information on revenue and expenditures for a certain number of U. S. cities.

602. U. S. Federal Reserve System. Board of Governors. **Flow of Funds in the United States, 1939-1953.** Washington, 1955. 390 p.

603. _____ . **Banking and Monetary Statistics.** Washington, 1943. 979 p.

Presents a basic reference work on all banking and monetary activities of the Federal Reserve banks and their members including information on production and movement of gold and international finance development. Uses data from 1914 to 1941, which should be revised.

MONOGRAPHIC TREATISES
(A selected list of standard works which include
numerous bibliographical citations)

604. Andreades, Andreas Michael. **History of the Bank of England 1640 to 1903.** Translated by Christabel Meredith. With a preface by H. S. Foxwell. 3rd ed. London, P. S. King, 1935. 455 p.

Bibliography: p. 429-446.

605. Ashton, Thomas Southcliffe, and Sayers, R. S. eds. **Papers in English Monetary History.** Oxford, Clarendon Press, 1953. 167 p.

Contains eleven essays written by six authors on various aspects of banking and monetary history of Great Britain. Index of persons is included.

606. Balogh, Thomas. **Studies in Financial Organization.** Cambridge, Eng., University Press, 1950. 319 p. (National Institute of Economic and Social Research. Economic and Social Studies, 6).

This study is "a fragment of an international enquiry into the working of the Western European monetary and banking systems and capital markets undertaken in 1939" (Pref.) Index.

607. Beckhart, Benjamin Haggott, ed. **Banking Systems.** New York, Columbia University Press, 1954. 934 p.

"A successor volume to Foreign banking systems, edited by H. P. Willis and H. Beckhart." Describes the various banking systems in sixteen major countries of the world.

608. Clapham, Sir John Harold. **Bank of England: a History.** Cambridge, University Press, 1958. 2 v.

Contents: v. 1. 1694-1797; v. 2. 1797-1914. With an epilogue; The bank as it is. Includes an index.

609. Copeland, Morris Albert. **A Study of Moneyflows in the United States.** New York, National Bureau of Economic Research, 1952. 338 p.

This is "the product of a lifetime of probing into the meaning and significance of money, and of delving into and improving statistical material essential of how money does, in fact, flow through our economy." (Introd.) New statistical economic measurements, and new monetary theory are introduced. Many tables, charts and general index are included.

610. Coppieters, Emmanuel. **English Banknote Circulation, 1694-1954.** Foreword by R. C. Hawtrey. Louvain, Louvain Institute of Economic and Social Research, 1955. 171 p.

Describes the role which bank notes played in the history both of English currency and of English banking from the first tentative issues of the Bank of England to the present time. Includes nine statistical tables, five pages of references (besides many footnotes) and an index. Bibliography: p. 161-166.

611. Crowther, Sir Geoffrey. **Outline of Money.** Rev. ed. London, Nelson, 1948. 417 p.

612. Del Mar, Alexander. **A History of Money in Ancient Countries,** from the Earliest Times to the Present. New York, B. Franklin, 1968. 358 p.

613. Dewey, Davis Rich. **Financial History of the United States.** 8th ed. London, Longmans, Green, 1922. 567 p. (American Citizen Series).

This is an account of Federal finances from the Colonial period to the 1916's.

614. Dougall, Herbert. **Investments.** 8th ed. Englewood Cliffs, N. J., Prentice-Hall, 1968. 586 p.

First ed. published by D. F. Jordan under title: Jordan on Investments, Seventh ed. by D. F. Jordan and H. E. Dougall published 1960 under title: Investments. Presents new developments in taxation, legal and financial aspects. Includes a new chapter on valuation of securities; explains all media of investments including their analysis and their place in investment programming. References cite important works for further study.

615. Edey, Harold C. **National Income and Social Accounting,** by Harold C. Edey, Alan T. Peacock and Ronald A. Cooper. 3rd rev. ed. London, Hutchinson University Library, 1967. 207 p.

Divided into three parts: 1. The framework of social accounting (includes: the nature of national income and social accounting and national income accounts) 2. Some applications of social accounting: with a further consideration of techniques; 3. Further analysis.

616. Friedman, Milton, and Schwartz, Anna J. **A Monetary History of the United States, 1867-1960.** Princeton, Princeton University Press, 1963. 860 p. (National Bureau of Economic Research Studies in Business Cycles, 12).

Discusses the money factor and its role in economical and political development of the United States during the covered period. This work traces changes in the stock of money from the end of the Civil War to 1960, examines the causes for the changes, and analyzes the influence of the stock of money on American history. A detailed subject index is included.

617. Goldsmith, Raymond William. **A Study of Savings in the United States.** Princeton, Princeton University Press, 1955-56. 3.v.

Provides a comprehensive quantitative description and an analysis of savings in this country in the years 1897 to 1949. Bibliography at end of each volume.

618. Gurley, John G. and Shaw, Edward S. **Money in the Theory of Finance.** Washington, D.C., Brookings Institution, 1960. 371 p.

The authors develop for the first time "a theory of finance that encompasses the theory of money, and a theory of financial institutions that includes banking theory." (Introd.) Glossary and index are included.

619. Hawtrey, Sir Ralph George. **Currency and Credit.** 3rd ed. London, Longmans, Green, 1928. 477 p.

Expounds the main theory of currency and credit of the pre-war (First World War) conditions in pt. 1 and illustrates it by historical chapters in pt. 2. Includes a detailed index.

620. Hicks, Ursula Kathleen (Webb) **British Public Finances, Their Structure and Development, 1880-1952.** London, Oxford University Press, 1958. 225 p. (The Home University Library of Modern Knowledge, 227).

Contents: 1. The growth of the public authorities; 2. The forms of public expenditure; 3. The adjustment of the tax structure; 4. Local government in the fiscal system; 5. Budget balance and national balance; 6. Loan finance and debt management. Bibliography: p. 215-220.

621. Holzman, Franklyn D. **Soviet Taxation: the Fiscal and Monetary Problems of a Planned Economy.** Cambridge, Mass., Harvard University Press, 1955. 376 p. (Russian Research Center Studies, 16).

The Soviet tax policy and praxis with the framework of the Soviet fiscal and monetary policy. Discusses various theoretical topics of taxation. Includes numerous statistics. Bibliographical references included in "Notes" p. 333-369.

622. Jevons, William Stanley. **Investigations in Currency & Finance.** New York, A. M. Kelley, 1964. 428 p. (Reprints of Economic Classics). Reprint of 1884 ed.

This volume is a collection of papers, mostly reprints, on money, prices, commercial fluctuations, value of gold, commercial crises, money markets, currency, cover prices, etc. Numerous tables and diagrams accompany the text. Fifty two page bibliography section lists items from 1568 to 1882 in chronological order. Bibliography: p. 363-414.

623. Keynes, John Maynard. **Monetary Reform.** New York, Harcourt, Brace, 1924. 227 p.

This treatise of the famous English economist is divided into five chapters: (1) The consequences, (2) Public finance and changes in the value of money, (3) The theory of money and the foreign exchanges, (4) Alternative aims in monetary policy, (5) Positive suggestions for the future regulation of money. Index is included.

624. Keynes, John Maynard. **A Treatise on Money.** London, Macmillan, 1958. 2 v.

Contents: v. 1. The pure theory of money subdivided into bk. 1. The nature of money, bk. 2. The value of money, bk. 3. Fundamental equations of money, bk. 4. The dynamics of the price-level. v. 2. The applied theory of money, bk. 5. Monetary factors and their fluctuations, bk. 6. The rate of investment and its fluctuations, bk. 7. The management of money. Index is included.

625. Kuznets, Simon Smith, and Jenks, Elizabeth. **Capital in the American Economy; its Formation and Financing.** A Study by the National Bureau of Economic Research. Princeton, Princeton University Press, 1961. 664 p. (National Bureau of Economic Research. Studies in Capital Formation and Financing, 9).

Deals with long term trends in capital formation and financing in the United States, taking under consideration main sectors of the national economy: agriculture, mining, manufacturing, public utilities, government, and nonfarm real estate. The analysis for each sector summarizes the trends in capital formation from 1870, and financing from 1900, and the factors determining those trends. A wealth of statistical material in form of tables with diagrams is included. General index is added.

626. McCulloch, John Ramsey. **A Select Collection of Scarce and Valuable Tracts on Money.** New York, A. M. Kelley, 1966. 637 p. (Reprints of Economic Classics) First published 1856.

Contains fourteen essays on metallic money. The oldest is the speech of Sir Robert Cotton before the Privy Council in 1626. The second oldest and very important is "A Discourse of coin and coinage," by Rice Vaughan, published in 1675, written between 1630 and 1635. It is the earliest tract in English, giving a general view of the origin of money, the material used for coinage, its forms, and proportions, its uses and abuses. The most valuable treatise in this collection is an anonymous Essay on money and coins in two parts published in 1757-58 by Joseph Harris (supposed author). Tablets of Greek and Roman money are included.

627. Meyer, John Robert, and Glauber, Robert R. **Investment Decisions, Economic Forecasting and Public Policy.** Boston, Division of Research Graduate School of Business Administration, Harvard University, 1964.

Reviewing the more important theories concerning business investment behavior, the authors test the theories adequacy in terms of evidence of twelve postwar years, and then they introduce a more complex and elective "accelerator-residual funds" theory which should be more useful. New statistical techniques are developed to solve known but difficult problems. Their study is a part of a broader program of research in the area of "Profits and the Functioning of the Economy" financed by the Rockefeller Foundation.

628. Mints, Lloyd Wynn. **A History of Banking Theory in Great Britain and the United States.** Chicago, University of Chicago Press, 1945. 319 p.

Among other topics, the book contains chapters discussing the beginning of banking theory in Great Britain, early American writers, British opinion from 1821-1860: the controversy between the currency and banking schools, agitation for banking reform, and a brief survey of banking literature since 1913. Subject and name indexes are added. Bibliography : p. 288-307.

629. Musgrave, Richard Abel, and Peacock, Alan T. eds. **Classics in the Theory of Public Finance.** London, Macmillan, 1962. 244 p.

Reviews a long debate among Continental (European) economists on public finance, which lasted for some forty years, (1880 to 1920). Presents a sample of voluminous literature on that subject. The arrangement of material is chronological. The main topic is taxation in theory and application. Index of names is included.

630. Orsinger, Roger. **Banks of the World.** Translated by D. G. Ault. London, Macmillan, 1967. 299 p.

Contents: 1. Historical survey of banking operations. 2. The development of banking in various countries (France, England, Austria, Italy, Vatican, Belgium, Holland, Switzerland, Spain, U. S., Canada, Japan, Communist Bloc). 3. The seven international banking and financial institutions of Washington. 4. The banks and European integration. 5. The 110 most important commercial banks in the world. 6. The 475 century-old banks of the world.

631. Patinkin, Don. **Money, Interest, and Prices; an Integration of Monetary and Value Theory.** 2nd ed. New York, Harper and Row, 1965. 708 p.

The central point of this study is the working of monetary forces in the commodity markets. Bibliography: p. 675-692.

632. Reimann, Guenter and Wigglesworth, Edwin F. eds. **The Challenge of International Finance.** New York, McGraw-Hill, 1966. 1017 p. (McGraw-Hill Series in International Development).

Covers the entire system of postwar international finance, focusing on seven major world financial centers and the free gold markets. Includes a "Directory of foreign commercial financing" giving information on over 1300 major institutions with names of executives, addresses and other data. Bibliography: p. 957-969.

633. Riegel, Robert and Miller, Jerome S. **Insurance Principles and Practices.** 5th ed. Englewood Cliffs, N. J., Prentice-Hall, 1966. 867 p.

634. Robertson, Sir Dennis Holme. **Money.** 4th ed. Chicago, University of Chicago Press. 1962. Reprinted. 187 p. (The Cambridge Economic Handbooks).

Presents a thorough analysis of the economic role of money, describing the general principles of money in an enterprise society and contemporary monetary institutions. The book, written in a clear and understandable style, has been widely used as a textbook in unversities and colleges.

635. Scott, Ira Oscar. **Government Securities Market.** New York, McGraw-Hill, 1965. 239 p.

Analyses the important operations in United States securities, discussing policies and practices of the primary dealers. A large portion of references accompany the text. Bibliography: p. 179-225.

636. Thorn, Richard S. ed. **Monetary Theory and Policy; Major Contributions to Contemporary Thought.** New York, Random House, 1966. 672 p.

This work is a collection of classical writings in the field of the theory and policy of money, which previously have been published in various economic journals during the last fifteen years.

637. Trescott, Paul B. **Money, Banking, and Economic Welfare.** 2nd ed. New York, McGraw-Hill, 1965.

Designed as a text book for undergraduate and graduate courses in money and banking, this study stresses the importance of economic theory in this field. The treatment is presented rather from a liberal arts point of view than from business. An index is included.

638. Triffin, Robert. **Our International Monetary System: Yesterday, Today and Tomorrow.** New York, Random House, 1968. 206 p.

Investigates monetary history from 1815 to the present, indicating the future prospects for reform. Divided into two parts: 1. The evolution of the international monetary system: 1815-1965; 2. Reform plans and negotiations. Bibliography: p. 197-201.

639. Wicksell, Knut. **Interest and Prices (Geldzins und Güterpreise) A Study of the Causes Regulating the Value of Money.** Translated from the German by R. F. Kahn, with an introd. by Bertil Ohlin. London, Macmillan, 1936. 219 p.

In twelve chapters author discusses the quantity theory, purchasing power of money and prices, velocity of circulation of money, the interest rate, international price relationship and the practical proposals for the stabilization of the value of money.

CHAPTER FOUR

COMMERCE & MARKETING

GUIDES TO INFORMATION

640. Carpenter, Robert N. **Guidelist for Marketing Research and Economic Forecasting.** New York, American Management Association, 1966. 112 p. (A.M.A. Research Study 73).

This is an annotated guide to publications which could be of interest for marketing researcher and economic forecaster. Cited are numerous indexes, bibliographies, catalogs and directories of directories. The 1966 edition of this bibliography is an outgrowth of two earlier listings.

640a. Coman, Edwin Truman. **Sources of Business Information.** Rev. ed. Berkeley, University of California Press, 1964. 330 p.

An annotated manual and a reference guide to selected sources, covering: general references, accounting, advertising, automation, banking, economic, finance, industries, insurance, international trade, management, marketing, real estate, statistics, etc. Includes checklist of sources at end of most of the chapters. Chapter 16, A basic bookshelf, has a list of basic reference material for a private business library. A detailed general index is included.

641. Davinson, Donald. **Commercial Information; a Source Handbook.** Oxford, Pergamon Press, 1965. 164 p.

A useful guide to commercial reference sources, with an emphasis on Great Britain.

642. Dun and Bradstreet, Inc. **Market Guide of Discounter and Mass Merchandisers.** New York, 19 — Semiannual.

643. Editor & Publisher. **Market Guide.** v. 1 — 1924 — New York. Annual. Title varies.

A very useful business information guide covering more than 1,500 cities in the United States and Canada, giving current data about population, income, commerce, industries, retail trade, etc.

644. Frank, Nathalie D. **Market Analysis: a Handbook of Current Data Sources.** New York, Scarecrow Press, 1964. 268 p.

Attempts "to provide a guide to the understanding of marketing information, its origins and retrieval. No attempt has been made to create an exhaustive bibliography or to encompass all sources of interest to the broad area of marketing research" (Introd.) An extensive index is included.

645. Harvey, Joan M. **Statistics-Europe: Sources for Market Research.** Kent, CBD Research, 1968. 170 p.

Provides up-to-date information on published statistics and shows the availability of unpublished materials.

646. **Industrial Marketing, Media Market Planning Guide.** 1963 — Chicago, Advertising Publishers, 1963 —

647. Klein, B. and Company, New York. **Directory of Mailing List Houses. 7th ed.** New York, 1969. 347 p.

648. Library Association. County Libraries Group. **Readers' Guide to Books on the Business World.** London, 1952. 51 p.

649. Maltby, Arthur. **Economics and Commerce; the Sources of Information and their Organization.** London, C. Bingley. 1968. 239 p.

650. Market Research Society. **Statistical Sources for Market Research.** London, Market Research Society in association with the Oakwood Press, 1957. 32 p. (Its Publications, no. 2).

Provides very useful introductory guide to the government statistical sources in Great Britain.

651. **Marketing Information Guide. March 1954** — Washington, U. S. Dept. of Commerce. Monthly.

Title varies: v. 1-7, Distribution Data Guide. This annotated guide includes materials of federal, state, local, foreign governments, also of international and private organizations. Subject indexes are issued semiannually as supplements.

652. National Sales Executives, Inc., New York. **Sources of Information for Sales Executives and Specialists in Marketing.** Prepared by the Committee on Bibliography for Sales Management. New York, 1954. 23 p.

653. Romaine, Lawrence B. **A Guide to American Trade Catalogs, 1744-1900.** New York, R. R. Bowker, 1960. 422 p.

An important list of trade catalogs arranged in classes giving location of items.

654. Special Libraries Association. Business and Finance Division. Committee on Sources of Commodity Prices. **Sources of Commodity Prices.** Compiled by Paul Wasserman. New York, Special Libraries Association, 1959. 170 p.

Updates the Price Sources published by the U. S. Dept. of Commerce in 1931. This work presents a project undertaken by the Business and Finance Division of the Special Libraries Association.

655. Special Libraries Association. New York Chapter. Advertising and Marketing Group. **Guide to Special Issues and Indexes of Periodicals.** New York, 1962. 125 p.

Aids in location of specialized data and statistics in business, technical, and consumer periodicals. The included periodicals (ca. 800) are arranged alphabetically giving information about supplements, indexes, frequency, and some other data. Subject index is included.

656. U. S. Bureau of Foreign and Domestic Commerce. **Market Research Sources; a Guide to Information on Domestic Marketing.** 1st — 1927 — Washington, U. S. Govt. Print Off., (Its Domestic Commerce Series).

Title varies: 1926-30, Market Research Agencies; a Guide to Publications.

657. U. S. Business and Defense Services Administration. Office of Distribution. **Guides to Information Sources for Education in Distribution.** Washington, 1961. 33 p.

Intended to introduce materials and sources on marketing subjects, emphasizing the government and business sources.

658. U. S. Dept. of Commerce. **Business Service Check List.** v. 1 — July 5, 1946 — Washington, U. S. Govt. Print. Off. Weekly.

BIBLIOGRAPHIES (CURRENT)

659. **Tables of Contents of Selected Advertising and Marketing Publications.** v. 1 — April 1967 — Princeton, N.J., Marketing Communications Research Center. Monthly.

Designed as a monthly compilation of table of contents of selected serials (journals) and a few proceedings of conferences, meetings, etc., to serve as a convenient reference tool to advertising and marketing literature in English language.

660. U. S. Dept. of Commerce. Library. **United States Department of Commerce Publications;** compiled under the direction of Wanda Mae Johnson, Librarian. Washington, U. S. Government Print Office., 1952. 795 p. — Supplement 1951/52 — Washington, U. S. Government Print Office. Annual.

Cumulations of the Business Service Check List issued by Dept. of Commerce. This is a selected list of publications in print and those out of print which have research value. First section provides general information regarding distribution of publications currently available and location of publications no longer available for distribution. Section II contains a selected listing of publications by each bureau and office. In Section III is a detailed alphabetical subject index. The Supplement contains a selected list of publications issued from October 1950 to December 1952.

BIBLIOGRAPHY (RETROSPECTIVE)

660a. Advertising Federation of America. Bureau of Research and Education.
Books for the Advertising and Marketing Man; a Classified Bibliography on
Advertising, Marketing, Selling, and Related Subjects. Rev. ed. New York,
1957. 37 p. (Supplement, 1958. 15 p.)

660b. Advertising Research Foundation. **A Bibliography of Theory and
Research Techniques in the Field of Human Motivation.** New York, 1956.
117 p.
    Presents an extensive coverage of books and periodical articles on human
motivation.

661. Barcelona. Cámara Oficial de Comercio y Navagación. Biblioteca.
Catàlogo de la Bibliòteca por Orden Alfabetico de Autores. Barcelon, Tip.
La Academica de Herederos de Serra y Russell, 1946. 546 p.
    A Spanish bibliography on commerce, arranged alphabetically by author.

662. **A Bibliography for Students of Retailing,** by Charles M. Edwards, Jr.,
and others. New York, B. Earl Puckett Fund for Retail Education, 1966. 163 p.

663. **Bibliography on Marketing to Low-Income Consumers.** Washington,
U. S. Dept. of Commerce, Business and Defense Services Administration,
U. S. Govt. Print. Off., 1969. 49 p.

664. Buzzell, Robert Dow. **Basic Bibliography on Mathematical Methods in
Marketing:** Chicago, American Marketing Association, 1962. 62 p. (A.M.A.
Bibliography Series, no. 7).

665. Cole, Arthur Harrison. **Measures of Business Change; Baker Library
Index,** with the assistance of Virginia Jenness and Grace V. Lindfords.
Chicago, Irwin, 1952. 444 p.
    This annotated bibliography is divided into two main parts. (1) National
measure of change, which covers index numbers of business commodity prices,
construction costs, employment and finance; (2) Regional and local measures,
covering various regions and places of the U. S. In all, 449 entries are listed.
Included are: list of indexes in order of presentation, reference list of basic
sources, and a general index.

666. Chute, Aaron Hamilton. **A Selected and Annotated Bibliography of
Retailing.** Austin, Bureau of Business Research, University of Texas, 1964.
112 p. (University of Texas, Bureau of Business Research. Bibliography
Series, no. 5. rev.)
    Originally published under title: A Selected and Annotated Bibliography
of Literature on Retailing.

667. Clarke, George Timothy. **Bibliography of Advertising and Marketing Theses for the Doctorate in United States Colleges and Universities, 1944 to 1959.** New York, Advertising Educational Foundation, 1961. 28 leaves.

Lists three hundred dissertations arranged alphabetically by title under subjects.

668. Dunn, Albert H. **Annotated Bibliography on Field Sales Management.** New York, Sales on Marketing Executives-International, 1967. 42 p.

669. Frank, Nathalie D. **Current Sources of Information for Market Research,** a Selected and Annotated Bibliography; Presented at American Management Association Marketing Orientation Seminar, New York, 1954. 29 p.

670. Gt. Brit. Stationery Office. **Commerce and Industry and H.M.S.O.:** a Selection of Government Publications for the Businessman. London, 1966. 31 p.

An annotated list arranged in 15 sections, mostly of informative nature for businessmen.

671. Gunther, Edgar and Goldstein, Frederick A. **Current Sources of Marketing Information; a Bibliography of Primary Marketing Data.** Chicago. American Marketing Association, 1960. 119 p. (A.M.A. Bibliography Series, no 6).

This is an annotated guide of about 1,200 titles (books, periodicals, documents, reports). The arrangement is by subject, then by branch of industrial or commercial activity.

672. Hamburg, Welt-Wirtschafts-Archiv. Bibliothek. **Bibliographie zur Marktforschung:** 1072 Titel mit Signaturen der Bibliothek. Bibliography on Market Research: 1072 Titles with Call Numbers of the Library. Hamburg, 1955. 108 p.

673. Hertfordshire, Eng. Country Technical Library Service. **A Select Bibliography on Computer Applications in Commerce and Industry,** compiled by C. R. Randall. Hatfield, Herts., Hatfield College of Technology, 1963. 52 p.

A useful list for business and commerce libraries, for special librarians and students of business administration.

674. Hollander, Stanley C. **A Special Interest Bibliography on Discount Selling, Retail Price-Cutting and Resale Price Controls.** Chicago, American Marketing Association, 1956. 52 p. (A.M.A. Bibliography Series, no. 3).

675. Holloway, Robert J. **A Basic Bibliography on Experiments in Marketing.** Chicago, American Marketing Association, 1967. 45 p. (A.M.A. Bibliography Series, no. 14).

676. Humpert, Magdalene. **Bibliographie der Kameral Wissenschaften.** Köln, Schroeder, 1937. 1184 p. (Kölner Bibliographische Arbeiten, 1).

This German bibliography on commerce covers the period from 1520-1850 and is one of the best for historical material.

677. Kelley, Eugene J. and others. **Marketing Management; an Annotated Bibliography.** Chicago, American Marketing Association, 1963. 71 p. (A.M.A. Bibliography Series, no. 8).

678. Lawrence, Richard M. ed. **Sources of Information for Industrial Market Research.** With Special Reference to the Chemical Process Industries. New York, Chemical Industries 1947. 97 p.

679. Mallen, Bruce E. and Litvak, I. A. **A Basic Bibliography on Marketing in Canada.** Chicago. American Marketing Association, 1967. 119 p. (A.M.A. Bibliography Series, no. 13).

680. Marks, Norton E., and Taylor, Robert M., comps. **Physical Distribution and Marketing Logistics;** an Annotated Bibliography. Chicago, American Marketing Association, 1966. 125 p. (A.M.A. Bibliography Series, no. 11).

681. Massie, Joseph. **Bibliography of the Collection of Books and Tracts on Commerce, Currency, and Poor Law, (1557-1763).** Formed by Joseph Massie. . Transcribed from Lansdowne muscript MXLIX with historical and bibliographical introd. by William A. Shaw. London, G. Harding, 1937. 173 p. (Reprint 1967).

682. Massy, William F. **Planning in Marketing; a Selected Bibliography.** Cambridge, Mass., M.I.T. 1962. 56 p.

An annotated list of most important publications in this field. It includes books, periodicals, articles, and reference material of recent origin. No index.

683. Megathlin, Donald E. and Schaeffer, Winnifred E. **A Bibliography on New Product Planning.** 2nd ed. Chicago, American Marketing Association, 1966. 62 p. (A.M.A. Bibliography Series, no. 5).

684. New York University. Graduate School of Business Administration. **Bibliography of Graduate Theses in the Field of Marketing,** Written at U. S. Colleges and Universities, 1950-1957. New York, 1957. 92 p.

685. Rathmell, John M. **A Bibliography of Personal Selling.** Chicago, American Marketing Association, 1966. 50 p. (A.M.A. Bibliography Series, no. 12).

686. Revzan, David Allan. **A Comprehensive Classified Marketing Bibliography.** Berkeley, University of California Press, 1951. 2 pts. (California

University Bureau of Business and Economic Research Publications).

Contents: pt. 1. Books published through 1949; pt. 2. Government publications, University research monographs, and articles in professional journals, published through 1949.

687. Sheparovych, Zenon B. **Quantitative Methods in Marketing; a Selected Annotated Bibliography,** compiled and edited by Zenon B. Sheparovych, Marcus Alexis and Leonard S. Simon. Chicago, American Marketing Association, 1968. 86 p. (American Marketing Association. Bibliography Series, no. 15).

688. Staudt, Thomas A. and Lazer, William, comps. **A Basic Bibliography on Industrial Marketing.** East Lansing, Mich., American Marketing Association, 1958. 233 p. (A.M.A. Bibliography Series, no. 4).

689. Texas University. Distributive Education Dept. **Distributive Education Bibliography,** Including: Instructional Material from States; books; periodicals; material from trade associations, pamphlets and booklets. Issued by the University of Texas, Division of Extension, Distributive Education Dept. in cooperation with Texas Education Agency, Distributive Education Service, Austin, 1954. 206 p. (Supplement, 1957. 134 p.)

690. Thompson, Ralph Burnham. **Selected and Annotated Bibliography of Marketing Theory.** Austin, Bureau of Business Research, University of Texas, 1958. 27 p. (Bureau of Business Research, University of Texas. Bibliography Series 14).

691. U. S. Library of Congress. Map Division. **Marketing Maps of the United States;** an Annotated Bibliography. 3rd rev. ed. Compiled by Walter W. Ristow. Washington, 1958. 147 p.

692. U. S. National Archives. **Preliminary Inventory of the Records of the Price Department of the Office of Price Administration (Record group 188).** Compiled by Meyer H. Fishbein, Walter W. Weinstein, and Albert W. Winthrop. Washington, 1956. 272 p. (Its Publication no. 57-3. Preliminary Inventories, no. 95).

693. Wales, Hugh G. and Ferber, Robert. **A Basic Bibliography on Marketing Research.** 2nd ed. Chicago, American Marketing Association, 1963. 182 p. (A.M.A. Bibliography Series, no. 2. 1963 rev.)

Supersedes the 1956 ed. Presents a detailed annotated list of literature, arranged by major areas of marketing research.

694. Warsaw. Szkola Główna Handlowa. Biblioteka. **Katalog Biblioteki; Nauki Ekonomiczne: Handlowe.** Opracowal Andrzej Grodek. Warszawa, 1945. 941 p. Title transl. Library Catalog: Economic and commerce sciences.

695. Wild, J.E. **The European Common Market and European Free Trade Association.** 3rd rev. ed. London, Library Association, 1962. 62 p. (Special Subject List, no. 35).

Lists books, pamphlets, reports, periodical articles, bibliographies, and reading material. Some entries are annotated. Name and subject indexes.

DICTIONARIES AND ENCYCLOPEDIAS

696. Graham, I. **Encyclopedia of Advertising.** 2nd ed. New York, Fairchild, 1969. 512 p.

Includes some 1200 entries in classified arrangement.

697. Herbst, Robert. **Dictionary of Commercial, Financial and Legal Terms Pertaining to Trade and Industry,** Including Terms Used in Importing, Manufacturing, Distributing and Marketing, as well as those used in banking, stock exchange dealings, credit, foreign exchange, taxation, and customs, traffic including land, sea, and air transport, insurance and mail services, economics, social science, and politics, and covering, in particular, the special terminology as used in all fields of private and public law including legislative, executive, and judicial branches of government. 2nd ed. Lucerne, Thali, 1962-66. 3 v.

698. Hanson, John Lloyd. **A Dictionary of Economics and Commerce.** London, Macdonald & Evans, 1965. 401 p. illus.

Most of over 4,000 entries refer to principles, theory and applied economics. Includes many cross references.

699. Motta, Guiseppe. **Dizionario Commerciale: Inglese-Italiano, Italiano-Inglese.** Economia, legge, finanza (amminstrazione, banca, borsa, assiourszione, scami, commercio estero e marittimo, transporti, dogane, ecc.) Milano, C. Signorelli, 1961. 1050 p.

A useful English-Italian and Italian-English dictionary of commercial terms.

700. Nemmers, Erwin Esser and Janzen, Cornelius C. **Dictionary of Economics and Business.** Paterson, N.J., Littlefield, Adams. 1959. 326 p.

700a. **Pitman's Business Man's Guide: a Comprehensive Dictionary of Commercial Information.** 14th ed. by L. T. Nelson, London, Pitman, 1967. 346 p.

DIRECTORIES

(This is a highly selective listing of directories in this area. For a more comprehensive coverage consult *International Business and Foreign Trade: A Guide to Information Sources* (Gale, 1968). For more current imprints, published during 1969, consult *American Reference Books Annual* (Libraries Unlimited, 1970 —).

701. Adler, Max Kurt. **Directory of British Market Research Organizations and Services.** London, C. Lockwood, 1965. 88 p.

702. Advertising Research Foundation. **Directory of Organizations which Conduct Motivation Research.** New York, 1954. 127 p.

703. Advertising Research Foundation. **Directory of Research Organization Members.** New York, 1968 — 1 v. (Loose-leaf).

704. Bradford, Ernest Smith. **Survey and Directory of Marketing Research Agencies in the United States and the World.** New York, C. E. Burckel, 1944 — Annual. Subtitle varies.

A comprehensive listing of agencies and persons engaged in marketing, advertising, economic and personnel research, community and public opinion surveys, and other activities in related fields. The first list is arranged by cities, the second list by the type of research activity.

705. **British Rate and Data's Directories and Annuals.** London, MacLean & Hunter, 19 — Annual.

Lists directories and annuals by titles with subject index. Presents a useful supplement to Current British Directories. Part of Standard Rate and Data Service (International Editions).

706. Dun and Bradstreet, Inc. **Middle Market Directory.** 1964 — New York. Annual.

Lists about 25,000 companies with a net worth of $500,000 to $1 million in alphabetical geographical and product sections.

707. Henderson, George Poland and Anderson, I. G. **Current British Directories,** 1966-7. 5th ed.

Contents: 1. Local directories; 2. Specialized directories; 3. International directories; 4. Directories of the British Commonwealth and South Africa; Index; Publisher's addresses.

708. **Kelly's Directory of Merchants, Manufacturers and Merchants Including Industrial Services.** London, 1880 —

709. **Kompass; Register of British Industry and Commerce.** 1st — 1962 — Croydon, Eng., Kompass Register.

710. **MacRae's Blue Book.** 76th ed. Western Springs, Ill., MacRae's Blue Book Co., 1969. 4 v.

A directory of American Manufacturers. Volume one is corporations index. The remaining volumes provide a classified directory of products.

711. **Poor's Register of Directors and Executives, United States and Canada.** New York: Standard and Poor's Corp., 1928 — Annual with three supplements yearly.

Arrangement is alphabetical by corporation, with a product index, industrial index, and register of directors. Brief biographical sketches are given.

712. Selka, K. R. ed. **Europ Production.** Darmstadt, Europ Export Edition, 1966 — Annual.

Lists over 450,000 entries of manufacturers in 17 European countries. Includes indexes of products in English, French, Italian, German and Spanish.

712a. **Standard Directory of Advertisers.** Jan. 1916 — Skokie, Ill., etc. National Register Pub. Co., Frequency varies. Title varies: 1916-19, Standard Register of National Advertising; 1920 — Standard Advertising Register.

Formed in 1964 by merger of Standard Advertising Register, and McKittrick Directory of Advertisers. Lists 17,000 companies.

713. U.S. Dept. of Commerce. **Business Service Check List.** v. 1 — July 1946 — Washington, U.S. Govt. Print. Off., Weekly.

714. **World Trade Data Yearbook,** New York, Business Abroad, 1957 — Annual.

715. **World Who's Who in Finance and Industry.** 16th ed. Chicago, Marquis, 1969. 787 p.

In addition to providing biographical sketches, this publication lists principal businesses and their executives.

HANDBOOKS
(Most handbooks included in this section provide additional bibliographical references)

715a. Aspley, John Cameron. **Sales Manager's Handbook.** 11th ed. rev. Chicago, Dartnell, 1968. 1151 p.

Brings a wealth of useful information for sales people particularly in sales organization, method of selling, training of salesmen, markets, surveys and research. Glossary of marketing terms is included.

716. Aspley, John Cameron. **The Sales Promotion Handbook.** 5th ed. rev. Chicago, Dartnell, 1966. 1080 p.

This is a companion volume to author's Sales Manager's Handbook.

717. Frey, Albert W. ed. **Marketing Handbook.** With the assistance of Gerald Albaum. 2nd ed. New York, Ronald Press, 1965. 1 v.

This compilation presents a comprehensive reference work on marketing facts, methods, principles, theories, and techniques written by numerous experts in their fields.

718. Stephenson, James. **Principles and Practice of Commerce.** 6th ed., by J. L. D. Ciano. London, Pitman, 1965. 616 p.

INDEXES

719. **Business Periodicals Index.** New York, H. W. Wilson, 1958 –

For annotation see entry no. 98.

720. Davenport, Donald Hills, and Scott, Frances V. **An Index to Business Indices.** Chicago, Business Publications, 1937. 187 p.

This is a guide to most important business and statistical indexes of the United States, in two parts: 1. Finding index, and 2. Description of indexes. Now only of historical interest.

721. King, Robert L. **An Annotated Index to the Proceedings of the American Marketing Association Conferences. '55/'66.** Chicago, American Marketing Association, 1966. 163 p. (A.M.A. Bibliography Series, no. 10).

722. **Research Index.** Wallington, Surrey, Business Surveys, 1965 – Semi-monthly.

This is an index to about 130 British business, economic and trade periodicals and to the nations newspapers and to the noteworthy articles which appear in them.

ATLASES

723. Rand McNally. **Commercial Atlas and Marketing Guide.** 100th ed. New York, 1969. 611 p.

An excellent annual atlas of the United States and the world covering: a general information, agriculture, communications, manufacturing, populations, trade, transportation, state maps and statistics, etc. Emphasis is on the U. S. less extensively is treated Canada and the rest of the world. Well indexed.

724. Business International Corporation. **Information System.** New York, 195 — Weekly.

This business service publishes a weekly newsletter reporting in international developments in the field of business and commerce on most countries of the world. In each issue is a brief business outlook on a different country. In addition, Business International publishes a number of specialized publications, e.g. Business Europe, Business Latin America, Investing, Licensing and Trading Conditions Abroad, etc. A master cumulative index to all publications is issued quarterly.

725. Hauser, Philip Morris, and Leonard, William R. eds. **Government Statistics for Business Use.** 2nd ed. New York, Wiley, 1956. 440 p. (Wiley Publications in Statistics).

Designed as a guide to statistics for management,production and marketing needs. Each chapter has been written by a specialist giving reference sources. The general index is included.

726. Standard Rate and Data Service, **Consumer Markets.** Chicago, 1919 — Annual.

Market surveys are arranged by state, country and city. Each issue includes statistical data on income, household, trading areas, gives information on rates, advertising media of radio, T.V., newspapers, and serial publications.

727. U. S. Bureau of Labor Statistics. **Wholesale Prices and Price Indexes,** 1945-5 — Washington, U. S. Govt. Print Office, 1957 — Annual. (Its Bulletin no. 1214, 1235, etc.)

Some issues, (1954-56, 1958) include "Bibliography" listing bulletins and reprints covering wholesale prices from the year 1900. The Bureau also issued a series; Wholesale prices, 1922-1951-52. Contains: price movements, wholesale price indexes for major commodity groups, by stage of processing, etc., references and regional office directory.

728. U. S. Bureau of the Census. **Census of Business,** 1933 — Washington, Govt. Print Office, 1934 — Frequency varies. Number and title of volumes vary.

Contents for 1963 ed.: v. 1. Retail trade summary statistics; v. 2. Retail trade area statistics; v. 3. Major retail center statistics (Large metropolitan areas) v. 4. Wholesale trade summary statistics; v. 5. Wholesale trade area statistics; v. 6. Selected services summary statistics; v. 7. Selected services area statistics.

729. U. S. Office of Business Economics. **Business Statistics; Statistical Supplement.** 1951 — Biennial. Washington, U. S. Govt. Print Off.

Designed as a supplement to Survey of Current Business; this biennial provides statistical tables giving monthly or quarterly data and some annual averages.

MONOGRAPHIC TREATISES

(This is a sample of the voluminous literature on this subject. Most works listed here include extensive bibliographies).

730. Britt, Steuart Henderson and Boyd, Harper W. **Marketing Management and Administrative Action.** New York, McGraw-Hill, 1963. 772 p. (McGraw-Hill Series in Marketing and Advertising).

Presents a very valuable collection of 70 articles in this field. Stressed is the theme that marketing is the unifying agent for all activities of the business search for profit and survival.

731. Brown, Lyndon O. **Marketing and Distribution Research.** 3rd ed. New York, Ronald Press, 1955. 561 p.

Presents a comprehensive study of marketing and distribution research including methods and techniques, various types of analyses and investigations. This work may be very helpful for student and research worker in this field.

732. Davies, Antony Hawes and Palmer, O. W. **Market Research and Scientific Distribution.** London, Blanford Press, 1957. 362 p.

733. Ferber, Robert, and Wales, Hugh G. eds. **Motivation and Market Behavior.** Homewood, Ill., Irwin, 1958. 437 p.

Discusses various interpretations and attitudes toward the study of motivation, and different approaches to solve the problems in human behavior. The organization of material goes from general discussion in part 1, through psychological approach in part 2, and non-psychological survey techniques in part 3, to other techniques in final part 4. General index is included. Bibliography: p. 402-429.

734. King, William R. **Quantitative Analysis for Marketing Management.** New York, McGraw-Hill, 1967. 574 p.

Discusses the decision problems in marketing management, emphasizing the methodology of analysis rather than the technical aspects. The first four chapters of the book deal with the general ideas and theories, the last seven chapters offer an approach to apply those ideas and models into practice.

735. Luck, David Johnston and others. **Marketing Research.** 2nd ed. Englewood Cliffs, N. J., Prentice-Hall, 1961. 541 p.

Presents functions, techniques and applications of research to marketing problems. Discusses such topics as performance analysis, motivation, operations research, case problems, electronic data processing, data collection methods and others.

736. McCulloch, John Ramsey. **Early English Tracts on Commerce; from the Originals of Mun, Roberts, North and Others.** Cambridge, Economic History Society, 1952. 663 p.

Included tracts are of great rarity. The first, A Discourse of Trade from England unto the East Indies, published in 1621 is the oldest one. The last one entitled Considerations on the East India Trade, published in 1701 is the newest one.

736a. McNair, Malcolm Perrine and Hansen, Harry L. **Readings in Marketing.** 2nd ed. New York, McGraw-Hill, 1956. 559 p.

737. Minnesota. University. Library. James Ford Bell Collection. **Merchants and Scholars; Essays in the History of Exploration and Trade.** Collected in memory of James Ford Bell and edited by John Parker. Minneapolis, University of Minnesota Press, 1965. 258 p.

This collection of essays, "diversified in its contents, is intended as a contribution and an encouragement to research into many areas of knowledge. . . In acquiring source materials and in assisting in the publication of the results of research into the history of European commercial expansion, the James Ford Bell Collection hopes to continue the ancient tradition of cooperation between the merchant and the scholar." (Introd.)

738. Reid, Margaret Gilpin. **Consumers and the Market.** 3rd ed. New York, Crofts, 1942. 617 p.

This textbook is an outgrowth of a course in "Consumer marketing" given at the Iowa State College. Intended to enlighten consumers about the practical issues of marketing. Included are indexes of authors and of subjects. Selected bibliography and suggested questions and problems: p. 582-600.

739. Stanton, William J. **Fundamentals of Marketing.** 2nd ed. New York, McGraw-Hill, 1967. 743 p.

A practical, basic, and analytical understanding of how and why marketing operates in American business today. Written largely from the "micro" viewpoint of marketing executives in an individual firm, the text presents marketing as a total, interacting system of business activity designed to plan, promote, and distribute want-satisying goods and services to household consumers and industrial users.

CHAPTER FIVE

INTERNATIONAL ECONOMICS
Foreign Trade & Exchange: Exports, Imports
(See also Commerce and Marketing)

GUIDES TO INFORMATION

740. Bank of America. **International Trade Information; a Man on the Spot Guide.** New York, 1964 — Looseleaf.

A useful guide for exporter and importer on various aspects of international trade, such as: export letters of credit, patents, capital sources, credit, insurance, world export-import controls.

741. Chamber of Commerce of the United States. **Foreign Commerce Handbook; Basic Information and a Guide to Sources.** 16th ed. Washington, D.C., 1967. 184 p.

Describes the activities and services in the field of foreign trade of U.S. government agencies, and of related intergovernmental organizations and private U.S. business organizations. Includes sources of information on special topics; lists American chambers of commerce in foreign countries and local chambers of commerce.

742. **Concise Guide to International Markets.** London, International Advertising Association, U. K. Chapter, 1966. Looseleaf.

Supplies information on marketing and advertising conditions on geography, population, education, currency, income and industry in foreign countries.

743. Dun and Bradstreet, Inc. **International Market Guide; Continental Europe.** V. 1 — 1961 — New York.

744. Dun and Bradstreet, Inc. **International Market Guide; Latin America.** v. 1 — 1938 —

Title varies: 1938-59, Latin America sales index; 1960, Latin America Market Guide.

745. Hulm, Mary, W. **Importation of Goods; a Buyer's Guide to Import Procedures.** London, Purchasing Officers Association, 1956. 29 p.

746. **International Information Service.** Chicago, Library of International Relations, 1962 — Quarterly.

This is a guide to publications on economic, political and social conditions in various countries of the world. It lists books, pamphlets, reports and periodicals in subject arrangement. Includes directory of cited periodicals and a geographic index.

747. **International Reference Handbook of Services, Organizations, Diplomatic Representation, Marketing, and Advertising Channels.** New York, World Trade Academy Press. 1954 —   Title varies: 1-3, 1954 —

This International Reference Handbook covers the whole of the U. S. and about 120 foreign countries. Arrangement is alphabetical by country.

748. **Overseas Marketing Survey;** a Guide to over 80 Expert Markets. 2nd enl. ed. London, Business Publications, 1949. 389 p.

749. U. S. Bureau of Foreign Commerce. **A Guide to Foreign Business Directories.** Washington, U. S. Governments Print Office, 1955. 132 p.

Aimed to help businessmen in identifying the names of persons or companies of commerce and industry in foreign countries. The data in this guide are based on reports submitted by the Foreign Service of the United States. The book is divided into two parts. Part one, Country Directories, contains the titles of directories in the free world arranged in alphabetical order under country's name. Part two, International Directories published in the United States, lists directories alphabetically by industry, trade or profession. Indexes are included.

750. U. S. Bureau of Foreign Commerce. **Guides for the Newcomer to World Trade.** Prepared by Paul E. Pauly and F. Preston Forbes. Washington, U. S. Govt. Print. Off., 1957. 20 p.

Presents a brief but highly selected list of books, pamphlets, reports and other material which are essential for the beginner in the study of international trade.

751. U. S. Bureau of Foreign Commerce. **Sources of Information on Foreign Trade Practice.** Washington, 1959. 47 p.

752. U. S. Bureau of the Census. **Guide to Foreign Trade Statistics.** Washington, 1969. 139 p.

Describes the publications on foreign trade statistics of the U. S. Bureau of the Census, of the U. S. Dept. of Commerce and of Bureau of Customs Offices.

BIBLIOGRAPHIES (CURRENT)

753. Contracting Parties to the General Agreement on Tariffs and Trade. **GATT Bibliography, 1947-1953.** Geneva, GATT Secretariat, 1954.

754. _____. Supplement. 1st —   1954/June 1955 —   Annual.

755. Martinstetter, Hermann. **Internationale Bibliographie des Zollwesens.** Konstanz, Industrie-Verlag C. Gehlsen, 1954. 189 p. (Supplement, 1957).

756. U.S. Bureau of International Commerce. **International Business Publication Checklist.** 19 — Washington, D.C., Dept. of Commerce. Irregular.

In addition to listings of publications of the Dept. of Commerce, this checklist includes publications on international trade of other governmental and nongovernmental agencies.

BIBLIOGRAPHIES RETROSPECTIVE

757. Ball, Joyce, and Gardella, Roberta, comps. **Foreign Statistical Documents;** a Bibliography of General International Trade, and Agricultural Statistics, Including Holdings of the Stanford University Libraries. Stanford, Calif., Hoover Institution on War, Revolution and Peace, 1967. 173 p.

Lists official, statistical documents in country arrangement.

758. Bromley, D. W. **What to Read on Exporting.** 2nd ed. London, Library Association, 1966. 68 p. (Special subject list no. 42).

A useful list on foreign trade, markets, marketing research, advertising, packaging, etc. Includes directory of publishers' addresses, and an author, title and subject index.

759. Contracting Parties to the General Agreement on Tariffs and Trade. International Trade Centre. **Compendium of Sources; International Trade Statistics;** an analytical compilation of foreign trade statistics published by international agencies and national governments to world over, with an introduction on their use in market research. Geneva, GATT International Trade Centre, 1967. 150 p.

760. Hamburg. Welt-Wirtschafts-Archiv. Bibliothek. **Ausländische Adress-Bücher;** 893 Titel mit Signaturen der Bibliothek. 2. Ausg., Stand. Juni 1953. Ausgearbeitet von Anny Schmidt. Hamburg, 1953. 116 p.

Contains 893 titles of foreign address books of commercial firms.

761. Mostecky, Vaclav. **Doing Business Abroad; a Selected and Annotated Bibliography of Books and Pamphlets in English.** Cambridge, Mass., Harvard University, Law School Library, 1962. 88 p.

762. Organization for Economic Cooperation and Development. Library. **Conférence des Nations Unies sur le Commerce et le Dévelopment. United Nations Conference for Trade and Development.** Paris, 1965. 58 p (Its Bibliographie speciale analytique, 5 (42).

763. _____. **International Monetary System. Système Monétaire International.** Paris, 1967. 130 p. (Its Special annotated bibliography, 16).

764. Organization for Economic Cooperation and Development. Library. **Payments Internationaux. International Payments.** Paris, 1964. 51 p. (Its Bibliographie Speciale Analytique, 4 (41).

765. _____. **Les Rélations Commerciales Est-Ouest. East-West Trade Relations.** Paris, 1966. 95 p. (Its Bibliographie speciale analytique, 7 (44).

766. Schloss, Henry H. and Breswick, William N. **A Selected and Annotated Bibliography of International Trade.** Austin, 1951. 28 p. (Texas University, Bureau of Business Research. Bibliography, no. 9).

767. Stewart, Charles F. and Simmons, George B. **A Bibliography of International Business.** New York, Columbia University Press, 1964. 603 p.

Over 8,000 items (books and articles from 120 journals) on international business are selected, excluding foreign language publications. All material has been divided into four parts: 1. Comparative business sytems; 2. Government and international operations; 3. The firm in international operations; 4. Nations and regions.

768. U. S. Library of Congress. Legislative Reference Service. **Free Trade, Tariff Legislation and Common Markets for the Western Hemisphere;** a collection of excerpts and selected references. Washington, U. S. Govt. Print. Off., 1962. 70 p.

This is a basic study of free trade references for the Western World countries.

769. U. S. Library of Congress. Reference Dept. **International Economic and Social Development;** a selective background reading list, prepared for the National Conference on International Economic and Social Development, April 7-9, 1952. Washington, 1952. 55 p.

770. Wheeler, Lora J. ed. **International Business and Foreign Trade.** Information Sources, Detroit, Gale Research, 1966. 221 p.

A useful guide to source materials and basic reference works.

DICTIONARIES & ENCYCLOPEDIAS

771. **Eksportno-Importnyi Slovar.** Glavnyi red. B.T. Kolpakov. Moskva. Vneshtorgizdat, 1952-54. 3 v.

This Russian encyclopedic dictionary gives explanations in longer or shorter articles to thousands of commercial terms related to foreign trade. Terms are translated into several languages. Texts are supplemented with numerous tables and illustrations.

772. **Exporters' Encyclopaedia: Containing Full and Authentic Information Relative to Shipments for Every Country in the World.** New York, Exporters' Encyclopaedia Corporation, 1st ed. 1904 —

Annual with supplementary bulletins to keep it up-to-date.

773. Henius, Frank. **Dictionary of Foreign Trade.** 2nd ed. New York, Prentice Hall, 1947. 959 p.

The aim of this dictionary is to interpret the meaning of foreign trade terms, usages, practices, procedures, and abbreviations. The book is composed of four parts: the Abbreviations, the Dictionary (main body) Weights and measures, and the Specimen forms (arranged alphabetically by subject).

DIRECTORIES

774. **American Register of Exporters and Importers,** New York, 1946 — Annual.

775. **Anglo American Trade Directory.** 1962/63 — London, American Chamber of Commerce in London. Annual.

776. Benko, William John. **Business Around the World;** World Trader's International Directory and Handbook. New York, 1963.

777. _____. **International Importer's Trade Directory.** New York, 1960. 1 v.

778. Bottin. **Bottin International: International Business Register.** Anuario del Comercio Exterior. Internationales Handelsregister. 1947 — Paris, Annuaire du commerce Didot-Bottin. Annual.

779. **British & International Buyers & Sellers Guide.** 19 — Glasglow, C. G. Birn.

780. **Canadian Trade Index.** Toronto, Canadian Manufacturer's Ass'n. Annual.

781. **Directory of Active Foreign Buyers.** v. 1 — 1960 — New York, Journal of Commerce.

782. **Directory of American Firms Operating in Foreign Countries.** Compiled by Juvenal L. Angel. 1955/56 — New York, World Trade Academy Press, 1955 — Annual.

Divided into two parts: pt. 1. Geographical distribution by country; pt. 2. Alphabetical list of corporations giving United States addresses.

783. **The Directory of British Exporters.** 1951 — London, Benn Bros. Biennial.

784. **Directory of United States Import Concerns.** 1951 — New York.

785. **International Yellow Pages.** ` 1963/64 — Rochester, N. Y. Reuben H. Donnelley Telephone Directory Co., Annual.

Presents a classified product and service listing of more than 538,000 companies in 136 countries. The basic informations are given about each country such as, the capital, currency, language, population, commerce and trade.

786. Khungar, T. C. **Khungar's Directory of Trade Directories of the World.** Contains nearly 2,100 titles showing number of pages, price, particulars in brief and addresses of their publishers. Delhi, Bharat Directories Corp. 1961 —

787. **Marconi's International Register.** 64th ed. London, Marconi, International Code Co., 1964. 1623 p.

Lists alphabetically principal firms having international interests.

788. **Owen's Commerce & Travel & International Register. . . : Africa, Middle East & Far East, with international trade list.** London, Owen's Commerce & Travel, 1954 — Annual. Title varies.

This is not only a trade directory but also an information source about the countries of Africa, Middle and Far East, giving statistical data, figures and maps. All sectors of national economy (agriculture, commerce, industry, population) education, emmigration and immigration, health, etc. are included.

788a. **Sell's International Register.** 1961 — London, Business Directories. Annual.

789. **Trade Directories of the World.** 1st — 1952 — New York, Croner Publications. v. Title varies: 1952, Croner's World Register of Trade Directories.

A loose-leaf handbook containing the latest information on all business and trade directories in the United States and foreign countries, kept up-to-date by an amendment service. Divided into five main sections: Europe, Africa, Americas, Asia, Australasia, and subdivided by countries, the Register lists title of directories in an alphabetical order. Indexes of trades, professions and countries are included.

790. U. S. Bureau of Foreign Commerce (1953-1961). **A Directory of Foreign Advertising Agencies and Marketing Research Organizations for the United States International Business Community.** (Compiled by Helen Biggane). Washington, 1959. 135 p.

791. U. S. Bureau of Foreign Commerce. **A Directory of Foreign Organizations for Trade and Investment Promotion.** Washington, 1961. 108 p.

792. **Westminster Directory of the World.** London, Tamar Publishing Co., 1968. 564 p.

HANDBOOKS

793. Bureau of National Affairs, Washington, D. C. **International Trade Reporter.** Washington, 1954-56. 2 v. (Looseleaf).

794. _____. **Export Shipping Manual. Steamship Services Supplement.** Washington, 1960. 130 p.

795. _____. **Export Shipping Manual. Shipping Services Supplement.** Ocean, cargo-air cargo. 2nd ed. Washington, 1965. 125 p.

796. Dartnell Corporation. **The Dartnell International Trade Handbook** by Gerard R. Richter and others. Leslie Llewellyn Lewis, editor. 2nd ed. Chicago, 1965. 1023 p.

797. Evitt, Herbert E. **A Manual of Foreign Exchange.** 5th ed. London, I. Pitman, 1960. 260 p.

Explains various terms, concepts and procedures of foreign exchange emphasizing more the technical aspects of international transactions than the economic factors.

798. **Gallatin Annual of International Business.** 1965 — New York, American Heritage, 1965 —

Designated for American executive doing business abroad to be an information source about business and economic conditions in various countries except the United States. Kept up to date by the bi-weekly Gallatin Letter.

799. Lybrand, Ross Bros. & Montgomery. **International Reference Manual.** New York, 1966. 1 v. (Looseleaf).

Provides valuable information to management about such topics as forms of corporate organization, accounting, labor laws, taxation tariffs, and other data in various countries of the world. Updated annually.

800. Overseas Development Institute, London. **The Less Developed Countries in World Trade; a Reference Handbook** by Michael Zammit Cutajar and Alison Franks. London, 1967. 209 p.

Intended to present the facts about the export trade of less developed countries, the policies of the major industrialized countries affecting this trade, and the work and the policies of two international institutions, the General Agreement on Tariffs and Trade (GATT) and the U. N. Conference on Trade and Development (UNCTAD).

801. Stanley, Alexander O. **Handbook of International Marketing:** How to Export Import and Invest Overseas. New York, McGraw-Hill, 1963. 680 p.

Written in a clear style this work provides a compendium of tested practices in overseas marketing. Applying a step-by-step formula it shows similarities and differences between domestic and international marketing techniques. This handbook lays down precise guidelines for an effective operational activity in overseas trade.

802. Walton, Leslie Eugene. **Foreign Trade and Foreign Exchange;** their Theory and Practice. London, Macdonald & Evans, 1956. 264 p.

REPORTS & SURVEYS

803. Barclays Bank D. C. O. **Overseas Survey. . .;** covering the trade and economic conditions which prevailed during the year. . . in the overseas territories in which the Barclays Group of Banks is represented. London, 19 — Annual.

A valuable survey of over 40 countries and regions mostly in Africa and West Indies with illustrations, statistical tables and maps.

804. International Monetary Fund. **Annual Report.** Washington, 1946 —

This is a very important annual publication which widely covers all phases of international monetary cooperation, current monetary problems and developments.

805. **International Reports on Finance and Currencies.** New York, International Reports, Inc.

Reports weekly on current monetary trends and conditions throughout the world, financial prospects, exchange conditions and rates, free market gold prices, trends of silver and platinum prices. Includes also a liquidity for 88 countries.

806. Morgan Guaranty Trust Company of New York. International Banking Division. **Doing Business Abroad;** Summary of Regulations Affecting Trade, Investment and Foreign Exchange. New York. Looseleaf.

Informs about the basic regulations on international trade and investments. Up-dated by replacement leaves sent to subscribers.

807. Organization for Economic Cooperation and Development. **Overall Trade by Countries.** Series A. Paris, 1965 —

Provides detailed information on international trade among OECD countries including Yugoslavia.

808. _____. **Commodity Trade Analysis by Regions.** Series B, Paris, 1963 —

809. Organization for Economic Cooperation and Development. **Trade by Commodities.** Paris, 1960 —

Provides detailed information on imports and exports of various commodities among OECD member countries and some non-members.

810. U. S. Agency for International Development. **Index to Catalog of Investment Information and Opportunities.** Washington, D. C., U. S. Govt. Print Off., 1966. 124 p.

Includes three types of reports: 1. specific investment opportunity in a particular country, 2. economic and technical information about certain industries in a country, 3. relating to the country as a whole.

811. U. S. Bureau of International Commerce. **Foreign Markets Report Service.**
Covers many subjects and ranges in various sizes.

812. U. S. Bureau of Internation Commerce. **World Trade Directory Reports.** Washington, D. C.

813. U. S. Dept. of Commerce. **Market Share Reports.** Washington.

Publishes a series of reports indicating the United States share of world markets. Issued in: 1. Commodity series and Country series, giving dollar value of each imported and exported commodity.

814. U. S. Dept. of Commerce. **Trade of United States, Western Europe, Canada, and Japan in Manufactured Products 1961/62.** Washington, 1964. 387 p.

Surveys exports and imports for 45 products manufactured in the U.S., Canada, OECD member countries, and Japan providing a comparative study of international trade.

815. U. S. Tariff Commission. **Summaries of Trade and Tariff Information.** Prepared in terms of the tariff schedules of the United States. Washington, 1966 —

A multivolume work containing basic information on production, consumption and international trade of various United States products. Each commodity shows U. S. tariff treatment, domestic production and consumption, exports and imports, foreign production and trade, and its uses.

816. **World Monetary Reform: Plans and Issues.** Edited by H. G. Grubel, London, Oxford Univ. Press, 1964. 446 p.

A very useful guide to international liquidity.

817. Allen, Roy George Douglas, and Ely, J. Edward. **International Trade Statistics.** New York, Wiley, 1953. 448 p.

"The objective. . . is to describe and appraise the principles and practices under which the statistics are compiled that the user of the statistics will recognize the limitations of the data and take advantage of their strong points." (Introd.) Contents: pt. 1. Basic characteristics of the statistics; pt. 2. Important derived uses of the statistics; pt. 3. Statistics of individual countries. Bibliography: p. 417-439.

818. **Direction of International Trade.** v. 1 — 1950 — New York. Annual.

Joint publication of United Nations (Statistical Office). International Monetary Fund, International Bank for Reconstruction and Development. (Statistical Papers, series T.) Statistical tables arranged mainly by country.

819. **Exporter's Yearbook.** 1st — 1917 — London, Syren and Shipping.

Title varies: - 1922, Syren and Shipping International Mercantile Diary & Year Book; 1923-51, International Mercantile Diary & Year Book.

Provides a wealth of information on export trade of Great Britain, Commonwealth of Nations and other countries in the world, and such topics as: area, population, principal ports, banks, holidays, weights and measures, postal information, commerce, etc.

820. Food and Agriculture Organizations of the United Nations. **Trade Yearbook. Annuaire du Commerce. Anuario de Comercio.** v. 12 — 1958 — Rome, 1959 —

Formerly Yearbook of Food and Agricultural Statistics, pt. 2.

821. International Monetary Fund. **Balance of Payments Yearbook.** 1946/47 — Washington.

Continuation of the Annual Balance of Payments, issued 1926-45, by the Secretariat of the League of Nations.

822. Organization for Economic Cooperation and Development. **Foreign Trade Statistical Bulletins.** Paris, 1959 —

Series A: Overall trade by countries. Quarterly. Series B: Commodity trade: analysis by main regions. Quarterly. Series C: Commodity trade: detailed analysis by S.I.T.C. items.

823. Organization for Economic Cooperation and Development. **Sources of Statistics for Market Research.** Paris, 1961-64. 6 v.

Reports statistical data for each OECD country on the production consumption and trade of various products. Chart forms are also used.

824. Organization for Economic Cooperation and Development. **Statistical Bulletins; Foreign Trade.** 1960 — Paris, O.E.C.D.

Supersedes the Organization for European Economic Cooperation. Statistical bulletin on foreign trade. Issued in three series: Series A (semi-monthly) Overall trade, by origin and destination; Series B (quarterly) Analytic abstracts; Series C (quarterly) Trade by commodities.

825. _____. **Statistics of Balance of Payments, 1950-1961.** Paris, 1964. 134 p.

Includes bibliography. Brings statistical data for all member countries and some non-member comparing their data to seventeen standard balance of payments indicators.

826. United Nations. Statistical Office. **Commodity Trade Statistics,** by groups of the Standard International Classification. v. 1 — Jan./Mar. 1951 — New York.

827. _____. **World Trade Annual.** New York, Wasker, 1964 — Annual.

Surveys the international trade in figures of many countries of the world. The arrangement is by country subdivided by commodity giving the amount and value in dollars of imports and exports for each product. Products are listed by Standard International Classification number.

828. _____. **Yearbook of International Trade Statistics.** 1950 — New York. Annual.

Continues the Statistical Yearbook of the League of Nations. Contains: 1. Summary tables for world trade and tables for individual countries (143 countries in 1965 edition). The figures are taken from the official government sources published by the governments of the countries concerned. For each country the following tables are used: (1) An historical table for the last thirty years, (2) Import and export tables, and (3) Tables of trade by principal countries of provenance and destination.

829. U. S. Bureau of the Census. **Foreign Commerce and Navigation of the United States.** Washington, U. S. Govt. Print. Off., 1965. 871 p.

Covers the official statistics on foreign trade of the U. S. between 1946 to 1963. Export and import data are prepared by commodity and by continent and country of destination.

830. **Vneshnaia Torgovlia Soiuza S.S.R.; Statisticheskii Obzor.** 19 — Moskva, Vneshtorg. Annual.

Title transl: Foreign Trade of the U.S.S.R.; Statistical Survey.

831. **World Trade Data Yearbook.** New York, Business Abroad, 1957 —
Annual.

Provides important information on finance, commerce, marketing,
communications and transportation including various directories of international
trade organizations and other useful data.

MONOGRAPHIC TREATISES

(A selected list of monographic works containing bibliographical listings)

832. American Economic Association. **Readings in the Theory of International Trade.** Philadelphia, Blakiston Co., 1949. 637 p. (The Series
of Republished Articles on Economics, v. 4).

The main objective of this collection is to bring together the best
essays and articles in this field which could be useful in the instruction
of senior and graduate students in economics. The articles are clustered
under main headings related to international commerce. Classified
bibliography of articles: p. 555-625.

833. Angel, James W. **The Theory of International Prices.** Cambridge,
Mass., Harvard University Press, 1926. 571 p. Reprinted by A. M. Kelley,
1965.

Traces the historical development and synthesis of price doctrines
in the more important economic literatures. Examines the results
reached by various authors, and draws up a positive formulation of the
main theory. Bibliography: p. 535-556.

834. Ashley, Percy Walter Llewellyn. **Modern Tariff History: Germany-
United States-France.** 3rd ed. New York, Dutton, 1920. 365 p.

Attempts "to provide a brief, so far as possible, unpartisan sketch
of the development of tariff policy in Germany, the United States,
and France and of the forces, political and economic, which have
determined its course". Bibliography at the end of each part.

835. Ashworth, W. **Short History of the International Economy since
1850.** 2nd ed. London, Longmans, Green, 1962. 295 p.

Concentrates on two principal fields of study. The first deals with the
nations and their economics which showed a dominant influence on the course
of world economic history since the nineteenth century. The second is
concerned with international economic relations. Bibliography: p. 283-290.

836. Chalmers, Henry. **World Trade Policies: the Changing Panorama, 1920-
53;** a Series of Contemporary Periodic Surveys Foreword by J. B. Condliffe.
Berkeley, University of California Press, 1953. 546 p.

Presents a series of periodic surveys (mostly annuals) of the foreign trade
policies and practices of various countries from 1920 to 1953. The surveys

deal with changes in tariffs, import restrictions, exchange controls and other aspects of the international commerce policies.

837. Ellsworth, Paul Theodore. **International Economy.** Rev. ed. New York, Macmillan, 1959. 513 p.

Intended to provide advanced students with the theoretical equipment necessary to an analytical understanding of the problems of international economic relations. An index is included.

838. Haberler, Gottfried. **Survey of International Trade Theory.** Princeton, International Finance Section, Dept. of Economics and Sociology, Princeton University, 1955. 68 p. (Special Papers in International Economics).

"A translation from the German, by W. Michael Blumenthal, of the article 'Aussenhandel (Theorie)' in Handwörterbuch der Sozialsissenschaften, 1954. Revised and enlarged by the author." Bibliography: 57-68.

839. Letiche, John Marion. **Balance of Payments and Economic Growth.** New York, Harper, 1959. 378 p.

Presents a critical study of the theory of the balancing of international payments. In the first part entitled The balancing of international payments the author deals with the historical origins of modern doctrines, and an analytical account of classical and modern theories. In the second part, the case studies, with application of this generalized theory and analyzing relationship between economic growth and international equilibrium, are discussed. Bibliography: p. 321-364.

840. McGuire, Edward B. **British Tariff System.** 2nd ed. rev. and enl. London, Methuen, 1951. 365 p.

Presents an account of the tariff of the United Kingdom without advocating any particular policy, emphasizing however, the more permanent features. An index is included.

841. Myrdal, Gunnar. **An International Economy; Problems and Prospects.** New York, Harper, 1956. 381 p.

Examines the present state of international economic relations within the non-Soviet world. The principal idea of this study is "more closely integrated free-world economy" (Pref.) Bibliography: p. 367-373.

842. Ohlin, Bertil Gotthard. **Interregional and International Trade.** Rev. ed. Cambridge, Mass., Harvard University Press, 1967. 324 p. (Harvard Economic Studies, v. 39).

Presents "a theory of international trade, which was first published in 1933, in a somewhat abbreviated and updated form to bring it into line with recent developments." (Pref.) Terminology has been modernized, the outdated empirical material has been eliminated. A general index is added.

843. Schmitthoff, Clive Maximilian. **Export Trade; the Law and Practice of International Trade.** 4th ed. London, Stevens, 1962. 469 p.

"The aim of this book is to give a concise account of the law and practice of international trade" (Pref.) Contents: pt. 1. The international sale of goods; pt. 2. Representatives abroad; pt. 3. Matters incidental to exporting; pt. 4. Government regulation of exports. An index is added;

844. Taussig, Frank William. **Tariff History of the United States.** 8th ed., including a consideration of the tariff of 1930. New York, Putnam, 1931. Reprinted 1966. 536 p.

Covers the period from colonial times to the Tariff Act of 1930. Index is included.

845. Viner, Jacob. **The Customs Union Issue.** New York, Carnegie Endowment for International Peace, 1950. 221 p. (Carnegie Endowment for International Peace. Division of International Law. Studies in Administration of International Law Organization, no. 10).

Discusses the possibilities and limitations of customs unions as a method of regulating international commercial relations, also reviews the economics practical aspects, and prospects of custom unions. Included are: list of conventions, decrees, etc., and an index. Bibliography: p. 171-211.

846. Viner, Jacob. **Studies in the Theory of International Trade.** New York, Harper, 1937. 650 p.

A historical approach in appraisal of the modern foreign trade theory, which attempts to find out the forgotten or overlooked material worthy of inclusion, to trace the origin and development of the established doctrines, and to examine current controversies in economical, classical and neo-classical literature. Bibliography: p. 602-631.

847. Whale, Philip Barrett. **International Trade.** London, T. Butterworth, 1939. 255 p. Reprinted 1967.

Examines most important factors of international trade such as for example: foreign exchange rates, balance of payments, protection and regulation of international trade, commercial treaties and tariffs, the prospects of international trade, etc. Bibliography: p. 253-254.

848. Woytinsky, Wladimir S. and Woytinsky, E. S. **World Commerce and Governments; Trends and Outlook.** New York, Twentieth Century Fund, 1955. 907 p.

Deals with the commodities exchange among nations, with transportation within and among the countries, with governments and their various functions and actions, supranational organizations and international cooperations. 291 statistical tables and 166 figures (diagrams, charts) are attached to support the text. The general index is included. Bibliography: p. 863-888.

CHAPTER SIX

AGRICULTURAL AND LAND ECONOMICS; ECONOMIC GEOGRAPHY

GUIDES

849. Berry, Brian Joe Lobley, and Hankins, Thomas D. **A Bibliographic Guide to the Economic Regions of the United States;** a Report Prepared for the Commission on Methods of Economic Regionalization of the International Geographical Union. Chicago. University of Chicago, Dept. of Geography, 1963. 101 p. (Chicago University, Dept. of Geography Research, Paper no. 87).

This guide focuses upon the economic regions of the United States that appear in the American literature of the last half century. It includes books, pamphlets and articles.

850. California. University. Giannini Foundation of Agricultural Economics. Library. **Important Sources of Information for Work in Agricultural Economics, with special emphasis on California.** 9th ed. Berkeley, 1956. 108 p.

851. Frauendorfer, Sigmund von. **Survey of Abstracting Services and Current Bibliographical Tools in Agriculture, Forestry, Fisheries, Nutrition, Veterinary Medicine and Related Subjects.** München, BLV Verlagsgesellschaft, 1969. 192 p.

852. Library Association. County Libraries Group. **Reader's Guide to Books on Agriculture.** 4th ed. London, 1968. 58 p. (Its Readers' guide, new series, no. 102).

853. Lock, C. B. Buriel. **Geography: a Reference Handbook.** Hamden, Conn., Archon, 1968. 178 p.

854. Mikheev, Nikolai Mikhailovich. **Bibliograficheskie Ukazateli Sel'-skokhoziaistvennoi Literatury. 1783-1954 gg.** Moskva, Gos. izd-vo sel' khoz litry, 1956. 191 p.

Translated: Bibliographical Guides to Agricultural Literature, 1783-1954. Presents a standard guide to bibliographies in agriculture covering a fairly long period.

855. Minto, S. C. **How to Find Out in Geography.** New York, Pergamon Press, 1966. 99 p.

A handy handbook describing standard reference sources in geography, including material in economic geography.

A quick reference guide to the study of geography, including many important reference titles in the field of economic geography.

856. Wright, John K. and Elizabeth T. Platt. **Aids to Geographical Research; Bibliographies, Periodicals, Atlases, Gazetteers and Other Reference Books.** 2nd ed. rev. New York: Columbia University Press, 1947. 331 p.

Selective guide, including material in many languages, emphasizing American geography with descriptive annotations. The appendix is a classified index of American geographers, geographical libraries, and institutions. Includes author, title, and subject index. Outdated but still useful.

BIBLIOGRAPHIES (CURRENT)

857. **Bibliography of Agriculture.** v. 1 — July 1942 — Washington, D. C., Dept. of Agriculture Library. Monthly.

Supersedes six agricultural bibliographies published by various branches of the Dept. of Agriculture. Lists current literature on agriculture received by the National Agricultural Library. Arrangement is alphabetical by subject listing books, pamphlets, periodical articles, government documents, reports, etc. Foreign language publications are also included.

858. Canada. Dept. of Agriculture. Economics Division. **List of Published Material, 1930-1956,** by members of the Economics Division. Ottowa, 1957. 64 p.

859. _____. **Supplement.** 1957/62 — Annual. cumulated every few years.

Lists entries by the subject in alphabetical arrangement and in chronological order within each subject. "The place of publication has been omitted; in the majority of cases it is Ottawa. The name of the issuing agency is included only if it is not the Economics Division." (Pref.) No index is included.

860. **Forschungsgesellschaft für Agrarpolitik und Agrarsoziologie. Forschungsarbeiten aus Agrarökonomik und Ländlicher Soziologie.** 1 — Folge; 1945/57 — Bonn.

Translated: Research works in agricultural economics and rural sociology.

861. **Referativnyi Zhurnal; Geografiia.** Svodnyi tom. 1956 — Moskva, Akademiia nauk S.S.S.R., Institut nauchnoi informatsii. Monthly.

Title translated: Reference journal; Geography 1956 — Lists books, periodical and newspaper articles on economic and physical geography, and related subject in Russian and other languages. Subject, geographic and author annual indexes.

862. **Das Schrifttum der Bodenkultur.** 1 — Jahrg. Mai 1948 — Wien, Österreichischer Fachzeitschriftenverlag. Bimonthly.

Translated: The Literature of agriculture.

863. U. S. National Agricultural Library. **Library List.** no. 1 — May 1942 — Washington, 1942 —

This is an annotated bibliography of selected references in various fields of agriculture including agricultural economics; it is international in scope. Each issue is dedicated to particular topic. Includes monographs, pamphlets, articles, documents and reports. Author indexes are included.

BIBLIOGRAPHIES (RETROSPECTIVE)

864. Ball, Joyce. **Foreign Statistical Documents; a Bibliography of General International Trade and Agricultural Statistics; Including Holdings of the Stanford University Libraries,** ed. by Joyce Ball and compiled by Roberta Gardella. Stanford, Calif., Hoover Institution in War, Revolution, and Peace, Stanford University, 1967. 173 p. (Hoover Institution Bibliographical Series 28).

Material is arranged alphabetically by country, then by type of publication in following order: general statistics — annuals and bulletins, trade statistics — annual and bulletins, agricultural statistics, and annual reports of agricultural departments. Each item is listed in reverse chronological order with the latest material first.

865. Bazhanova, Elena Vasil'evna. **Sovetskii Narod za Krutoi Pod"em Sel' skogo Khoziaistva S.S.S.R.: Bibliograficheskii Ukazatel'.** Moskva, Fundamental' naia b-ka obshchestv. nauk Akad, nauk S.S.S.R., 1955-57. 2 v.

Title translated: Soviet people struggling to raise productivity of agriculture in the U.S.S.R.; a bibliographical guide. Contains 7178 entries of books, reports and periodical articles (including newspapers) in Russian and other languages of the Soviet Union.

866. Denman, Donald Robert. **Bibliography of Rural Land Economy and Landownership, 1900-1957;** a Full List of Works Relating to the British Isles and Selected Works from the United States and Western Europe, by Donald R. Denman, J. F. Q. Switzer and O. H. M. Sawyer. Cambridge, Dept. of Estate Management, Cambridge University, 1958. 412 p.

Lists books, articles, reports, periodicals and thesis on rural economy, with emphasis on Great Britain. The material is arranged into two main lists: 1. Classified works and 2. Alphabetical list of authors — English works, and Foreign works. Includes a subject index.

867. **Ekonomika i Organizatsiia Sel'skokhoziaistvennogo Proizvodstva;** Rekomendatel'nyi ukazatel' Literatury. Sostavitel' G. K. Donskaia.

Redaktor A. M. Bochever. Moskva, Kniga, 1966. 49 p.

Translated title: Agricultural economics and farm management; a reference guide to literature.

868. Food and Agriculture Organization of the United Nations. **Bibliography on Land Tenure.** Bibliographie des Régimes Fonciers. Bibliografia Sobre Tenencia de la Tierra. Rome, 1955. 386 p.

Presents a comprehensive bibliographical work in cooperation with the University of Wisconsin supported by the United Nations, International Labor Office and Unesco.

869. Food and Agriculture Organization of the United Nations. **Bibliography on the Analysis and Projection of Demand and Production. 1963.** Rome, 1963. 279 p. (Its Commodity Reference Series, 2).

870. Hannay, Annie Murray (Macgregor). **Land Ownership; a Bibliography of Selected References,** compiled by Annie M. Hannay, Donald W. Gooch and Marie L. Gould. Washington, U. S. Govt. Print. Off., 1953. 293 p. (U. S. Dept. of Agriculture. Bibliographical Bulletin, no. 22).

871. International Institute of Agriculture. Library. **International Bibliography of Agricultural Economics,** v. 1 – 8. 1938-1946. Rome. Quarterly.

Title and text also in French and German.

872. London. University. Centre for Urban Studies. **Land Use Planning and The Social Sciences, a Selected Bibliography.** Literature on town and country planning and related social studies in Great Britain, 1930-1963. London, 1964. 44 p.

873. Mezhov, Vladimir Izmailovich. **Krestianskii Vopros v Rossii.** Polnoe sobranie materialov dlia istorii krest' ianskogo voprosa na iazykakh russkom i inostrannykh, napechatanykh v Rossii i zagranitsei, 1764-1864. St. Petersburg, Tip. Min-va vnutr. diel, 1865. 421 p. Translated: The peasant question in Russia. Collected materials for the history of peasant question in Russian and foreign languages issued in Russia and in foreign countries, 1764-1864. This annotated bibliographical guide contains about 2,800 entries in Russian and ca 500 in foreign languages. It covers not only agricultural matters of Russia but includes also history of European peasantry and American agricultural history.

874. _____. **Zemskii i Krest'ianskii Voprosy.** Bibliograficheskii ukazatel' knig i statei vyshedshikh po pervomu voprosu s samogo nachala vvedeniia v deistvie zemskikh uchrezhdenii i ranee, po vtoromu s 1865g. vplot' do 1871g. St. Petersburg, 1873.

Translated: Agrarian and peasant question. Designed as a supplement to author's previous bibliographical work covering the period of 1865-71.

875. Singleton, Carey Bryan. **Agricultural Rents in Theory and Practice; an Annotated Bibliography.** Washington, U. S. Dept. of Agriculture, Economic Research Service, Farm Economic Division, 1962. 81 p. (U. S. Dept. of Agriculture. Miscellaneous publication, 901).

Divided into four chapters: 1. Introduction, 2. American contribution to rent theory, 3. British contributions and 4. Other contributions. Includes an author index.

876. U. S. Bureau of Agricultural Economics. **Agricultural Economic and Statistical Publications.** Washington, 1952. 83 p.

877. U. S. Dept. of Agriculture. Economic Research Service. Farm Production Economics Division. **Publications Containing Recent Farm Enterprise Input-Output Data.** Washington, 1963. 42 p.

878-887 are omitted.

888. U. S. National Archives. **Writings Relevant to Farm Management in the Records of the Bureau of Agricultural Economics,** Compiled by Vivian Wiser. Washington, 1963. 80 p. (Its Publication no. 63-16. Special Lists, no. 17).

DICTIONARIES ENCYCLOPEDIAS & HANDBOOKS

889. Stamp, Laurence Dudley, and Gilmour, S. Carter. **Chisholm's Handbook of Commercial Geography.** Entirely Rewritten. 18th ed. London, Longmans, Green, 1966. 918 p.

Chisholm's Handbook was first published in 1889 and since then became a standard reference work in many countries of the world. The material is arranged by commodities, by geographical areas, subdivided by countries. Many statistical tables and some maps accompany text. Index.

INDEXES AND ABSTRACTS

890. **Biological and Agricultural Index, a Cumulative Subject Index to Periodicals in the Fields of Biology. Agriculture and Related Sciences.** 1964 — New York, Wilson, 1964 — v. 50 — Monthly.

Supersedes Agricultural Index. Lists by subject in alphabetical order, articles published in English language periodicals. The list of periodicals indexed is included in each issue of the index.

891. Forschungsgesellschaft für Agrarpolitik und Agrarsoziologie. **Übersicht über Agrarpolitische und Agrarsoziologische Aufsätze.** Bonn, 1954 —

Title translated: A survey over agro-political and agro-sociological articles.

892. **Geographical Abstracts. C. Economic Geography.** London, Dept, of Geography, London School of Economics, 1966 —

Covers books, pamphlets, papers, reports, newspaper, and periodical articles on agriculture, fishing, forestry, manufacturing, mineral resources, service industries, transport, commerce, regional and urban studies. Includes a comprehensive annual subject index to all four parts of Geographical abstracts.

893. **Tropical Abstracts;** compiled from world literature on tropical and subtropical agriculture. Amsterdam, Royal Tropical Institute, 1946 — v. 1 — Monthly.

Includes numerous abstracts on economic aspects of various branches of tropical agriculture including forestry and fishery.

894. **World Agricultural Economics and Rural Sociology Abstracts.** v. 1 — 1959 — Amsterdam, North-Holland Co. Quarterly. Title also in French, German and Spanish.

Prepared by the Commonwealth Bureau of Agricultural Economics, Oxford, and published by Commonwealth Bureau and the International Association of Agricultural Libraries and Documentalists. Worldwide in scope it contains abstracts of books, pamphlets & periodical articles on agricultural economics and rural sociology, written by the specialists. Detailed indexes of authors, subjects and geographical are included.

SURVEYS AND STATISTICS

895. **Commodity Yearbook.** 1st — 1939 — Commodity Research Bureau, Inc. New York.

Surveys around one hundred agricultural & mineral commodities, supplying statistical data for each one. The arrangement is alphabetical by commodity.

896. Food and Agriculture Organization of the United Nations. **The State of Food and Agriculture;** a Survey of World Conditions & Prospects. 1947 — Washington, etc. Annual.

Reviews the recent world food and agriculture situation providing extensive statistical data. Extra feature of each issue is an inclusion of an interesting special topic.

897. Food and Agriculture Organization of the United Nations. Commodity Division. **FAO Commodity Review.** 1961 — Rome. Annual.

Contains: pt. 1, a General review, which is a summary of developments in international commodity markets during a previous year and early months of referred year; pt. 2, consists of a series of chapters analyzing the current situation and outlook for all of the major agricultural commodities including forest and fisheries products.

898. Russia (1923 — U.S.S.R.) Tsentral'noe statisticheskoe uprevlenie. Otdel statistiki sel'skogo khoziaistva. **Sel'skoe Khoziaistvo SSSR; Statisticheskii sbornik.** Moskva, Gosstatizdat, 1960. 665 p.

Agriculture in the U.S.S.R., a statistical collection. Presents a very extensive compilation of statistical data on Soviet agriculture.

899. U. S. Dept. of Agriculture. **Agricultural Statistics.** 1936 – Washington, Govt. Print Office. Annual.

Presents a reliable reference book on agricultural production, supplies, consumption, facilities, prices, costs, and profits. The historical data goes back for the last 10 years. All material is divided into eleven chapters, subdivided into smaller units. Detailed index is included.

MONOGRAPHIC TREATISES

900. Benedict, Murray Reed. **Farm Policies of the United States 1790-1950; a Study of Their Origins and Development.** New York, Twentieth Century Fund, 1953. 548 p.

American farm policy has always been a major political and economic issue, though with industrial growth of the U.S. the primaries of agriculture in the American economy have declined. The main idea of this work is to bring into clear perspective the historical development of farm policies and the results of those policies on farm people and the national economy. General index is included.

901. Black, John Donald. **Economics for Agriculture;** Selected Writings. Cambridge, Harvard University Press, 1959. 719 p. (Harvard Economic Studies, v. 111)

The book is divided into thirteen parts, dealing with production economics, land use, marketing, cooperation, prices, consumption, population and food supply, agricultural economics and policy.

902. Heady, Earl Ord. **Economics of Agricultural Production and Resource Use.** New York, Prentice-Hall, 1952. 850 p.

"Emphasis is on fundamentals in respect to production and resource relationships, the conditions under which efficiency is attained, and the behavior patterns of persons who serve as managers and demonstrators of agricultural resources." (Pref.)

903. Lösch, August. **The Economics of Location.** Translated from the 2nd rev. ed. by William H. Woglom with the assistance of Wolfgang F. Stelper. New Haven, Conn., Yale University Press, 1954. 520 p.

Following von Thünen's famous "Ring theory" author proposes to consider space as a main factor of all economic activities. He discusses theory and problems of location, economic regions, trade and practical examples based on American data. Numerous references are attached as footnotes.

904. Mellor, John William. **The Economics of Agricultural Development.** Ithaca, Cornell University Press, 1966. 403 p.

Presents a comprehensive, well documented treatment of the economic aspects of agricultural development in the less developed countries.

905. Mighell, Ronald L. **American Agriculture: Its Structure and Place in the Economy.** For the Social Science Research Council in Cooperation with the U. S. Dept. of Agriculture. New York, Wiley, 1955. 187 p. (Census Monography Series).

Assesses the role of agriculture in the economy of the United States using statistical data of the 1950 census of agriculture.

906. Schultz, Theodore William. **The Economic Organization of Agriculture.** New York, McGraw-Hill, 1953. 374 p.

Discusses the role of agriculture as an important factor which can make considerable contribution to economic development and stability. Numerous tables, maps, and figures supplement the text.

907. Thünen, Johann Heinrich von. **Der Isolierte Staat. Isolated State;** an English edition of Der Isolierte Staat. Translated by Carla M. Wartenberg. Edited with an introduction by Peter Hall. Oxford, Pergamon Press, 1966. 1 v. 304 p. Abridged and translated from the 2nd German ed.

Presents the famous classic of agricultural economics which had a tremendous influence on both sciences — the agriculture and economics.

CHAPTER SEVEN

INDUSTRY AND TRANSPORTATION

Industry

GUIDES TO INFORMATION

908. Chamber of Commerce of the United States of America. Dept. of Manufacture. **Guide to Listings of Manufacturers;** where to find the names, locations and products of manufacturers. Washington, D.C., 1962. 19 p.

Provides a listing of directories and suggests methods of locating firms.

909. Chamber of Commerce of the United States of America. State Chamber of Commerce Service Dept. **Sources of State Information and State Industrial Directories.** Washington, 1958. 18 p.

Brings a valuable list of available directories and instruction how to locate difficult sources of information on states.

910. **Guide to American Directories.** New York, McGraw-Hill. 1954 — Prepared by B. Klein. Title varies: — 1958. Guide to American directories for compiling mailing lists. Subtitle for 6th ed; A Guide to the major business directories of the U. S. covering all industrial, professional and mercantile categories.

A very detailed and useful guide, emphasizing a wide range of directories on various trades and professions which exist in the U.S. indicating what kind of information could be obtained from those directories. The arrangement is alphabetical by subject.

911. **Industrial Marketing, Media Market Planning Guide. 1963** — Chicago, Advertising Publishers, 1963 — Semi-annual. Title varies.

Presents basic data on many classifications and subclassifications of industrial and trade markets, giving information about numerous business publications, describing services of many business papers, listing the national trade associations, supplying digests of market analyses.

912. Lewis, Howard Thompson. **Where to Find It: Bibliography of Industrial Purchasing.** 3rd ed. New York, Literature Review Committee, National Committee for Professional Development, National Association of Purchasing Agents, 1961. 50 p.

Presents information data as to locating and evaluating industrial materials.

913. Sherman, Morton. **Industrial Data Guide.** New York, Scarecrow Press, 1962. 368 p.

914. U. S. Dept. of Commerce. **Business Service Check List.** v. 1 — July 5, 1946 — Washington, U. S. Govt. Print Off. Weekly.

915. Waer, David Kent Wentworth. **Common Market Antitrust; a Guide to the Law, Procedure and Literature.** The Hague, M. Nijhoff, 1964. 67 p.

Presents the extensive literature on this topic listing books and periodical articles arranged by authors and language (English, French, Dutch, German, Italian). Gives the sources of antitrust laws and other legal aspects.

BIBLIOGRAPHIES (CURRENT)

916. National Industrial Conference Board. **Cumulative Index of N.I.C.B. Publications.** New York, 1950-54 — Title varies.

Designed as a subject index to articles, reports and papers in N.I.C.B. journals on economics, business, personnel administration, public affaris, etc.

917. **Referativnyi Sbornik; Ekonomika Promyshlennosti.** 1960 — Moskva, Akademiia nauk S.S.S.R. In-t. nauch. informatsii. Monthly.

Translated title: Reference collection; industrial economics. This is a bibliographical monthly bulletin of selected books, articles and reviews in Russian and foreign languages. Includes annual indexes.

BIBLIOGRAPHIES (RETROSPECTIVE)

918. Akademiia nauk S.S.S,R. Sektor seti spetsiial'nykh bibliotek. **Bibliografiia po Voprosam Razmeshcheniia i Raionirovaniia Promyshlennosti S.S.S.R., 1901-1957.** (Sostavitel' T.S. Guchek, Otv. red. A. E. Probst). Moskva, Akademiia nauk S.S.S.R., 1960. 355 p.

Title translated: Bibliography of location and regions of industry in the U.S.S.R., 1901-1957. Includes more than 4,000 items of which about 3,950 were published after 1917. Listed are books, dissertations, periodical articles, papers of learned journals, etc. An author and title index is included.

919. Brodskaia, A. B. **Voprosy Tekhnicheskogo Progressa v Promyshlennosti S.S.S.R.;** Knizhanaia i Zhurnal'naia Literatura za 1945-1956gg. Moskva, Fundamental'naia b-ka obshchestv. nauk Akad. nauk S.S.S.R., 1958.171 leaves.

Title translated: Questions of technological progress in the Soviet industries; monographic and periodical literature for the period of 1945-1956.

Contains 1,750 entries of books, dissertations, papers and articles in Russian and other languages.

920. Deutsches Industrieinstitut, Cologne. **Veröffentlichungen des Deutschen Industrieinstituts, 1951-1961.** Köln, Deutsche Industrie-verlags-Gmb H, 1961. 65 p.

Publications of the German Industry Institutes.

921. Hamburg. Welt-Wirtschafts-Archiv. **Verzeichnis der Fest- und Denkschriften von Unternehmungen und Organisation der Wirtschaft.** Hamburg, 1961. 566 p. (Its Veröffentlichung).

Includes over 4,000 Festschriften and histories of firms located in the Archiv; international in scope. Entries are arranged by 1. author or personal name, 2. the name of the firm, and 3. geographical name.

922. Harvard University. Graduate School of Business Administration. Baker Library. **Studies in Enterprise; a Selected Bibliography of American and Canadian Company Histories and Biographies of Businessmen.** Lorna M. Daniels, compiler. Boston, 1957. 169 p.

An expanded edition of Business Biographies and Company Histories, compiled by Baker Library in 1948. A very useful list of industries and biographies of individuals related to industrial firms. Three indexes (Subject, author and periodicals) are included.

923. Huffschmid, Jörg. **Bibliographie Konzentration and Konzentrationspolitik, Bibliography Concentration and Concentration Policy. 1960-1966.** Bearb. von Jörg Huffschmid, Jörg Michaelis und Wolf-Rudiger Plan. Mit einer Einführung von Helmut Arndt. Berlin, Duncker u. Humbolt (1967). 284 p. (Schriftenreihe des Institus für Konzentrationsforschung an der Freien Universitat Berlin, Bd. 1).

This is a German bibliography on monopolies, industrial trusts and their politics.

924. John Crerar Library. Chicago. **A List of Books on the History of Industry and Industrial Arts.** January, 1915. Prepared by Aksel G. S. Josephson. Detroit, Gale Research Co., 1966. 486 p. Reprint of the 1915 ed.

This is an annotated bibliography of publications issued in Western languages. History of economics is also included. Entries are arranged alphabetically under main subject headings.

925. _____. **Selected References on Industrial Development.** Prepared in cooperation with the Office of Technical Services, Dept. of Commerce. Washington, Technical Aids Branch, Office of Industrial Resources, International Cooperation Administration, 1961. 140 p.

926. Oklahoma. University Library. **The Harry W. Bass Collection in Business History in the University of Oklahoma Library,** as of February 20, 1956. Norman, 1956. 76 p.

927. Riley, Vera, and Allen, Robert Loring. **Interindustry Economic Studies.** Baltimore, Published for Operations Research Office, the Johns Hopkins University, by the Johns Hopkins Press, 1955. 280 p. (Johns Hopkins University. Operations Research Office. Bibliographic Reference Series, no. 4. Programming for Policy Decision, v. 2).

Interindustry economic analysis is relatively a new field in economics developed in the last thirty years. The literature is located in books, periodicals, pamphlets and other publications. This comprehensive bibliography of interindustry research has alphabetical arrangement under six arbitrarily chosen headings. A detailed author, title and issuing agency index is included.

928. Stanford Research Institute. International Development Center. **Small Industry; an International Annotated Bibliography.** Compiled by Marian Crites Alexander-Frutschi. Glencoe, Ill., Free Press of Glencoe, 1960. 218 p.

Includes 1,100 mostly recently published items, books, pamphlets, reports, and articles according to a classified arrangement. An author index and directory of publishers and periodicals are added.

929. United Nations. Library. **Bibliography on Industrialization in Underdeveloped Countries.** New York, 1956. 216 p. (Its Bibliographical Series, no. 6).

930. United Nations. Statistical Office. **Bibliography of Industrial and Distributive-Trade Statistics.** 3rd ed. New York, 1967. 139 p. (Statistical papers, ser. M, no. 36, Rev. 3).

Presents an annotated list of references, arranged by continents, then by countries in form of tables. Covers construction, manufacturing, mining, production of electricity and gas.

931. _____. **Input-Output Bibliography, 1955-1966,** by Charlotte Taskier. Harvard Economic Research Project. New York, United Nations, 1961. 222 p. (ST/SAT/7).

This is a sequel to Interindustry Economic Studies by Vera Riley and Robert Allen (1955). It consists of over 600 titles of books, documents and periodical articles in many languages.

932. _____. **Input-Output Bibliography, 1960-1963.** New York, 1967. 259 p.

Includes ca. 1,000 entries in 23 languages.

933. _____. **Input-Output Bibliography, 1963-1966.** New York, 1967. 259 p.

Contains about 1,500 references in many languages.

934. U. S. Dept. of State. Library Division. **Industrial Plants in the United**

States; a Selected Bibliography of their Expansion and Trends, 1942-1952. Washington, 1953. 91 p. (Its Bibliography no. 74).

935. U. S. International Cooperation Administration. Office of Industrial Resources. **Industrialization and Economic Development. Literature Recommendations.** Washington, 1960. 29 p.

936. Wilson, Fern L. **Wilson's Index of Publications, by University Bureaus of Business Research.** Cleveland, Press of Western Reserve University, 1951. 303 p.

Aimed to locate thousands of unbiased, factual business and industrial studies published by research departments in many universities or colleges which, because of limited edition would have been lost for many users. Those studies are in the fields of economics, commerce and industry.

DICTIONARIES & ENCYCLOPEDIAS

937. Pinner, H. H. ed. **World Unfair Competition Law; an Encyclopedia.** Leyden, A. W. Sijthoff, 1965. 2 v. (1008 p.). (The Protection of Intellectual and Industrial Property Throughout the World; a Library of Encyclopedias.)

Divided into 82 titles in alphabetical order, then subdivided by country. Most articles are signed. A very detailed Index in English, French, German, Italian and Spanish has been planned for the third supplementary volume.

938. Prentice-Hall, Inc., **Directors' and Officers' Encyclopedic Manual,** prepared by the editorial staff of Prentice-Hall, Inc. New York, 1955. 641 p.

939. Roberts, Harold Selig. **Roberts' Dictionary of Industrial Relations.** Washington, BNA Incorporated, 1966. 486 p.

"Labor-management relations has over the years developed a language peculiar to its needs and problems." (Introd.) The growth of automation, the new technical processes, the new job description, the unionization among employees, the labor legislation, all have been responsible for creation of new words, pharases, and new vocabulary. Bibliography: p. 472-486.

DIRECTORIES

940. Dun and Bradstreet, Inc. **Dun's Reference Book of Corporate Managements. ments.** 1st — 1967 — New York.

941. _____. **Reference Book of Manufacturers.** Oct. 1965 — New York.

Issued as a supplement to Dun's Reference Book.

942. Federation of British Industries. **FBI Register of British Manufacturers.**
1924 — London, Thomas Skinner, 1924 — .

Publication suspended 1940/41-1946/47. Included material is divided
into many sections such as: products and services, language glossaries, alphabetical directory of FBI firms, trade associations, brands and trade names. etc.

943. **Kelly's Directory of Merchants, Manufacturers and Merchants Including
Industrial Services.** London, 1880 — Annual.

This Directory is specially designed for simplicity and quick reference.
The Index to Trade, which is issued as a separate booklet provides an easy
guide to over 10,000 classified headings in both volumes.

944. **Kompass; Register of British Industry and Commerce.** 1st — 1962 —
Croydon, Eng. Kompass Register.

945. **MacRae's Blue Book** 1929 — Chicago, MacRae's Blue Book Co. Annual.

At the present issued in four volumes. Volume 1 contains an alphabetical list of companies and a trade name section; volumes 2-4 are classified
product listing.

945a. **Poor's Register of Directors and Executives, United States and Canada.**
New York, Standard and Poor's Corp. 1928 — Annual with supplements
three times a year.

An excellent source of locating names of representatives of the companies
(executives, directors, managers). The main part is arranged alphabetically
by name of corporation, supplemented by a product and industrial index, and
a list of directors.

946. Roberts, Harold Selig. **Who's Who in Industrial Relations.** Honolulu,
Industrial Relations Center, College of Business Administration, University of
Hawaii, 1966 — 67. 2 v.

Introduces an alphabetical listing of persons who are involved in
matters of labor-management relations in the U.S. and Canada.

947. **Thomas' Register of American Manufacturers.** New York, Thomas Pub.
Co., 1900 — Annual.

Now in 4 vols. Contents: v. 1-3. Product classification. v. 4. List of
manufacturers, trade names, and commercial organizations. Index, Product
finding guide to contents, and index to advertisers.

948. U. S. Small Business Administration. **Research and Development: a
List of Small Business Concerns Interested in Performing Research and
Development.** Washington, 1960 — Annual.

Lists 2,674 business concerns which are interested in research and development; divided under 33 major categories with many subdivisions.

949. **World Who's Who in Commerce and Industry.** 1st — Chicago, Marquis-Who's Who, 1936 — Biennial.

Divided into two parts: 1. The Roster of ranking executives; career sketches of leading businessmen and others noteworthy in the field of commerce and industry; II. The indexed catalog of principal businesses. About 30,000 individuals identified with commerce and industry and more than 9,000 leading firms are listed.

SURVEYS AND STATISTICS

950. **The Annual Review of British Industry.** 1958 — London, A. Wingate.

951. **Beerman's Financial Year Book of Europe.** London, Beerman, 19 — Annual.

952. **Industry Surveys.** New York, Standard and Poor's Co. 1900 —

This is a two volume loose-leaf service analyzing various industries and their major companies. Divided into numerous industry sections, each one subdivided into two parts: (1) a current analysis with the short-term outlook (3-4 months) and (2) a recent statistics with a basic analysis emphasizing the long-run trends and issued once a year.

953. Organization for Economic Cooperation and Development. **Industrial Statistics. Statitiques Industrielles.** Paris, 1900/55 — Paris. Issued in the series statistical bulletins.

Offers a statistical presentation for O.E.C.D. member countries and some selected other countries of production, consumption and foreign trade in energy sources, minerals and their industries, chemicals, fertilizers, pulp and paper, textiles and others. The included appendix provides some more statistics for the world and some major industrial countries.

954. **The Scope Year Book of Industry, Trade and Finance.** 1950 — London, Annual.

955. Spencer, Vivian Eberle. **Raw Materials in the United States Economy, 1900-1961.** Washington, U.S. Dept. of Commerce, Bureau of the Census, 1964. 139 p. (U.S. Bureau of the Census. Working Paper, no. 6) Bibliographical footnotes.

Presents revised and updated statistical data in form of tables, diagrams and textual essays on production, consumption, trade, prices, etc. of raw materials which are classified according to producing industry and use.

956. United Nations. Statistical Office. **The Growth of World Industry, 1938-1961; National Tables.** LaCroissance de l'Industrie Mondiale, 1938-1961; Tableaux par pays. New York, United Nations, 1963. 849 p.

"A more current and expanded version of pt. 2 of Patterns of Industrial Growth, 1938-1959." (Introd.) In English and French. Included are numerous tables of industrial production for approximately one hundred countries and regions.

957. United Nations. Statistical Office. **World Energy Supplies, 1929/50** — New York, 1952 — (Its Statistical Papers, ser. J) Annual.

Covers 170 countries, giving data on production, trade, and consumption of energy per year. Included data are for coal, coke, oil, gas, electricity and some others.

958. U.S. Bureau of the Census. **Annual Survey of Manufactures.** 1949/50 — Washington, U.S. Govt. Print Off.

Provides estimates of the value of shipments for the U.S. during one year of about one thousand classes of manufactured products. The purpose of those surveys is to show the key measures of manufacturing activity for industry groups and important industries.

959. _____. **Census of Manufacturers. 1958.** Washington, Govt. Print Office, 1962. 3 v.

From 1810-1900 published decennially; from 1904-1919 at five year intervals and from 1921-1939 at two-year intervals, and again from 1948 has been published every fifth year. Arrangement is by industry and area. Includes data on products, materials, employment, capital expenditure, payrolls, etc.

960. _____. **Census of Mineral Industries, 1967.** Washington, Govt. Print Office, 2 v.

Published in two volumes presenting the final results of the 1963 Census of mineral industries. Volume one, Summary and industry statistics, provides information in tabular form for various groups of mineral industries. Detailed statistics are shown by geographic region, by state and by type of operation. Volume two: Area Statistics, contains separate chapters for each of 48 states and one chapter for Delaware, Maryland and District of Columbia. Each of fifty industries is presented by data.

961. _____. **Current Industry Reports.** 1st — Washington, D.C. n.d. Frequency varies. Title varies: Facts for industry.

Contains statistical information on production, sales, shipments and other activities of various industrial commodities.

MONOGRAPHIC TREATISES
(A Selected List of Monographs Containing Comprehensive Bibliographies)

962. Alderfer, Evan Brenner and Michl, H. E. **Economics of American Industry.** 3rd ed. New York, McGraw-Hill, 1957. 710 p.

Aimed to present an introductory survey of the principal manufacturing industries in the United States.

963. Allen, George Cyril and Donnithorne, Audrey. **Western Enterprise in Far Eastern Economic Development:** China and Japan. London, Allen & Unwin, 1962. 291 p.

Describes the beginning of Western enterprise in those two countries, the character and forms of that enterprise, the relationship with the native economies, and finally the effect of the Western impact upon the commercial and industrial life of both countries. An index is included. Bibliography: p. 272-279.

964. _____. **Western Enterprise in Indonesia and Malaya;** a Study in Economic Development. London, Allen & Unwin, 1957. 321 p.

This is another monographic study with a good basic bibliography.

965. Baer, Werner, **Industrialization and Economic Development in Brazil.** Homewood, Ill., Irwin, 1965. 309 p. (Yale University. Economic Growth Center Publications).

Discussed in this study are: the structural changes in Brazil's economy during the years of 1947-1961, and the process of industrialization and its effects on other sectors of national economy. The appendices supplement the text with a wealth of statistical data on Brazilian economy, reviewing the reliability of the data used in this monograph. Bibliography: p. 203-208.

966. Bryce, Murray D. **Industrial Development; a Guide for Accelerating Growth.** New York, McGraw-Hill, 1960. 282 p.

Brings together the economic, financial and management techniques of industrial development, which can be used in any region of the world intending to increase the rate of industrial growth. Three major subject fields are covered: 1. Approaches to industrialization in a developing economy; 2. The development of industrial projects; 3. The financing of industrial projects. Includes an index. Selected bibliography: p. 273-276.

967. Chandler, Alfred Dupont. **Strategy and Structure; Chapters in the History of the Industrial Enterprise.** Cambridge, M.I.T. Press, 1962. 463 p. (M.I.T. Press Research Monographs).

Presents a comparative study of the administrative history of U.S. industry, based on a detailed analysis of four large companies: General Motors, duPont, Sears and Standard Oil. Bibliographical references included in "Notes": p. 399-453.

968. Clark, John Bates. **Essentials of Economic Theory as Applied to Modern Problems of Industry and Public Policy.** New York, Macmillan, 1907. 566 p.

Examines the role and the general application of static laws in an industrial society, discusses the effects of different changes, economic friction, the role of monopolies, the laws of economic dynamics, the law of population, of accumulation of capital, problems of transportation and the important issues of a national economy. Index.

968. Clark, Victor Selden. **History of Manufactures in the United States;** With an introd. by Henry W. Farnam. New York, Published for the Carnegie Institution of Washington, by McGraw-Hill, 1929. 3 v.

This is a revised edition of History of Manufactures in the United States 1607-1860, published 1916. A new material has been added so that time period has been covered until 1929. Bibliography: v. 3. p. 400-442.

969. Davis, Ralph Currier. **Industrial Organization and Management.** 3rd ed. New York, Harper, 1957. 953 p.

Designed as a standard text book on industrial management with very good presentation of theory and practice in a clear and logical sequence.

970. Filipetti, George. **Industrial Management in Transition.** Rev. ed. Homewood, Ill., Irwin, 1953. 344 p. (Irwin Series in Industrial Engineering and Management).

Reviews the development from various sources: books, periodicals and recent reports giving very good summary in this topic.

971. Glover, John G. and Lagai, Rudolph L. eds. **The Development of American Industries: Their Economic Significance.** 4th ed. New York, Simmons-Boardman, 1959. 835 p.

Designed as a cooperative effort of 36 industries (in the present edition) in writing the history of the development of the major American industries in the past two centuries. "Each chapter in the book is the joint product of some of the best minds in the particular industry covered, and is a scholarly and accurate history of the industry." (Pref. to 1st ed.) Includes an index.

972. Jewkes, John, and others. **The Sources of Invention.** London, Macmillan, 1958. 428 p.

Attempts to answer such questions as: where and under what conditions have industrial invention arisen in modern times? What is an important invention? Who is the inventor in any particular case? In the second part of the book the summaries of case histories with references are presented. The general index is included.

973. Kerr, Clark, and others. **Industrialism and Industrial Man; the Problems of Labor and Management in Economic Growth.** Cambridge, Harvard University Press, 1960. 331 p.

This volume is a part of the Inter-university Study of Labor Problems in Economic Development. It discusses the problems of industrial society in the age of a total industrialization, the interrelationships between managerial elite and working classes, their organizations, and at the end the pluralistic industrialism.

974. Lave, Lester B. **Technological Change, Its Conception and Measurement.** Englewood Cliffs, N.J., Prentice-Hall, 1966. 223 p. (Prentice-Hall Series in Mathematical Analysis of Social Behavior).

Examines the role of technological change as related to economic theory and econometrics; also reviews the related literature, summarizing the various measures and their estimates of technological change in various sectors of many countries. An index is added. Bibliography: p. 207-220.

975. Research Conference on Industrial Relations and Economic Development, Geneva, 1966. **Industrial Relations and Economic Development;** edited by Arthur McRoss. London, published for the International Institute for Labour Studies, by Macmillan, 1966. 413 p.

"Literature on industrial relations and economic development." p. 321-406.

976. Singer, Eugene M. **Antitrust Economics: Selected Legal Cases and Economic Models.** Englewood Cliffs, N.J., Prentice-Hall, 1968. 276 p.

Illuminates the basic issues in antitrust by presenting an analysis of law cases and economic models.

977. Thorelli, Hans Birger. **The Federal Antitrust Policy: Origination of an American Tradition.** Baltimore, Johns Hopkins Press, 1955. 658 p.

Covers thoroughly the wide field of U.S. antitrust policy, presenting historical (genesis) economic, social, constitutional and political background, the legal aspects of the Sherman act, the trust problem in Congress, 1890-1903, summary-conclusions and appraisal. Indices of cases cited, of persons and of subjects are included. Bibliography: p. 617-639.

978. Vance, Stanley. **American Industries.** New York, Prentice-Hall, 1955. 626 p.

Transportation
(Communication; Public Utilities)

GUIDES TO INFORMATION

979. **ABC Goods Transport Guide.** London, Illiffe, 1954 — (January and July).

Includes roads, railways, air, sea canals; gives services, indicating frequency and facilities.

980. Evanston, Ill. Transportation Center at Northwestern University. **A Reference Guide to Metropolitan Transportation; an Annotated Bibliography.** Evanston, Ill., 1964. 42 p.

600 titles are entered under five main headings: metropolis, local transit, traffic and periodicals.

981. Metcalf, Kenneth Nolan. **Transportation: Information Sources; an Annotated Guide to Publications, Agencies, and other Data Sources Concerning Air, Rail, Water, Road, and Pipeline Transportation.** Detroit, Gale Research Co., 1965. 307 p. (Management information guide, 8).

Aimed to cover all aspects of transportation. Only sources written in English language are covered. The collected material is listed in 9 sections. Includes two indexes: author-title-source, and subject.

BIBLIOGRAPHIES (CURRENT)

982. **Current Literature in Traffic and Transportation.** v. 1 — Jan./Feb. 1960 — Evanston, Ill., Library, Transportation Center at Northwestern University. Semimonthly (irregular). Supersedes Current literature in transportation.

Lists in an alphabetical subject arrangement books, pamphlets, reports, government documents and periodical articles from domestic and foreign journals. Also includes listings of periodicals and of publishers with addresses.

983. National Research Council. Highway Research Board. **Publication Index. 1921-49** — Washington.

984. **Zheleznodorozhnaia Literatura S.S.S.R.;** Ezhegodnik. 1940 — Moskva, Transzheldorizdat. Annual.

Title translated: Railway literature of U.S.S.R.; a yearbook. Contains books, dissertations, papers, periodical articles and book reviews in Russian and other languages of the Soviet Union. Includes special sections on railway economics.

BIBLIOGRAPHIES (RETROSPECTIVE)

985. Ad Hoc Committee of Librarians for "Sources of Information in Transportation." **Sources of Information in Transportation.** Compiled by Ruth F. Blaisdell and others. Evanston, Ill., Published for the Transportation Center at Northwestern University by the Northwestern University Press, 1964. 262 p.

Emphasis is given to sources concerned with the U.S. national highway program. Publications of only local interest have been omitted. Foreign publications, especially, periodicals have been included, but the priority is given on those of Canada, England, Australia, and other English speaking countries.

986. Bureau of Railway Economics, Washington, D.C. **Railway Economics; a Collective Catalogue of Books in Fourteen American Libraries.** Chicago, Published for the Bureau of Railway Economics by the University of Chicago Press, 1912. 446 p.

A classified catalog with index of names.

987. Canada, Bureau of Statistics. Library. **Bibliographical List of References to Canadian Railways, 1829-1938.** Ottawa, 1938. 99 p.

Includes 1179 entries of books and journals supplying information about location of copies.

988. **Ekonomika Zheleznodorozhnogo Transporta S.S.S.R.;** Bibliograficheskii Ukazatel'. Pod red. V. A. Dmitrieva. Moskva. Transzheldorizdat, 1958. 64 p. (Tsentr. nauch.-tekhn. b-ka M-va putei Soobshcheniia S.S.S.R.)

Translated title: Economy of the railway transportation in the U.S.S.R.; a bibliographical guide. Contains 404 annotated entries of books and articles published during 1952-57 period. Includes an author index.

989. European Communities. Commission. **Bibliographie sur les Transports dans l'Intégration Europeenne. . .** Luxembourg, Services des publications des Communautes europennes, 1967. 119 p. Multi-lingual.

Bibliography of transportation in European community.

990. Lee, Robert R. **Engineering-Economic Planning of Transportation Facilities: a Selected Bibliography** by Robert R. Lee, Gerald A. Fleischer and Fincent J. Roggeveen. Stanford, Calif., Stanford University, Project on Engineering-Economic Planning, 1961. 104 leaves.

Provides a worthy list of publications on transportation emphasizing the economic administrative, and political factors of transport planning.

991. Rogerson, I., ed. **History of Transport.** Cheltenham, Gloucestershire Technical Information Service, 1965 (Reprinted 1966). 46 p. (Bibliographical Series, 4).

992. _____. **History of Transport, a Second List.** Cheltenham, Gloucestershire Technical Information Service, 1966. 24 p.

Compilation of books and some periodical articles; divided into four sections: 1. General; 2. Water transport; 3. Land transport; and 4. Air transport. Includes name index.

993. Siddall, William R. **Transportation Geography; a Bibliography.** Manhattan, Kansas State University Library, 1964. 49 1. (Kansas State University of Agriculture and Applied Science, Manhattan Library. Bibliography Series, no. 1).

Under four main headings: general, transportation facilities, regional studies and recent additions, are entered books and articles in English published between 1950-1963.

994. Soltman, Theodore J., and Hacke, Sarah D. eds. **Selected Bibliography for Transportation Planning.** Pittsburgh, Pittsburgh Area Transportation Study, 1964. 81 p.

Includes current books, pamphlets, reports and articles on transportation planning in a subject arrangement. This is a valuable bibliography for persons interested in this field.

995. Thomson, Thomas Richard. **Check List of Publications on American Railroads before 1841;** a union list of printed books and pamphlets, dealing with charters, by-laws, legislative acts, speeches, debates, land grants, officers' and engineers' reports, travel guides, maps, etc. New York, New York Public Library, 1942. 250 p.

"Reprinted with additions from the Bulletin of New York Public Library of January-July-October, 1941."

996. U.S. Library of Congress. Reference Dept. **Soviet Transportation and Communications; a Bibliography;** compiled by Renee S. Janse. Washington, 1952. 330 p.

This is a comprehensive, partly annotated bibliography of Russian and non-Russian sources on transportation and communications in the U.S.S.R. Emphasis is on material published after 1930. Bibliography is divided into two parts: 1. Transportation and 2. Communication. Includes a detailed author index.

997. Virginia Council of Highway Investigation and Research. **Forecasting and Estimation; a selected Annotated Bibliography with Special Emphasis on Methodology,** supplemented by a section of annotated entries, by Marvin Tummins, consultant, and William R. Trevor. In cooperation with the U.S. Bureau of Public Roads, Charlottesville, 1961. 96 p.

The function of long service-life of highways facilities requires a lengthy planning and construction period based on forecasts and estimates. This bibliography is the first step in such forecasting study. In part I the annotated entries are listed by subject. Part II contains a list of unannotated entries. Includes two indexes.

998. Wolfe, Roy I, and Hickok, Beverly, comps. **An Annotated Bibliography of the Geography of Transportation.** Berkeley, Cal., 1961. 61 I. (California, University Institute of Transportation and Traffic Engineering. Information Circular, no. 29).

Listed are books in geography and on the economics of transportation with an emphasis on works performed by geographers in the United States and Canada, and less in Great Britain and Germany. Also the geographical literature of other countries is included. No cross references are given.

999.   Zhabrov, A. A. **Annotirovannyi Ukazatel' Literatury na Russkom Iazyke po Aviatsii i Vozdukhoplavaniiu za 50 Let, 1881-1931.** Teoriia; Tekhnika; Stroitel'stvo; Ekonomika; Statistika; Istoriia; Mirnoe priminenie. Moskva, Gosavitsionnoe i avtotraktornoe izd-vo, 1933. 312 p.

Translated: An annotated guide to literature in Russian in avaiation and air flights in 50 years (1881-1931); Theory, technology, construction, economics, statistics, history, peaceful application. Contains 2,535 entries of books and periodical articles in Russian. An author index is included.

DICTIONARIES, ENCYCLOPEDIAS & HANDBOOKS

1000.   **Dr. Gablers Verkehrs-Lexikon.** Hrsg. von Walter Linden unter Mitwirkung von zahlreichen Fachleuten aus Verkehrswissenschaft und - praxis, Wiesbaden, Dr. Gabler, 1966. 1834 columns, 47 p.

This is a German encyclopedic dictionary of transportation.

1001.   **Moody's Public Utility Manual.** 1954 — New York, Moody's Investors Service. Annual. Supersedes Moody's Manual of Investments: American and Foreign. Public utility securities.

1002.   **Moody's Transportation Manual:** Railroads, Airlines, Shipping, Traction, Bus and Truck Lines. American and Foreign 1954 — New York, Moody's Investors Service. Annual. Supersedes Moody's Manual of Investments: American and Foreign Railroad Securities (later Transportation).

DIRECTORIES

1003.   **Custom House Guide.** 1 — 18 — New York, Import Publications. Annual with monthly supplements. Title varies.

Supplies various informations for each port of entry, such as: custom house brokers, steamship lines and agents, warehouses, foreign consuls, chambers of commerce, port authorities, U.S. Customs Tariff Act, customs regulations, etc.

1004.   **Directory of Railway Officials & Year Book.** v. 1 — 1950/51 — London, Tothill Press, etc. Annual. Supersedes Universal Directory of Railway Officials and Railway Yearbook (1933/34-1950) and the Universal Directors of Railway Officials (1895-1933).

In addition to railway information in Great Britain and Ireland it includes a brief survey of railroads in various countries of the world.

1005.   Dun & Bradstreet, Inc. **Motor Carrier Directory, Listing Carriers with $50,000 or More Gross Annual Revenue.** 1963 — Washington, Trine Associates.

This is an automotive transportation directory for the U.S.

1006.   **The Globe World Directory for Land, Sea and Air Traffic.** 1st — 1948 —
Copenhagen, Globe Directories.

1007.   **International Telephone Directory.** Paris, 1954 — Annual.
        Covers over one hundred countries including some smaller about
which there is limited amount of information available. Entries are arranged
by countries and subarranged by subject.

1008.   **Lloyd's Register of Shipping.** 18 — London, Wyman and Sons, etc.
Annual.
        "Founded 1780. Reconstituted 1834. United with the Underwriters'
registry for iron vessels in 1885". Title varies: 18 — 1913, Lloyd's register
of British and foreign shipping.

1009.   **Mass Transportation. Directory.** 19 — Chicago, Kenfield-Davis
Pub. Co.

1010.   **Ports of the World.** London, Shipping World, 1946 — v. 1 — Annual.
        Lists alphabetically ports by country, giving the locations, name and
information as to population, port facilities, charges, export, import, etc.
There is a separate section for the United Kingdom.

1011.   **The Shippers Directory of National and State Agencies, Associations
and Organizations** in or Correlated with the Motor Transport Field and Related
Data. 1951 — Chicago, Curtis and Stewart. Annual.

1012.   **Shipping World Year Book and Who's Who.** Edited by Sir Archibald
Hurd, 1883 — London, Shipping World, 1883 — Annual.
        Offers a very important information source regarding merchant
marine, in particular: statistical data, directories of ship builders, ship owners,
repairers, marine equipment suppliers, marine engine builders, shipping
organizations, and who's who in the shipping world.

1013.   U.S. Bureau of Customs. **Merchant Vessels of the United States**
(including yachts and government vessels) v. 1 — 1866/67 — Washington,
Govt. Print Office. Annual.
        Lists in alphabetical order names of ships giving: the size, tonnage,
curricula of ship, the owner, home port, etc.

1014.   **Who's Who in Railroading in North America.** 14th ed. New York,
Simmons-Boardman, 1959. 703 p.
        Title varies: 1885-1930, The Biographical Directory of Railway Officials
of America.

ATLASES

1015.　**Lloyd's Maritime Atlas Including a Comprehensive List of Ports and Shipping Places of the World.** Compiled and edited by the shipping editor at Lloyd's. 4th ed. London, Lloyd's 1961. 99 p.

SURVEYS & STATISTICS

1016.　United Nations. Economic Commission for Europe. **Annual Bulletin of Transport Statistics for Europe.** 1949 — New York, 1950 — Annual.

1017.　U.S. Civil Aeronautics Board. **Handbook of Airline Statistics, United States Certificated Air Carriers.** 1938-42 — Annual (irregular). Title varies: 1938-48, Annual airline statistics. . .

　　　　Designed as a useful statistical information source of American air transport including financial data, chronology of events, comparison of air with other transportation means and a glossary of air-transport terms.

1019.　U.S. Federal Aviation Agency. **F.A.A. Statistical Handbook of Aviation** 1944 — Washington.

　　　　Title varies: 1944-58. Statistical Handbook of aviation, etc. Provides statistical data on airports, the federal airway system, aircraft production and export, accidents, and other civil-aviation activities.

1020.　U.S. Interstate Commerce Commission. **Report on Transport Statistics in the United States.** v. 1 — 1887/88 — Washington, Govt. Print Office. Annual.

　　　　Title varies: 1887/1953, Annual Report on the Statistics of Railways in the United States.

MONOGRAPHIC TREATISES
(A Selected List of Monographs Including Comprehensive Bibliographies)

1021.　Barnouw, Eric. **A History of Broadcasting in the United States.** New York, Oxford University Press, 1966 —

　　　　Contents: v. 1. A Tower of Babel. Presents good documented history to 1933, including bibliography and an index.

1022.　Fogel, Robert William. **Railroads and American Economic Growth.** Baltimore, Johns Hopkins University Press, 1964. 296 p.

　　　　Presents a critical evaluation of the proposition that railroads were of dominant influence on American economic growth during the 19th century. The thesis is that railways far from being indispensible to American economic life, were not even important to it. Includes an index. Bibliography: p. 263-285.

1023.   Milne, Alastair Murray. **Economics of Inland Transport.** London, Pitman, 1955. 292 p.

1024.   United Nations Educational, Scientific and Cultural Organization. **World Radio and Television.** Paris, Unesco, 1965. 159 p.
        Describes radio and T.V. facilities in about two hundred countries using statistical data.

CHAPTER EIGHT

LABOR ECONOMICS
(Industrial and Labor Relations; Professions; Wages)

GUIDES

1025. Cornell University. New York State School of Industrial and Labor Relations. Labor Management Documentation Center. **Guide to the Records.** Ithaca, N.Y., 1963. 62 p.

1026. Naas, Bernard G. and Sakr, Carmelita S. **American Labor Union Periodicals; a Guide to their Location.** Ithaca, N.Y., Cornell University, 1956. 175 p.

"Published for the New York State School of Industrial and Labor Relations. . . for the Committee of University Industrial Relations Librarians." Lists over 1,700 labor union periodicals, located in twenty cooperating libraries.

1027. Special Libraries Association. Social Science Group. **A Source List of Selected Labor Statistics.** Rev. ed. New York, 1953. 113 p.

Listed are those statistical series on labor force, employment, un- employment, labor costs, turnover, wages, workmen's budgets, fringe benefits and costs of living, which are published more than once a year. The included material is entered in one of three sections: federal agencies, state agencies and non-governmental agencies. Includes subject and title indexes, addresses of agencies listed as compilers, and periodicals referred to, with publication information.

BIBLIOGRAPHIES (CURRENT)

1028. Argentine Republic. Ministerio de Trabajo y Seguridad Social. Departmento de Publicaciones y Biblioteca. **Boletin de Biblioteca.** July, 1956 — Buenos Aires. Monthly.

This is a monthly listing of literature on labor.

1029. Canada. Dept. of Public Printing and Stationery. **Canadian Govern- ment Publications Relating to Labour;** Sectional Catalogue no. 10. 1st — 19 — Ottawa, Queen's Printer.

Published in two parts: English and French. Lists publications first of the Dept. of Labor then of other government agencies including Parliament, Royal Commissions, Supreme Court and Unemployment Insurance Commission. Includes a detailed index.

1030.   Cornell University. New York State School of Industrial and Labor Relations. **Library Catalog.** Boston, Mass., G. K. Hall, 1967. 12 v.

1031.   _____. **Supplement.** 1st — Boston, G. K. Hall, 1967 —
    Provides a coverage of labor management relations, human relations in industry, labor economics, labor history, unions, and international labor conditions and problems from the late 18th century to the present. All books and a selected number of important pamphlets are in that dictionary catalog. Additionally, author and subject entries for selected articles from 150 periodicals have been included since 1952. There is a separate card file for the documents collection. The subject headings are similar to those used by L.C. This is the most comprehensive bibliography on industrial and labor relations.

1032.   Illinois. University. Institute of Labor and Industrial Relations. **Bibliographic Contributions.** no. 1 — 1952 — Champaign.

1033.   International Labor Office. Library. **Bibliographical Contributions,** no. 1 — 1949 — Geneva.
    The aim of this mimeographed series is to note the resources of the International Labor Office Library. The scope is international as to the subjects, authors and language.

1034.   Madrid. Centro de Estudios Sindicales. **Selección de Publicaciones Internacionales.** 1 — Madrid, 1958 —

1035.   **Manpower Research: Inventory.** 1966/67 — Washington, U. S. Govt. Print Off.

1036.   Princeton University. Industrial Relations Section. **Bibliographical Series no. 61** — Princeton, N.J., 1939 —
    Continues the numbering of its Report which divided to form the above and its Research report series. This is an annotated bibliography containing most recent literature in the field of industrial and labor relations.

1037.   _____. **Outstanding Books on Industrial Relations.** 1949 — Princeton, N.J., 1950 — (Its Selected References, no. 31a, 50, etc.)

1038.   _____. **Selected References,** No. 1 — 1945 — Princeton, N.J. Irregular.
    Each issue under a special topic brings in alphabetical order an annotated list of books, pamphlets and periodical articles recently published. In March issue is included a list of "Outstanding Books on Industrial Relations."

1039.　U.S. Bureau of Labor Statistics. **Catalog of Publications: Bulletins, Reports and Releases. Periodicals:** Monthly labor review, Employment and earnings, Occupational outlook quarterly, Labor development abroad. Jan. 1946/ April 1947 — Washington. Semiannually. Title varies: 1946-63, Publications. Frequency varies: June 1947-63, monthly; Jan.-June 1964 — Semiannual.

1040.　_____. **A Catalogue of the Wage Studies of the Bureau of Labor Statistics.** 1941/46 —

1041.　_____. **A Directory of B.L.S. Studies in Industrial Relations.** 1953/58 —

1042.　_____. **A Directory of Industry Wage Studies and Union Scale Studies.** 1950/58 — Washington. Irregular.

1043.　U.S. Dept. of Labor. **Publications of the U.S. Department of Labor; Subject Listing.** 1948-1955 — Washington, U.S. Govt. Print Off.

1044.　_____. **Selected References for Labor Attaches;** a list of readily available materials. 1959 — Washington. Annual.

BIBLIOGRAPHIES (RETROSPECTIVE)

1045.　American Arbitration Association. **Arbitration Bibliography.** New York, 1954. 92 1.
　　　"A list of books, pamphlets, articles and unpublished manuscripts available for study and research in the Lucius Root Eastman Arbitration Library."

1046.　American Federation of Labor. Dept. of Education. **Labor's Library; a Bibliography for Trade Unionists, Educators, Writers, Students, Librarians.** 3rd ed. Washington, 1952. 109 p.

1047.　Association francaise pour l'accroissement de la productivité. **Bibliography on Productivity;** Project no. 233. Prepared by the National Centre of the French Association for the increase of Productivity and the European Productivity Agency. Paris, European Productivity Agency of the organization for European Economic Cooperation, 1956. 250 p.

1048.　Blum, Albert A. **An Annotated Bibliography of Industrial Relations and the Small Firm,** by Albert A. Blum with the assistance of Douglas M. Reid. Ithaca, N.Y., State School of Industrial and Labor Relations, Cornell University, 1960. 45 p. (Bibliography series, no. 3).
　　　Small firm is defined here as a unit having no more than 500 employees. The criterion for inclusion was the usefulness of the item for a busy executive. The arrangement is by subject and by author.

1049.   Brückmann, Kurt, et al. **Literatur für den Gewerkschaftsfunktionär;** eine Empfehlende Bibliographie. 2. erweiterte Aufl. Hrsg. von Bundesvorstand des F.D.G.B. and von der Deutschen Bücherei in Leigzig. Berlin, Tribüne, 1958. 219 p. (Sondern bibliographien der Deutschen Bücherei, 7).

Title translated: The literature for a labor union officer; a recommended bibliography.

1050.   California. University. University at Los Angeles. Institute of Industrial Relations. **Industrial Human Relations; a Selected Bibliography.** 6th revision, prepared by Irving R. Weschler. Los Angeles, 1959. 41 p.

1051.   Chamberlain, Neil W. **Source Book on Labor.** Rev. and abridged with the assistance of Richard Perlman, New York, McGraw-Hill, 1964. 382 p.

Contains various documents such as union constitutions, collective agreements, company statements relating to labor, laws and legislations, government reports, excerpts from congressional hearings, etc.

1052.   Chamberlin, Waldo. **Industrial Relations in Germany, 1914-1939; Annotated Bibliography** of Materials in the Hoover Library on War, Revolution, and Peace and the Stanford University Library, Stanford University, Calif., Stanford University Press, 1942. 403 p.

Divided into seven chapters: 1. Documents (Germany, U.S., Great Britain, International Labor Office, Miscellaneous). 2. Society Publications. 3. Newspapers and Periodical Publications. 4.-7. Monographs, Studies, and Articles. Includes an index.

1053.   Farrell, David M. **The Contracting out of Work: an Annotated Bibliography.** Kingston, Ont., Queens University. Industrial Relations Centre, 1965. 61 p. (Kingston, Ont., Industrial Relations Centre Bibliography Series, no. 1).

Contains books, articles, arbitration cases, reports, collected in two sections, the first one includes Canadian sources, the second lists American titles. Items are arranged within each section by subject. A certain number of entries are without annotations.

1054.   Folsom, Josiah Chase. **Agricultural Labor in the United States.** an Annotated Bibliography of Selected References. Washington, U.S. Govt. Print Off., 1953. 64 p. (U.S. Dept. of Agriculture. Library, Library List 59).

1055.   Gulick, Charles Adams, and others. **History and Theories of Working-class Movements; a Select Bibliography.** Berkeley, Bureau of Business and Economic Research and Institute of Industrial Relations, University of California, 1955. 364 p.

Lists articles, notes, and occasional documents from the English language journals. The main arrangement is by country, subject and author.

The last chapter entitled International deals with international labor organizations.

1056.   Hawaii. University, Honolulu. Industrial Relations Center. **Selected Bibliographies on Labor and Industrial Relations in Burma, Indonesia, Korea, Malaya, Singapore, Thailand.** Helen R. Shumaake, comp. Honolulu, Hawaii, 1962. 52 leaves.

These bibliographies are part of a series which began with the selected bibliographies on Australia, India, Japan, New Zealand and Philippines compiled in May 1961. All material is alphabetically arranged by the country, with following subarrangement: government publications, books, pamphlets, periodicals, unpublished materials, microfilm. Appendixes contain: List of periodicals cited and publisher's addresses.

1057.   Illinois University. Institut of Labor and Industrial Relations. **University of Illinois Library Resources in Labor and Industrial Relations,** by Ralph E. McCoy and Elizabeth O. Hogg. Urbana, 1949. 141 leaves.

1058.   International Labour Office. **Publications, 1954-1965.** Geneva, 1966. 64 p.

Arranged in sections alphabetically: 1. listed by subject, 2. Periodicals, 3. Documents and proceedings, 4. Miscellaneous. Includes an index and a list of depository libraries for I.L.O. Publications.

1059.   International Labour Office. Library. **Bibliographie des Sources de Documentation sur le Travail.** Bibliography of Research Sources on Labour Questions. Geneva, 1965. 129 p. (Bibliographical contributions, no. 24).

Material is arranged in six sections which are subdivided by country listing reference sources on labor.

1060.   _____. **Bibliography on Industrial Relations.** Geneva, 1955. 103 p. (Its Bibliographical Contributions, no. 10).

1061.   _____. **Bibliography on Labour Law.** Rev. ed. Geneva. 1958. 104 p. (Its Bibliographical Contributions, no. 13). In English and French.

Provides useful bibliography on labor, law and legislation in many countries. Included material is arranged by country. Author index is added.

1062.   _____. **Catalogue des Publications en Langue Francaise du Bureau International du Travail, 1919-1950.** Geneva, 1951. 411 p. (Its Contributions Bibliographiques, no. 6).

1063.   _____. **Supplement,** 1951-1955. Geneva, 1957. 88 p.

1064.   _____. **Catalogue of Publications in English of the International Labour Office, 1919-1950.** Geneva, 1951. 379 p. (Its

Bibliographic Contributions, no. 5).

Divided into two parts: (1) Titles and subjects, in one alphabet; (2) A Checklist arranged by conference, committee, or issuing agency, and by series.

1065.   Isbester, A. Fraser and others. **Industrial and Labor Relations in Canada: a Selected Bibliography.** Kingston, Ont., Queens University, Industrial Relations Centre, 1965. 120 p. (Kingston, Ont. Industrial Relations Centre. Bibliography Series, no. 2).

Lists the literature in collective bargaining, history and government of labor unions, labor force and unemployment, working conditions: hours, wages, and prices. All material in three sections.

1066.   Kaplun, S. I. **Ukazatel' Literatury na Russkom Iazyke po Nauchnoi Organizatsii Truda i Smezhnym Voprosam.** Izd. 2. Moskva, Voprosy truda, 1925. 421 p.

Title translated: A guide to literature in Russian language on scientific labor management. Includes 4,483 items: books, scholarly articles and papers for the period of 1917 to 1924.

1067.   LeClair, Marie J. **Bibliography on Labor in Africa, 1960-64.** Washington, U.S. Dept. of Labor, Bureau of Labor Statistics, U.S. Govt. Print Off., 1965. 121 p. (U.S. Bureau of Labor Statistics. Bulletin 1473).

1068.   McCoy, Ralph Edward and Gsell, Donald. **History of Labor and Unionism in the United States; a Selected Bibliography.** Champaign, 1953. 88 l. (Illinois University. Institute of Labor and Industrial Relations. Bibliographic Contributions, no. 2).

The arrangement is alphabetical by author. Emphasis is on a secondary material, such as books and pamphlets. Excluded are documentary sources, government publications, reports, proceedings of the conferences, periodicals, etc. The detailed subject index is included.

1070.   Michigan. University. Bureau of Industrial Relations. **A Selected List of Books and Periodicals in the Field of Personnel Administration and Labor-management Relations.** Ann Arbor. Graduate School of Business Administration, 1964. 26 p.

The included material is arranged under ten subject headings without annotations. Added is a list of serials and a directory of publishers.

1071.   Mundle, George F. **Industrial Relations Bibliographies; a Checklist.** Champaign, Ill., Institute of Labor and Industrial Relations, University of Illinois, 1965. 54 p. (University of Illinois. Institute of Labor and Industrial Relations. Bibliographic Contributions, no. 8).

Single items are arranged chronologically from 1893-1965, and series items are entered in an alphabetical order. Emphasis is on sources published in the U.S. Canadian and overseas publications are excluded. Author, title and subject indexes are included.

1072. Neufeld, Maurice F. **A Representative Bibliography of American Labor History.** Ithaca, N.Y., New York State School of Industrial and Labor Relations, Cornell University, 1964. 146 p.

The selected items represent a wide variety of types of materials. There are books more or less scholarly, theses, government publications, (documents, reports) union reports, management publications, articles from periodicals, learned and popular. Under various headings items are entered alphabetically by author title. Index is attached.

1073. Organization for European Economic Cooperation. European Productivity Agency. **Bibliography on Productivity.** Prepared by the National Centre of the French Association for the Increase of Productivity Agency. Paris, 1956. 250 p. (Project no. 253).

1074. Princeton University. Industrial Relations Section. **Incentive Wage Systems: a Selected Annotated Bibliography.** Princeton, N.J., Industrial Relations Section, Dept. of Economics and Sociology, Princeton University, 1955. 24 p. (Its Bibliographical Series, no. 83).

Consists of over one hundred titles (books and articles) dealing with this topic.

1075. _____. **A Trade Union Library, 1955.** Prepared by Martin Horowitz and Hazel C. Benjamin. 6th ed. Princeton, N.J., 1955. 58 p.

An annotated bibliography of books and government publications on industrial relations with a subject arrangement. Author index is included.

1076. Remizova, E. S. **Tvorcheskaia Initsiativa i Aktivnost' Trudiashchikhsia; kratkii bibliograficheskii ukazatel'.** Moskva, Profizdat, 1961. 97 p.

Translated: Labor's creative initiative and activity; a short bibliographical guide.

1077. Reynolds, Lloyd George and Killinsworth, Charles C. **Trade Union Publications; the Official Journals, Convention Proceedings, and Constitutions of International Unions and Federations, 1850-1941.** Baltimore, Johns Hopkins Press, 1944-45. 3 v.

Contents: v. 1 Description and Bibliography, v. 2-3 Subject Index. Presents the behavior of American trade unions in historical perspective, making accessible their rich reference sources. The most important undertaking in this work was the compilation of a subject index to official periodical publications, proceedings of the conventions of international unions and national federations.

1078.   Rose, Fred Duane. **American Labor in Journals of History; a Bibliography.** Champaign, Ill., Institute of Labor and Industrial Relations, University of Illinois, 1962. 87 p. (University of Illinois, Institute of Labor and Industrial Relations. Bibliographic Contributions, no. 7).

This is a supplement to the Labor History in the United States; a General Bibliography, by Gene S. Stroud and Gilber E. Donahue. It is limited to articles on labor history written in the United States historical periodicals. 903 items in 98 periodicals are selected. Journals listed are arranged in alphabetical and articles in each journal in chronological order. General and picture indexes are included.

1079.   Rosen, Ned and McCoy, Ralph E., comps. **Doctoral Dissertations in Labor and Industrial Relations, 1933-1953.** Champaign, 1955. 86 leaves. (University of Illinois. Institute of Labor and Industrial Relations. Bibliographic Contributions, no. 5).

1080.   Simpson, Keith and Benjamin, Hazel C. **Manpower Problems in Economic Development; a Selective Bibliography.** Princeton, N.J. Industrial Relations Section, Dept. of Economics and Sociology, Princeton University, 1958. 93 p. (Princeton University. Industrial Relations Section. Bibliographical Series, no. 85).

This is an annotated bibliography on manpower as a basic resource for economic development. The criterion for selection was on works of fundamental interest; most of the material is drawn from American experience.

1081.   Spatz, Laura (Huyett). **Productivity: a Bibliography.** November 1957. Washington, U.S. Dept. of Labor Statistics, 1958. 182 p. (U.S. Bureau of Labor Statistics. Bulletin no. 1226).

1082.   Stout, Ronald M. **Local Government In-Service Training; an Annotated Bibliography.** Albany, Graduate School of Public Affairs. State University of New York at Albany, 1968. 79 p.

1083.   Stroud, Gene S. and Donahue, Gilbert E. **Labor History in the United States; a General Bibliography.** Urbana, Institute of Labor and Industrial Relations, University of Illinois, 1961. 167 p. (Bibliographic contributions, no. 6).

This is a successor of the out of print History of Labor and Unionism in the United States: a Selected Bibliography, published by Ralph E. McCoy in 1953. The present bibliography has been expanded in scope including much more material than the McCoy's compilation. In one alphabetical listing are entered books, pamphlets, articles, reports, documents, etc. by author or the name of corporation. Subject index is included.

1084.   Sufrin, Sidney Charles, and Wagner, Frank Eugene. **A Brief Annotated Bibliography on Labor in Emerging Societies.** Prepared for the Pakistan project; Syracuse University, Maxwell Graduate School of Citizenship and Public Affairs, Center for Overseas Operations. Syracuse, N.Y., 1961. 64 p.

Lists titles of the recent literature on labor in English language related to the underdeveloped countries of non-Soviet bloc. The arrangement is by subject, subarranged by area and country. In addition the list of government reports, bibliographies, and major textbooks on economic development are included.

1085.   United Nations. Statistical Office. **Input-Output Bibliography, 1955-1960,** by Charlotte E. Taskier. Harvard Economic Research Project, New York, 1961. 222 p. (Its Document ST/STAT/7).

This is a sequel to Interindustry Economic Studies by Vera Riley and Robert Allen (1955). It consists of ca. 2,000 references to books, parts of books, articles, documents, reports, dissertations, proceedings of conferences in many languages. Some entries are annotated. Includes author and title index.

1086.   _____. **Input-Output Bibliography, 1960-1963.** New York, 1964. 159 p.

About 1,000 references.

1087.   _____. **Input-Output Bibliography, 1963-1966.** New York. 1967. 259 p.

About 1,500 references.

1088.   U.S. Bureau of Labor Statistics. **Foreign Labor Publications of the Bureau of Labor Statistics, 1945-June 30, 1962.** Washington, 1962. 29 leaves.

1089.   U.S. Civil Service Commission. Library. **Manpower Planning and Utilization in the Federal Government.** Washington, U.S. Civil Service Commission, 1963. 126 p. (Its Personnel Bibliography Series, no. 11).

1090.   U.S. Women's Bureau. **Employment of Older Women, an Annotated Bibliography;** Hiring Practices, Attitudes, Work Performance, by Jean A. Wells in the Division of Program Planning, Analysis and Reports. Washington, 1957. 83 p.

Supersedes an earlier publication issued by the Bureau under title: Bibliography on employment problems of older women.

1091.   _____. **Selected References on Equal Pay for Women,** 1947 — Washington.

1092.   Vradenburg, Juliet Cochran.   **The Guaranteed Annual Wage, an Annotated Bibliography of Source Material.** Stanford University, Calif., Stanford University Press, 1947. 101 p.

"The backbone material is source informations from pamphlets, brochures, and letters from the companies themselves, and where that has not been obtainable, from research organizations and industrial organs. (Pref.) Indexes of authors, of companies, and of subjects are included.

1093.   Witte, Irene Margarete.   **Bibliographie der Neueren Arbeits- und Betriebswirtschaftlichen Literatur des Auslandes.** Vorzugsweise der U.S.A. und Grossbritanien, mit Einem Namens- und Adressverzeichnis Einschlägiger Zeitschriften, Verlage Institute und Organisationen. Berlin, Duncker & Humblot, 1949. 170 p.

Translated: Bibliography of a more recent labor and management literature from foreign countries, particularly of the U.S. and Great Britain with a name and address index.

DICTIONARIES & ENCYCLOPEDIAS

1094.   **Careers Encyclopedia:** a work of reference upon some 220 occupations, for teachers, parents, school-leavers, undergraduates and employment, and employment officials. 5th ed. completely rev. London, Macmillan & Cleaver, 1967. 567 p.

Arranged alphabetically by career, giving essential informations about a given profession.

1095.   Casselman, Paul Hubert.   **Labor Dictionary; a Concise Encyclopedia of Labor Information.** New York. Philosophical Library, 1949. 554 p. Bibliography: p. 542-554.

1095a.   Lees-Smith, Hastings Bertrand, ed.   **The Encyclopaedia of the Labour Movement.** London, Caxton, 1928. 3 v.

1096.   U.S. Employment Service.   **Dictionary of Occupational Titles.** 3rd ed. Washington, Dept. of Labor, 1965. 2 v.

Contents: v. 1. Definitions of titles; v. 2. Occupational classification and Industry Index. Volume one identifies and defines a total of 35,500 titles in one alphabetical order, explaining: what gets done, how, and why. Volume two, which complements the first volume, classifies occupations according to categories, divisions and groups. A detailed explanation as to job classification is given in Introduction of v. 2. Added are: industry index, glossary, and an appendix with explanations.

DIRECTORIES

1097.   Angel, Juvenal Londono.   **Looking for Employment in Foreign**

Countries. 5th ed. rev. and enl. New York, World Trade Academy Press, 1961. 153 p.

Accompanying volume to author's National and International Employment Handbook for Specialized Personnel giving more information on employment in foreign countries.

1098.　Angel, Juvenal Londono. **National and International Employment Handbook for Specialized Personnel;** Practical Handbook for those Seeking Employment here and Abroad. 6th ed. New York, World Trade Academy Press, 1961. 308 p.

1099.　＿＿＿＿＿＿. **Student's Guide to Occupational Opportunities and their Lifetime Earnings.** New York, World Trade Academy Press, 1967. 312 p.

Presents estimates in the economic values of various grades of education, and various types of vocational training, for the present and for the future. Stresses the economic importance of education for every individual. A subject index is included. Bibliography; p. 299-303.

1100.　**International Labor Directory and Handbook.** 1950 — New York, Praeger, Editor: 1950 — D. D. Galbo. 1965 — J. Schuyler. Title varies slightly.

Designed as a useful information source on labor, its organizations, activities, publications, educational institutions, etc., in the U.S., Canada, Great Britain and other countries.

1101.　Roberts, Harold Selig. **Who's Who in Industrial Relations.** Honolulu, Industrial Relations Center, University of Hawaii, 1966-67. 2 v.

1102.　U.S. Bureau of International Labor Affairs. **Directory of Labor Organizations.** Rev. ed. Washington, D.C., 1959-63. 4 v. in 7. Looseleaf.

Contents: Africa, 1962 (1 vol.); Asia and Australasia, 1963 (2 vol.); Western Hemisphere excluding U.S. 1964 (2 vol.); Europe, rev. ed. 1965 — (2 vol.). Lists labor organizations in alphabetical arrangement by the country. Appendixes with lists of abbreviations, names, etc. are added.

1103.　U.S. Bureau of Labor Statistics. **Directory of National and International Labor Unions in the United States.** 1955 — Washington, D.C., Government Printing Off., 1955 — Biennial.

Unions in the United States; 1937-42. Directory of A.F.L. Unions, and Directory of C.I.O. Unions.

1104.　U.S. Bureau of Labor Statistics. **Occupational Outlook Handbook; Employment Information on Major Occupations for Use in Guidance.** 1st ed. — Washington, 1949 — (Its Bulletin, no. 1375). Biennial.

A useful guide to numerous occupations in the United States giving such informations as: kind of work, salary, working conditions and hours, where and how to apply, and other relating topics.

1105.   Who's Who in Labor; the Authorized Biographies of the Men and Women who Lead Labor in the United States and Canada, and of those who deal with Labor, 1946 — New York, The Dryden Press, 1946 —

Includes: a glossary of labor terminology, a chronology of labor legislation, a directory of labor press, a list of educational and research directors, and a list of the international labor unions.

HANDBOOKS

1106.   Aspley, John Cameron, ed. **Handbook of Employee Relations.** Chicago, Dartnell Corporation, 1957. 1391 p.

A successor to Industrial Relations Handbook. Discusses various phases of human relations in industry, banks, department stores, insurance companies, real estate, publishing houses, government and other places. Provides practical examples and suggestions how to handle labor disputes and contract negotiations, how to improve, supervision, production and the personal relations.

1107.   Commerce Clearing House. **Solutions to 3,500 Labor Problems.** Chicago, 1965. 2 v. Compiled by the Editorial staff of C.C.R.

Reviews the decisions of arbitrations in labor disputes in the past few years. The cases are arranged in alphabetical order by subject.

1108.   Peterson, Florence. **American Labor Unions, What they are and How they Work.** 2nd rev. ed. New York, Harper, 1963. 271 p.

Presents a valuable handbook of U.S. labor unions, their history, organizational structure, their government, their educations, welfare, and political activities, collective bargaining, relationships to employer, etc.

1109.   U.S. Dept. of Labor. **The American Workers' Fact Book.** Washington, 1960. 355, 40 p.

Designed as an elementary handbook on American labor and labor relations, providing many facts, statistical data, charts, and information about the U.S. Dept. of Labor.

1110.   Walch, John Weston. **Complete Handbook on Labor-Management Relations.** Portland, Me., 1965. 2 v.

INDEXES & ABSTRACTS

1111.   Cornell University. New York State School of Industrial and Labor Relations. Library. **Industrial and Labor Relations; Abstracts and Annotations.** 195 — Ithaca.

1112.   **Employment Relations Abstracts,** 1958 — Detroit, Information Service. Semimonthly. Supersedes Labor-personnel index, 1951 — 58.

Abstracts current books and about 120 periodicals; includes a detailed subject guide.

1113.   **Index to Labor Union Periodicals; a Cumulative Subject Index to Material from a Selected List of Newspapers and Journals Published by Major Labor Unions.** Ann Arbor, University of Michigan, Bureau of Industrial Relations, 1960 — v. 1 — Monthly.

Designed as an annotated index to about 50 periodicals with an annual cumulation.

1114.   **International Labour Documentation.** New Series. Geneva, International Labour Office, Central Library and Documentation Branch, 1949 — Weekly.

Presents abstracts of books, pamphlets and periodical articles; international in scope. Includes subject index; quarterly indexes of persons, corporate bodies, document numbers, geographical names and list of conferences.

1115.   **Occupational Index.** v. 1 — 1936 — Jaffrey, N.H., Personnel Service. Quarterly. Frequency varies: to 1940, monthly.

Presents a bibliography with abstracts of current publications on occupations. Author-title and subject indexes are included at the end of each volume.

1116.   U.S. Bureau of Labor Statistics. **Labor Development Abroad; Cumulative Index, 1956-63.** Washington, U.S. Govt. Print. Off., 1965. 67 p. (Its B.L.S. Report no. 292).

1117.   U.S. Bureau of Labor Statistics. **Subject Index of Bulletins Published by the Bureau of Labor Statistics, 1915-59.** Prepared by M. Frances Marshall and Gladys B. Wash. Washington, U.S. Govt. Print. Off., 1960. 102 p. (Its Bulletin no. 1281).

Provides a useful guide on basic labor statistics, working conditions, cost of living, etc. of the United States.

1118.   U.S. Bureau of the Census. **Alphabetical Index of Occupations and Industries,** 1960 Census of Population. Rev. ed. Washington, Govt. Print. Office. 1960. 649 p.

Issued with each decennial census, sometimes between censuses.

1119.   **University of Michigan Index to Labor Union Periodicals.** Jan. 1960 — Ann Arbor, Bureau of Industrial Relations, Graduate School of Business Administration, University of Michigan. Monthly with annual cumulations.

Presents good coverage of labor periodicals, alphabetically arranged by subject and name of union.

1120.   **The American Labor Yearbook,** 1916 —   Prepared by the Dept. of Labor Research of the Rand School of Social Science. New York, Rand School of Social Science. 1919/1920 — also designed v. 3 —

1121.   International Labor Office. **Yearbook of Labour Statistics.** Geneva, 1931 — Annual.

   Contains a summary of the principal labor statistics in 174 countries of territories. In 1965 ed. the included figures cover the last ten years. The data are drawn from national statistical sources, and are arranged under 10 main headings. At the end of each annual are included: References and sources used in compilation of data, and an Index of countries and territories. Text is in English, French and Italian.

1122.   **Labor Relations Yearbook.** 1965 —   Washington, Bureau of National Affairs.

1122a.   Labor Research Association. **Labor Fact Book.** New York, International Publishers, 1931 — Biennial (Irregular).

   Presents valuable informations on economics, social conditions, etc. of labor in America and abroad. Name and subject index is included.

1123.   Organization for Economic Cooperation and Development. **Wages and Labour Mobility;** a report by a group of independent experts on the relation between changes in wage differentials in the pattern of employment; with a foreword on the implications of the study for incomes policy by Pieter de Wolf. Paris, 1965. 258 p. (Its Economic studies).

   Surveys the wage structure and labor turn-over in OECD countries.

1124.   _____. **Supplement no. 1** — Paris, 1966 —

   Suppl. 1 is divided into two sections: the first contains abstracts of the economic literature dealing with this topic, the second describes labor markets and wages in Canada, France and Netherlands. Suppl. 2 deals with statistical data.

1125.   U. S. Bureau of Labor Statistics. **Employment and Earnings.** v. 1 — July, 1954 — Monthly.

   Supersedes Bureau's Employment and payrolls and its Hours and earnings, industry report.

   Provides a convenient source of current statistical information on weekly earnings, man-hour and payroll indexes. Of two major supplements one entitled Employment and earnings statistics for the United States, 1909-62 has been published in 1963, and another under title: Employment and Earnings Statistics for States and Areas, 1939-63 has been issued in 1964.

1126.   U.S. Bureau of Labor Statistics. **Employment and Earnings Statistics for States and Areas, 1939/63** — Washington, U.S. Govt. Print. Off. (Its Bulletin no. 1370). Annual. Each volume cumulative from 1939.

Surveys statistical data on employment and earnings divided among states and geographical areas during the period from 1939 to the present.

1127.   U.S. Bureau of Labor Statistics. **Employment and Earnings Statistics** for the United States, 1909-64. Washington, D.C., 1964. 662 p. (Its Bulletin, no. 1312-3).

Based on the 1957 Standard industrial classification. This bulletin presents detailed industry statistics of the U.S. nonfarm labor force. Included are monthly and annual averages on employment covering all employees, and average weekly and hourly earnings, overtime hours, and labor turnover rates.

1128.   _____. **Guide to Area Employment Statistics: Employment, Hours and Earnings, Area Definitions.** Washington, 1960. 227 p.

Aimed to provide useful statistical information on employment in various metropolitan areas of the United States.

1129.   _____. **Guide to Employment Statistics of B.L.S.: Employment, Labor Turnover, Hours and Earnings.** Washington, 1961. 134 p.

Provides the earliest data for which such statistics is available. Includes also definitions for each series.

1130.   _____. **Handbook of Labor Statistics, 1924/26-1950.** Supplement 1951. Washington, Govt. Print. Office, 1927-51. (Its Bulletin, no. 439, 491, 541, 616, 694, 916, 1016, 1016 suppl.)

Provides summaries from other publications of the Bureau and from some other government publications on the same and similar subjects.

1131.   _____. **History of Wages in the United States from Colonial Times to 1928.** Revision of Bulletin no. 499 with supplements 1929. 1933. Washington, Govt. Print. Office, 1934. 574 p. (Its Bulletin no. 6040.)

1132.   _____. **Labor Digest.** Washington.

Provides information on labor conditions in various countries of the world, surveying economic, political and social factors influencing labor, labor legislation, hours, wages, prices, standard of living and personnal relations in industries.

MONOGRAPHIC TREATISES
(A Selective List of Monographs Containing Additional Bibliographical Data)

1133.   Bancroft, Gertrude. **The American Labor Force, its Growth and Changing Composition.** For the Social Science Research Council in cooperation with the U.S. Dept. of Commerce, Bureau of the Census. New York, Wiley, 1958. 256 p.

Based on the wealth of official statistical data following topics are surveyed: economic activity of the population, trends in the labor force in 1890-1955, trends in the part time labor force, family employment patterns, and projections of the labor force to 1975.

1134.   Bloom, Gordon Falk, and Northrup, Herbert R. **Economics of Labor Relations.** 5th ed. Homewood, Ill., R. D. Irwin, 1965. 901 p. illus.

The textbook for students and teachers, written in clear, comprehensive and interesting style. It deals with the nature of labor problems, union history and government, collective bargaining, economics of the labor market, governmental wage regulation and the shorter workweek, economics of the search for security, government control of labor relations, some labor problems of the 1960's. Indexes of authors and subject are included.

1135.   Brown, Emily Clark. **Soviet Trade Unions and Labor Relations.** Cambridge, Mass., Harvard University Press, 1966. 394 p.

Bibliographical references included in "Notes": p. 339-381.

1136.   Brown, Ernest and Phelps, Henry. **The Economics of Labor.** New Haven, Yale University Press, 1962. 278 p. (Studies in Comparative Economics, 1).

A first-rate textbook on labor economics providing a large portion of references which would be of considerable value to labor economists. Emphasis is on the implications of basic economic theory and of certain statistical studies. Bibliography: p. 251-264.

1137.   Chamberlain, Neil W. and others. **History of Labor in the United States.** New York, Macmillan, 1935-36. 4 v.

A cooperative work of seven authors deals with the labor movement in the U.S. from the Colonial beginnings to 1932. More emphasized are labor conditions, philosophies and ideas than the structure, policies or history of individual unions. Bibliography: v. 2, p. 539-587; v. 3, p. 701-741; v.4, p. 639-661).

1138.   Cole, George Douglas Howard and Postgate, Raymond. **Common People, 1746-1946.** 4th ed. London, Methuen, 1949. (reprint 1956) 742 p.

Designed as a historical outline of "common people" in Great Britain from 1746 through 1946. Bibliography: p. 689-708.

1139.   _____. **Introduction to Trade Unionism.** London, Allen & Unwin, 1953. 324 p.

Discusses various phases of activity of British trade unions such as: collective bargaining, strikes, education, organization, etc. Includes an index. Bibliography: p. 308-312.

1140.   Cole, George Douglas Howard and Postgate, Raymond. **Short History of the British Workingclass Movement, 1789-1947.** New ed., compl. rev. and continued to 1947. London, G. Allen & Unwin, 1948, repr. 1960. 500 p.

Brings within a single work a general survey of the growth of the labor movement in all its phases, political, industrial and cooperative. Includes an index. Bibliographical references at end of each chapter.

1141.   Cook, Roy Anthony Paul. **Leaders of Labor.** Philadelphia, Lippincott, 1966. 152 p.

1141a.   **A Documentary History of American and Industrial Society.** Edited by John R. Commons and others. New York, Russell & Russell, 1958. 10 v.

A valuable source for the study of labor movement in the U.S. Contents: v. 1 - 2. Plantation and frontier. v. 3 - 4. Labor conspiracy cases. v. 5 - 10. Labor movement. Bibliography: v. 10, p. 142-155.

1142.   Dulles, Foster Rhea. **Labor in America, a History.** 2nd rev. ed. New York, Crowell, 1960. 435 p. (Growth of America ser.)

Presents an account of the rise of American labor from Colonial beginnings to the present days. Emphasis has been placed upon growth of national labor organizations such as National Labor Union, Knights of Labor, the A.F. of L. and the C.I.O. A general index is included. Bibliography: p. 414-422.

1143.   Flanders, Allen, and Clegg, H.A., eds. **The System of Industrial Relations in Great Britain,** its History, Law and Institutions. Oxford, B. Blackwell, 1954. 380 p.

Contents: 1. Social background; 2. Legal framework; 3. Trade unions; 4. Employers; 5. Collective bargaining; 6. Joint consultation. Includes also: Tables of Statutes and cases, and a General index.

1144.   Hicks, John Richard. **The Theory of Wages.** 2nd ed. London, Macmillan, 1964. 388 p.

This classic on wages continues to exert a considerable influence on economic thought. It examines the wage determination under competition effects of unemployment, demand and supply of labor, regulation of wages, the growth of power of trade unions, working hours and conditions.

1145.   Kindleberger, Charles Poor. **Europe's Postwar Growth; the Role of Labor Supply.** Cambridge, Harvard University Press, 1967. 270 p.

Analyzes the significance of labor movement from Greece, Italy, Portugal, Spain and Turkey into Germany, France, Switzerland and some other highly developed European countries. This is a well organized and documented study of recent economic trends in Europe. Includes an index.

1146.   Lebergott, Stanley. **Manpower in Economic Growth;** the American Record since 1800. New York, McGraw-Hill, 1964. 561 p. (Economics Handbook Series).

Presents a valuable study of manpower on economic growth of the United States since 1800. Part 1 reviews the distribution of labor among various regions and regions in the United States since the beginning of 19th century to the present. Parts 2 and 3 include plenty of new statistical data related to the nineteenth and twentieth centuries.

1147.   Long, Clarence D. **The Labor Force under Changing Income and Employment.** Princeton, Princeton University Press, 1958. 440 p. (National Bureau of Economic Research. General Series, no. 65).

Discusses the behavior of labor under various influences and conditions. Attempts to answer such questions as: Why people work? What is the relationship between labor supply and economics, labor force and income? The role of females in labor force, etc. Many tables, charts, diagrams with bibliographical references are included.

1148.   Madison, Charles Allan. **American Labor Leaders; Personalities and Forces in the Labor Movement.** 2nd enl. ed. New York, Ungar, 1962. 506 p.

Attempts to give a comprehensive and realistic account of the history of organized labor through a survey of the important trade unions and their famous leaders. Among those leaders there were idealists, utopian reformers, aggressive industrial unionists, marxists, communists and scrupulous opportunists. Bibliography: p. 475-491.

1149.   Menger, Anton. **The Right to the Whole Produce of Labor; the Origin and Development of the Theory of Labour's Claim to the Whole Product of Industry.** Transl. by M. E. Tanner, with an introd. and bibliography by H. S. Foxwell. London, Macmillan, 1899. 271 p.

Presents the main ideas of Socialism from a legal point of view. Bibliography of the English Socialist school: p. 189-267.

1150.   Miernyk, William H. **The Economics of Labor and Collective Bargaining.** Boston, Heath, 1965. 502

Contents: (1) History of American unionism. (2) Trade unions and public policy, (3) The structure, government, and objectives of trade unions, (4) Collective bargaining-process and issues, (5) Labor economics: the labor market and wage determination, (6) Manpower management the state of the American labor movement. Name and subject indexes are included. Bibliographical references at end of each chpater.

1151.   Millis, Harry Alvin and Montgomery, R. E. **Economics of Labor.** New York, McGraw-Hill, 1938. 3 v. (Business and Economics Publications).

Although these volumes are now out of print they present the most complete study of the economic and social problems of labor, therefore they are of a considerable value as a principal reference work in this field.

1152.   Moore, Wilbert Ellis. **Industrialization and Labor; Social Aspects of Economic Development.** Ithaca, N.Y., Cornell University Press, 1951. 410 p.

The field study in Mexico have been used for the investigation in economic development of the quantitative and qualitative supply of labor. The following topics are investigated: labor as factor in industrial development, from village to factories, morale and efficiency of workers, wages and the supply of industrial labor, Mexico: social and economic background, villages as potential labor supply, the Mexican factory worker. Bibliography: p. 365-398.

1153.   Morton, Arthur Leslie and Tate, George. **British Labor Movement, 1770-1920; a Political History.** New York, International Publishers, 1957. 313 p.

1154.   Oxford University, Institute of Statistics. **Economics of Full Employment; Six Studies in Applied Economics.** Oxford, B. Blackwell, 1945. 213 p. (Oxford. University Institute of Statistics. Monograph no. 2).

Contains six essays on full employment written by the specialists. Includes general index.

1155.   Reynolds, Lloyd George, and Taft, Cynthia H. **The Evolution of Wage Structure;** with a section by Robert M. Macdonald. New Haven, Yale University Press, 1956. 398 p. (Yale Studies in Economics, 6).

Divided into two parts: 1. Trade unionism and wage structure in the United States; 2. Studies in national wage structure. Part one deals with wages in a few major industries in the United States. Part two is concerned with a wage structure in France, Sweden, Great Britain, Canada and the United States. Includes an index. Bibliography: p. 385-392.

1156.   _____. **Labor Economics and Labor Relations.** 4th ed. Englewood Cliffs, N.J., Prentice-Hall, 1964. 568 p.

This updated edition covers various phases of labor economics including automation, labor legislation, depressed areas, Negro employment, etc. using comparative figures from other countries. This work is based on the author's original study and research.

1157.   Taft, Philip. **Organized Labor in American History.** New York, Harper, 1964. 818 p.

The text covers the development of unionism in the U.S. from 1827 when the first central labor union has been created until nineteenth sixties. It discusses the labor legislation, the role of U.S. government in the progress of the labor movement, influence of public opinion, immigration, the labor and politics and many other topics. Notes with bibliographical references: p. 711-790.

1158. Tiffin, Joseph and McCormich, Ernest J. **Industrial Psychology.** 5th ed. Englewood Cliffs, N.J. Prentice-Hall, 1965. 682 p.

Deals with the practical applications of psychology to the various human problems in industry, emphasizing the importance of a quantitative, scientific approach of human behavior in industry. Covers most recent research in this field.

1159. Twentieth Century Fund. **Employment and Wages in the United States,** by W.S. Woytinsky and associates. New York, 1953. 777 p.

Treats the various aspects of American labor such as: labor theories, relations, trends and facts. The work is divided into four parts: 1. Wage theory, trends and outlook; 2. The institutional setting; 3. Employment and unemployment; 4. Wages and earnings. The textual part is supported by numerous statistical tables.

1160. Ulman, Lloyd. **The Rise of the National Trade Union;** the Development and Significance of its Structure, Governing Institutions and Economic Policies. Cambridge, Mass., Harvard University Press, 1955. 639 p. (Wertheim Publications in Industrial Relations.)

Covers the period of the latter half of the nineteenth and the early years of the twentieth century. It brings together the facts about the development of union leadership and policies and which shows how the national unions became what they are.

1161. Webb, Sidney James and Webb, Beatrice. **Industrial Democracy.** London, Longmans Green, 1926. (1919 ed.) 929 p. Bibliography: p. 879-900. (Reprints of Economic Classics).

In this study authors describe in a systematic, detailed, realistic and objective way all forms of trade unionism, factory legislation and other forms of industry regulations in Great Britain. Nearly encyclopedic treatment of labor questions makes this work a valuable source of information for every student of labor economics. Includes a detailed general index.

1162. Wigham, Eric L. **Trade Unions.** 3rd impression (with revisions). London, Oxford University Press, 1963. 277 p. (The Home University Library of Modern Knowledge, 229).

Reviews the present situation of British trade unions, their history, their membership, their relationship with industries, with the state, with the world and with the future. Bibliography: p. 265-267.

1163. Yoder, Dale, and Heneman, Herbert G. **Labor Economics.** 2nd ed. Cincinnati, South-western Pub. Co., 1965. 824 p.

Authors names in reverse order in earlier edition. This text is only one part of the programmed introduction to labor economics contemplated by the authors. Emphasis is on theory. Three indexes: subject, authors, and of cases are included. Bibliographical footnotes of more than one thousand references.

1164.   Yoder, Dale. **Personnel Management and Industrial Relations.** 5th ed. Englewood Cliffs, N.J., Prentice-Hall, 1962. 667 p. (Prentice-Hall Industrial Relations and Personnel Series).

     Presents a comprehensive treatise on industrial relations, and administration, and relates these theories to management practice. Includes short case problems and references for further reading.

CHAPTER NINE

POPULATION AND STATISTICS

Population

GUIDES TO RESEARCH

1165.   Legeard, Claude. **Guide de Recherches Documentaires en Démographie.** Preface d'Alfred Sauvy. Paris, Gauthier-Villars, 1966. 322 p. table. 21 cm. (Documentation et Information).

1166.   Zelinsky, Wilbur. **A Bibliographic Guide to Population Geography.** Chicago: Univ. of Chicago, 1962. 257 p. (Dept. of Geography Research Paper no. 80).

International list of 2,588 items on all phases of population geography published since 1850. Geographically arranged, with regional classification and cross references.

BIBLIOGRAPHIES

1167.   Chasteland, Jean Claude. **Demographie; Bibliograpie et Analyse d'Ouvrages et d'Articles en Francais.** Paris, Editions de l'Institut national d'études demographiques, 1961. 181 p.

1168.   Demographic Training and Research Centre, Bombay. **A Select Annotated Bibliography on Population & Related Questions in Asia and the Far East.** New Delhi, U.N. Economic Commission for Asia and the Far East, 1963. 158, 61 p.

Has a classified arrangement. Classes A-M; M: Bibliographies and Yearbooks. Includes an author and subject indexes.

1169.   Eldridge, Hope Tisdale. **The Materials of Demography; a Selected and Annotated Bibliography.** Foreword by Dudley Kirk. New York, International Union for the Scientific Study of Population, 1959. 222 p.

Aimed to list and describe important publications on population. This compilation is limited to works published in recent decades, with the inclusion of some significant earlier works. Only works in English are listed. Includes an index.

1170.   France. Institut national de la statistique et des études économiques. Service de cooperation. **Bibliographie des Etudes Démographiques.** Relatives aux pays en Voie de Developpement (ouvrages parus depuis 1945). Mise à jour le 1er juillet 1961. Paris, 1961. 110 p.

1171.   Fuguit, Glenn Victor. **Dissertations in Demography, 1933-1963.**
Madison, Dept. of Rural Sociology, College of Agriculture, University of
Wisconsin, 1964. 72 p.

1172.   Mackensen, Rainer. **Bevölkerungsentwicklung und Wirtschaftswachstum.**
Population Growth and Economic Development. Ein Bericht über deutsche
Schriften seit 1950. Dortmund, Universität Münster, Sozialforschungsstelle,
1965. 108 p. (Materialien aus der Empirischen Sozialforschung, Heft 1).

German and English. Surveys the literature on population in German
language since 1950. Bibliography: p. 55-103.

1173.   Pokshishevskii, Vadim Viacheslavovich. **Geografiia Naseleniia v**
S.S.S.R. Moskva, 1966. 167 p. (Itogi Nauki: Geografiia S.S.S.R., vyp. 3).

Title translated: Population geography of the U.S.S.R. Table of
contents also in English; summary in English. Designed as a population
bibliography of the U.S.S.R.

1174.   Population Reference Bureau, Washington. **Bibliography on Popula-**
tion. Washington, 1966. 20 p.

A reference supplement to Population Bulletin, August 1966. Lists
262 items in 10 sections.

1175.   Stanford Research Institute. International Development Center.
Human Resources and Economic Growth, an International Annotated
Bibliography on the Role of Education and Training in Economic and Social
Development. Edited by Marian Crites Alexander-Frutschi. Menlo Park, Calif.,
Stanford Research Institute, 1963. 396 p.

Various materials, such as: books, pamphlets, periodical articles dealing
with the utilization and development of human resources, are entered under nine
major subject headings and 37 subheadings. Most of the included literature
is in English of the last decade.

1176.   Texas. University. Population Research Center. **International**
Population Census Bibliography. Austin, Bureau of Business Research,
University of Texas, 1965-67. 5 v. (Its Census Bibliography, no. 1 —)

1177.   _____. **Supplement 1968.** Austin, Bureau of Business
Research, University of Texas, 1968. 154 p. (Its Census Bibliography, no. 7).

Limited to population censuses only (census sources). Other types of
census reports (agriculture, housing, education, etc.) are included when they
are published in a series with the population censuses. The arrangement is
alphabetical by the country and chronological under country's name.

1178.   Thomas, Brinely. **International Migration and Economic Development: a Trend Report and Bibliography.** Paris, Unesco, 1961. 85 p. (Population and Culture).

   Assesses critically the theoretical and empirical research on international migration. Numerous biographies are included.

1179.   United Nations. Statistical Office. **Bibliography of Recent Official Demographic Statistics.** New York, 1954. 80 p. (Statistical papers. Series M, no. 18).

   Has an alphabetical arrangement by country.

1180.   U.S. Bureau of the Census. **The Population and Manpower of China:** an Annotated Bibliography, by Foreign Manpower Research Office, Bureau of the Census, under contract with Office for Social Science Programs, Air Force Personnel and Training Research Center, Air Research and Development Command. Washington, 1958. 132 p. (Its International Population Reports, Series P-90, no. 8).

1181.   U.S. Federal Council on Aging. **Federal Publications on Aging.** Selected Reports by Federal Agencies. Washington, 1958. 31 p.

   Presents an annotated and classified guide to government publications on aging.

1182.   Wisconsin, University. Center for Studies in Vocational and Technical Education. **Selected List of Acquisitions.** v. 1 – no. 1 – 1965 – Madison.

INDEXES

1183.   **Population Index.** v. 1 – Jan. 20, 1935 – Princeton, N.J., Office of Population Research, Princeton University. Quarterly.

   Each issue contains current items section, a lengthy bibliography section, an author index and the tables of statistics. Bibliography includes books, pamphlets, periodical articles, documents, etc.

SURVEYS & STATISTICS

1184.   Keyfitz, Nathan, and Flieger, Wilhelm. **World Population: an Analysis of Vital Data.** Chicago, University of Chicago Press, 1968. 672 p.

   This report is a product of a research program conducted at the Population Research and Training Center of the University of Chicago with the application of a computer. Presents in a tabular form official statistics on population making comparisons of mortality and fertility, analyzing the age distributions and infering the future trends. Bibliography: p. 667-671.

1185.   United Nations. Dept. of Economic and Social Affairs. **Population Studies,** no. 1 — New York, 1958 —

Each volume is dealing with a special topic or a special country. The purpose of each publication is to provide in convenient form some of the more important data required for the economic, demographic and social analyses of particular subject.

1186.   United Nations. Statistical Office. **Demographic Yearbook.** New York, 1949 — Annual.

In English and French. Surveys population, national origin, mortality, nuptiality, migration, divorce and other demographical topics of the world. Each issue presents special tables on one aspect of the topic. Supplemented by United Nations. "Statistical Papers," Series A: Population and Vital Statistics Reports.

1187.   United Nations. Statistical Office. **Population and Vital Statistics Reports,** v. 1 — Jan. 1949 — New York etc. 1950. — (Statistical Papers, ser. A). Quarterly.

1188.   U.S. Bureau of the Census. **Current Population Reports: Consumer Income.** Ser. P-60, no. 1 — 1948 — Washington.

Presents statistical data on income in relation to individuals, families, age, color, occupation, industry and trade, etc.

1189.   _____. **International Population Statistics Reports** - Series 90. Washington, U.S. Govt. Print. Off., 1952-65. 22 v.

Data on population of following countries are published: (1) The population of Germany and West Berlin, 1952. (2) The population of Israel, 1952. (3) The population of Czechoslovakia, 1953. (4) The population of Poland, 1954. (5). The population of Yugoslavia, 1954. (6) The population of Communist China, 1953. (6) The population of Manchuria, 1958. (8) The population and manpower of China: an annotated bibliography, 1958. (9) The population of Hungary (with list of sources). 1958. (10) The 1959 census of population of the U.S.S.R.: methodology and plans, 1959. (11) The labor force of the Soviet Zone of Germany and the Soviet Zone of Berlin, 1959. (12) The Soviet statistical system. Labor force recordkeeping and reporting, 1960. (13) The labor force of Czechoslovakia, 1960. (14) The labor force of Rumania, 1961 (P-60). (15) The size, composition and growth of the population of Mainland China, 1961. (16). Labor force of Bulgaria, 1962. (17) Soviet statistical system: labor force recordkeeping and reporting since 1957, 1962. (18) Labor force of Hungary, (1962). (19) Soviet mineral-fuels industries, 1925-58. 1963 . (20) Labor force of Poland, 1964 . (21) Non-agricultural employment in Mainland China, 1949-58. 1965. (22) Labor force of Yugoslavia, 1965 .

1190.   Bogue, Donald Joseph. **The Population of the United States.** With a special chapter on fertility by Wilson H. Grabill. Glencoe, Ill., Free Press, 1959. 873 p. (Studies in Population Distribution, no. 14).

Presents a great amount of statistical information based on the U.S. Bureau of the Census reports and other surveys and estimates. The main focus of this study covers the period 1950-1958, but the analysis goes many years back surveying the historical trends and making some forecasting for the future population development. A great portion of this work is concerned with the country's labor force, its achievements and its problems.

1191.   Field, James Alfred. **Essays on Population, and other Papers, Together with Material from his Notes and Lectures.** Compiled and edited by Helen Fischer Hohman. With a Foreword by James Bonar. Port Washington, N.Y., Kennikat Press, 1967. 440 p.

Represents author's reflections upon current issues and ideas regarding study of population. The chronological arrangement has been applied to show how author's thought over the years developed. Three chapters on other topics are added. Includes index. "Books and pamphlets on population in the library of James Alfred Field: p. 403-424."

1192.   Glass, David Victor, ed. **Introduction to Malthus.** New York, Wiley, 1953. 205 p.

Intended to provide a solid background for the study not only of Malthusian theory alone but for understanding the historical context in which this theory and conclusions have been formulated. Bibliography: p. 77-112.

1193.   Malthus, Thomas Robert. **First Essay on Population** (1798). With notes by James Bonar. London, Macmillan, 1966. 396 p. Reprint of 1926 ed.

Known as a theoretical essay first published in 1798 that provoked widespread argument. This shorter essay has a significant vigour of thought, clarity and sharpness of discussion which is not apparent in the second larger essay.

1194.   Olsson, Gunnar. **Distance and Human Interaction; a Review and Bibliography.** Philadelphia, Regional Science Research Institute, 1965. 112 p. (Bibliography Series, no. 2).

Contains: Introduction, the distance factor in location theory, the distance factor in economic migration theory and in diffusion models, gravity and potential models, concluding remarks and bibliography. Bibliography: p. 75-112.

1195.   Pearl, Raymond. **The Natural History of Population.** London, Oxford University Press, H. Milford, 1939. 416 p. (Heath Clark Lectures, 1937).

Designed as a study of human fertility in relation to the problems of population based upon the research material collected by the author. Bibliography contains about 700 titles, which is only a fraction of reference sources used by the author. 22 statistical tables are included in appendix. Bibliography, p. 356-398.

1196.   Spengler, Joseph John, and Duncan, Otis Dudley, eds. **Demographic Analysis, Selected Readings.** Glencoe, Ill., Free Press, 1956. 819 p.

     Bibliography: p. 785-813.

1197.   _____. **Population Theory and Policy: Selected Readings.** Glencoe, Ill., Free Press, 1956. 522 p.

     This is the companion volume to editors' Demographic Analysis: Selected Readings. It presents a collection of essays written by the specialists on population. Numerous selected references are provided for further study at end of many essays. Bibliography: p. 510-519.

1198.   Woytinsky, Wladimir S., and Woytinsky, E. S. **World Population and Production: Trends and Outlook.** New York, Twentieth Century Fund, 1953. 1268 p.

     This is a comprehensive treatise of world population, national resources and production. The work is divided into five parts: (1) Man and his enviornment (2) World needs and resources (3) Agriculture (4) Energy and mining (5) Manufactures. Includes alphabetical list of authors and general index. Bibliography: p. 1207-1250.

Statistics

     Here are entered general statistical reference works covering various data of a country, a continent, or of the whole world, including such types of publications as national censuses, statistical abstracts, and government statistical publications.

     Reference sources containing statistical data in one particular subject field are included in other chapters as subdivision of that subject; for example: Commerce − Statistics, Industry − Statistics, etc.

GUIDES & REFERENCE SOURCES

1199.   Andriot, John L. **U. S. Government Statistics** 3rd ed. Washington, Documents Index, 1961.

     An annotated guide to all federal publications containing statistical data.

1200.   Harvey, Joan M. **Sources of Statistics.** London, Bingley, 1969. 100 p.

     A guide to reference materials, primarily British. Includes chapters on population, vital statistics and migration, labor, production, trade, finance, prices, and transportation and communication.

1201.   Lewes, F.M.M. **Statistics of the British Economy.** London, Allen and Unwin, 1967. 200 p.

A good example of a guidebook to reference materials, limited to one country.

1202.   Verwey, Gerlof, and Renooij, D. C., **The Economist's Handbook; a Manual of Statistical Sources.** Amsterdam, Economist's Handbook, 1934. 1460 p. Supplement, 1937. 79 p.

Divided into two parts: (1) Subjects, with alphabetical index of all subjects; (2) Sources, classified by country, giving detailed information on name, price, and character of source, and an alphabetical index of all sources classified. The Supplement provides some additional source material and corrigenda.

1203.   Wasserman, Paul, ed. and others. **Statistics Sources.** Detroit, Gale Research, 1963. 288 p.

Covers American publications and organizations related to statistics in alphabetical subject arrangement, indicating the type of publications, period covered and frequency. Includes a comprehensive index of products, countries, etc.

BIBLIOGRAPHIES (CURRENT)

1204.   Buros, Oscar K. **Statistical Methodology Reviews,** 1933/38 — New York, J. Wiley. (Frequency varies).

Intended to assist research workers and statisticians to locate and evaluate the statistical methodology and published materials in all fields of statistical methods. The arrangement is alphabetical by author. Periodical directory and index, Publishers directory and index, indexes of titles, of names, and classified index of books are appended.

1205.   **Statistics Sources.** 1 — 1962 — Detroit, Gale Research. Monthly.

Supersedes Statistical Sources Review. Presents statistical sources in periodicals, books, pamphlets, yearbooks and government documents. The subject and title index is cumulated quarterly.

1206.   United Nations. Statistical Office. **List of Statistical Series. Collected by International Organizations. Dec. 1951** — New York. (Frequency varies).

BIBLIOGRAPHIES (RETROSPECTIVE)

1207.   "Bibliography" in 1963 Supplement to **United Nations Statistical Office. Monthly Bulletin of Statistics.** p. 238-54.

Includes very useful list of important government and central bank publications arranged by country.

1208.   Buckland, William Reginald, and Fox, Ronald A. **Bibliography of Basic Texts and Monographs on Statistical Methods, 1945-1960.** 2nd ed. Edinburgh, Published for the International Statistical Institute by Oliver and Boyd, 1963. 297 p.

Lists over 190 basic monographs in English on statistical methods and their applications, published between 1945 to 1960, including some important earlier works. Each entry is followed by a table of contents and extracts from reviews taken from 20 main statistical and allied periodicals published in English. The work is divided into 10 major fields of statistics, followed by list of journals consulted, list of publishers, supplementary list of book titles (1960-1962) and index of authors for books in text. Items in each chapter have an alphabetical arrangement.

1209.   Inter-American Statistical Institute. **Bibliography of Statistical Textbooks and Other Teaching Material.** Bibliografia de tratados y demas material de ensenanza de estadistica. 2nd ed. Washington, Pan American Union, 1960. 120 p.

1210.   Kendall, Maurice George and Doig, Alison G. **Bibliography of Statistical Literature.** New York, Hafner Pub. Co., 1962.

Contents: v. 1, 1950-1958. v. 2, 1940-1949. Lists 16,500 entries, books, pamphlets and periodicals mostly in Western languages. The entries are brief, giving author's surname and initials, a short title and short imprint. The planned 3rd volume should cover the years prior to 1940.

1211.   Lancaster, Henry Oliver. **Bibliography of Statistical Bibliographies.** Edinburgh, published for the International Statistical Institute by Oliver & Boyd, 1968. 103 p.

1212.   Organization for European Economic Cooperation. **Bibliographie des Périodiques Statistiques Cataloguées a la Bibliotheque.** 7 ed. Paris, O.E. E.C., 1957. 159 p.

Includes over one thousand statistical serials of various countries and areas and 122 periodicals of numerous international organizations. Not included are the economic or technical periodicals which publish statistical data.

1213.   Savage, I. Richard. **Bibliography of Nonparametric Statistics.** Cambridge, Mass., Harvard University Press, 1962. 284 p.

Lists in one dictionary arrangement books, pamphlets, and periodicals in many languages. Includes a list of literature searched.

1214.   Stillman, Minna. **Foreign Statistical Documents in Stanford Libraries, a Preliminary Survey.** n.p. 1959. 164 p.

1215.   U.S. Library of Congress. Census Library Project. **Statistical Bulletins; an Annotated Bibliography of the General Statistical Bulletins of Major Political Subdivisions of the World.** Prepared by Phyllis G. Carter. Washington, 1954. 93 p.

Lists the official general statistical bulletins issued by any country, colony, or territory in the world. Arrangement is alphabetical by country, according to continent. Annotated.

1216.   _____. **Statistical Year Books, an Annotated Bibliography of the General Statistical Yearbooks of Major Political Subdivision of the World.** Prepared by P. G. Carter. Washington, 1953. 123 p.

Arranged by continent, subarranged by area of country; entries are annotated, giving information on historical background, contents, and the location in Washington of the last five issues.

DICTIONARIES

1217.   Freund, John E., and Williams, Frank J. **Dictionary Outline of Basic Statistics.** New York, McGraw-Hill, 1966. 195 p.

Divided into two parts: (1) Dictionary of basic statistics, which is a list of terms with definitions, and (2) Statistical formulas. Bibliography: p. 193-195.

1218.   Inter American Statistical Institute. **Statistical Vocabulary.** 2d ed. Washington, Pan American Union, 1960. 83 p.

Title page and text in English, Spanish, Portuguese and French. Lists over 1,300 words in English and three other languages. Separate Spanish, Portuguese, and French indexes are included.

1218a.   Kendall, Maurice George, and Buckland, William R. **A Dictionary of Statistical Terms;** Prepared for the International Statistical Institute with the assistance of the UNESCO. 2nd ed. with combined glossary in English, French, German, Italian, Spanish. New York, Published for the International Statistical Institute, by Hafner Pub. Co., 1960. 575 p. (Reprint: Gale, 1969).

Provides lengthy definitions of terms with numerous illustrations. Some elementary terms which are self-explanatory are omitted. Divided into 6 parts: (1) Dictionary of statistical terms; (2) French-English glossary; (3) German-English; (4) Italian-English; (5). Spanish-English, and (6) Combined (revised).

1219.   Kurtz, Albert Kenneth, and Edgerton, Harold A. **Statistical Dictionary of Terms and Symbols.** New York, Hafner Pub. Co., 1967. 191 p.

DIRECTORIES & HANDBOOKS

1220.   Bruning, James L. and Kintz, B. L. **Computational Handbook of Statistics.** Glenview, Ill., Scott, Foresman, 1968. 269 p.

A useful handbook how to use and apply the statistical formulas.

1221.   **Directory of Statisticians and Others in Allied Professions, 1961.** Washington, American Statistical Association, 1962. 191 p.

Lists 9,400 members of the American Statistical Association, the Biometric Society, and the Institute of Mathematical Statistics, arranged alphabetically, giving dates, addresses, education and position of each person. A geographical section by state and city, and foreign by country is included.

1222.   United Nations. Dept. of Economic Affairs. **Directory of Economic and Statistical Projects:** a classified list of work completed, in progress or planned by United Nations and specialized agencies. 1948. 130 p.

1223.   United Nations, Statistical Office. **World Weights and Measures: Handbook for Statisticians.** prepared by the Statistical Office of the United Nations in collaboration with the Food and Provisional ed. New York, 1955. 225 p. (Its Statistical Papers, Ser. M. no. 21).

Presents a wealth of information on: international and national systems and units of weight and measure; national currencies arranged by country; comparison of national currencies to U.S. currency; unit weights of some commodities; indexes of weights and measures, abbreviations, and currencies.

1224.   U.S. Bureau of Labor Statistics. **B.L.S. Handbook of Methods for Surveys and Studies.** Washington, For sale by the Superintendent of Documents, U.S. Govt. Print. Off., 1966.   238 p. (Its Bulletin no. 1458).

YEARBOOKS & SURVEYS

1225.   **Globus-Jahrbuch des Deutschen Verlages; die Welt und ihre Länder in Politischer und Wirtschaftlicher Darstellung.** Berlin, Deutscher Verlag 19 —   (Irregular).

Presents statistically the various aspects of political, economic, financial, industrial and commercial conditions in various countries and areas of the world.   Includes indexes of subjects and of geographical names.

1226.   Organization for Economic Cooperation and Development. **General Statistics . Statistiques Generales.** Nov. 1950 —   Paris.   Bimonthly.

Contains a wealth of statistical information regarding population, labor force, production, commerce, business and finances of member countries including some non-members.   Supplemented by the Main Economic Indicators.   (Monthly).

1227.   **The Statesman's Yearbook: Statistical and Historical Annual of the States of the World.** London, Macmillian, 1864— illus., maps. Annual.

Lists in alphabetical arrangement countries of the world, their area, population, economic conditions, education, politics, valuable bibliography, and other statistical information.

1228.   United Nations. Statistical Office. **Compendium of Social Statistics, 1963.** New York, 1963. 598 p.

Presents statistical data on population, health, food consumption, education, housing, labor, income and expenditures, social security and cultural affairs in various countries of the world.

1229.   _____. **Monthly Bulletin of Statistics.** Bulletin Mensuel de Statistique, v. 1 —   Jan. 1947 —   New York.

Supersedes Monthly Bulletin of Statistics of the League of Nations. Covers the same subject range as its Statistical Yearbook.

1230.   _____. **Statistical Yearbook. Annuaire Statistique.** 1st — 1948 — New York. In English and French. Continuation of the Statistical Yearbook of the League of Nations.

Provides a convenient and comprehensive summary of international statistics. "It is the aim of the Yearbook tables to present for the various countries, over the period covered, time series which are as nearly comparable internationally as the available statistics permit". (Introd.) A country index is included.

STATISTICAL REFERENCES & REPORTS
IN VARIOUS COUNTRIES & AREAS
(Arranged Alphabetically by Continent, Region, or Country)

The Americas

1231.   Inter-American Statistical Institute. **Bibliography of Selected Statistical Sources of the American Nations, Bibliografia de Fuentes Estadistics Escogidas de las Naciones Americanas.** A Guide to the Principal Statistical Materials of the 22 American Nations, Including Data, Analyses, Methodology and Laws and Organization of Statistical Agencies. Washington, 1947. 689 p.

Annotations are given in two languages, English and the language of particular publication, Spanish, Portuguese or French. About 2,500 items are included in this work, mostly monographs, the rest: periodicals and journal articles. All material is divided into: (1) A Main List, (2) an Alphabetical Index, (3) Subject Index and (4) an Appendix in English and Spanish showing the subject classification scheme according to which the included material has been classified.

1232.   Pan American Union. Dept. of Statistics. **America en Cifras, 1945 —**
Pan American Union and Inter-American Statistical Institute, Washington, D.C.,
Secretaria General de la Organizacion de los Estados Americanos, 1966 —
        "America in figures" covers 21 American countries including Canada
and the U.S.A. giving statistical data on land, population, economy, cultural,
educational and other aspects of continent's life.

1233.   Pan American Union. **Statistical Compendium of the Americas 1969.**
Washington, 1969. 116 p.
        This first issue contains selected statistical data on all the member
states of the organization of American States, Canada, Guyana and Jamaica.

1234.   U.S. Library of Congress. Census Library Project. **General Censuses
and Vital Statistics in the Americas.** An annotated bibliography of the historical
censuses and current vital statistics of the 21 American republics, the American
sections of the British Commonwealth of Nations, the American colonies of
Denmark, France, and the Netherlands and the American territories and
possessions of the United States. Washington, U.S. Govt. Print Off., 1943.
151 p.
        Attempts to cover all official sources of demographic statistics in the
Western Hemisphere. Each section begins with a short historical sketch of
country's censuses and census publications.

Australia

1235.   Australia. Commonwealth Bureau of Census and Statistics. **Digest
of Current Economic Statistics.** Canberra, 1959 —   Monthly.
        Covers all possible phases of the national economy including building,
finance and national accounts.

1236.   Australia. Commonwealth Bureau of Census and Statistics. **Official
Yearbook of the Commonwealth of Australia.** Canberra, 1908 —   Annual.
        Arranged in many chapters, with text, tables, maps, an appended
statistical summary, and an analytical index.

Austria

1237.   Austria. Statistisches Zentralamt. **Statistisches Jahrbuch für die
Republik Österreich.** Vienna, 1950 —   Annual.
        Divided into more than thirty sections with an international part on
yellow colored paper. Supplemented by the monthly Statistische Nachrichten.

Belgium

1238.   Belgium. Institut National de Statistique. **Annuaire Statistique de
la Belgique.** Brussels, 1870 —   Annual.

Berlin

1239.　Berlin. Statistisches Landesamt. **Statistisches Jahrbuch Berlin.**
Berlin, Kulturbuchverlag, 19 —　Annual.

Supplies statistical data of all phases of life for West and East Berlin
including a special supplement of statistics for the Soviet Zone of Germany.

Canada

1240.　Canada. Bureau of Statistics. **Canada Year Book,** 1905 —　Ottawa.

Supersedes Statistical Year Book of Canada. An excellent source of
information regarding Canada's economic conditions. In more than 25 chapters
this official annual compendium gives a wealth of information on the institutions
and the economic and social development of Canada. Each volume includes
sources of official information, Canadian chronology, and the detailed index.

1241.　Canada. Bureau of Statistics. **Historical Catalogue of Dominion
Bureau of Statistics Publications, 1918 — 1960.** Ottawa, Queen's Printer,
1967. 298 p. Prepared by the staff of the D.B.S. Library, Canada Yearbook
Division.

Organized according to a special classification system of the Bureau,
this catalog lists all publications designed to provide statistical information for
the public with some small exceptions (special statements, press releases, restricted to internal or limited use). It is divided into two parts: 1. Publications
issued in the English language, and 2. Publications publiées en Francais.
Includes detailed indexes of titles.

1242.　Canada. Deptl of Public Printing and Stationery. **Canadian Government
Publications: Dominion Bureau of Statistics.** 1st — 1959 — Ottawa, Queen's
Printer.

Published in English and French. Each new edition brings up-to-date
and revises the listings contained in previous edition. Entries are arranged in
main subject groups giving full title, frequency and price. A combined title,
subject and commodity index is included.

1243.　Urquhart, M.C. and Buckley, K.A.H., eds. **Historical Statistics of
Canada.** Cambridge, Eng., University Press, 1965. 672 p. (Sponsored by
Canadian Political Science Association and Social Science Research Council
of Canada.)

Covers a wide range of statistical time series, along with material
describing the series, from 1867 to 1960. In addition to numerous tables,
each section provides textual parts which describe, explain and evaluate the
content of the individual time series. The material is arranged in 21 sections,
each one representing a special field of the national economy. A detailed index
is provided.

China

1244.   China. State Statistical Bureau. **Economic and Cultural Statistics of Communist China.** Washington, D.C., 1960. 187 p. (U.S. Central Intelligence Agency. Foreign Documents Division. Translation no. 737).

Translation of the Chinese original statistical publications.

Czechoslovakia

1245.   Czechoslovakia. Statni Urad Statisticky. **Statisticka Rocenka Ceskoslovenske Socialisticke Republiky.** Prague. SNTL. 19 —   Annual.

Statistical yearbook of the Czechoslovak Socialist Republic; text in Czech only.

Denmark

1246.   Denmark. Det Statistiske Dept. **Statistisk Arbogo.** Copenhagen, Munksgaard, 18 —   Annual.

Europe

1247.   U.S. Library of Congress. Census Library Project. **National Censuses and Vital Statistics in Europe, 1918 — 1939; an Annotated Bibliography,** with 1940-1948 Supplement. Prepared by Henry J. Dubester, Chief. Washington, 1948. Republished by Gale Research Co., Detroit 1967. 215, 48 p.

The arrangement is alphabetical by country, and chronological within the country. The Library of Congress serves as the main source for this bibliography. English translations of titles from foreign language publications are given in brackets immediately after the title. The titles of bilingual publications are given in both languages.

France

1248.   France. Institut National de la Statistique et des Études Economiques. **Annuaire Statistique de la France.** Paris, Imprimerie Nationale, etc. 1878 — v. 1 —   Annual.

Includes tables, diagrams, and textual comments. Supplemented by Bulletin Mensuel de Statistique, 1950 —   and quarterly cumulations.

Germany (East)

1249.   Germany (Democratic Republic) Staatliche Zentralverwaltung für Statistik. **Statistisches Jahrbuch der Deutschen Demokratischen Republik.** Berlin, VEB Deutscher Zentralverlag, 1956 —   Annual.

Organized in 27 sections, covers statistical data in a five-year period all administrative parts and units of East Germany. Also includes in a special green section the international and Comecon statistics.

Germany (West)

1250.   Deutsche Statistische Gesellschaft. **Bibliographie der Amtlichen Westdeutschen Statistik, 1945-1951.** München, 1952. 90 p. (Einzelschriften der Deutschen Statistischen Gesellschaft, Heft, Nr. 3).

Presents a bibliography of West German official government statistics for the period 1945-1951.

1251.   Germany (Federal Republic, 1949 -) Statistisches. Bundesamt. **Statisches Jahrbuch fur die Bundesrepublik** Deutschland, Stuttgart, Kohlhammer, 1952 — Annual.

Covers Federal Republic of Germany, the German Democratic Republic, the whole Berlin, the former eastern German territories; also section on international statics is included. Subject index and list of sources are added. Monthly supplements Wirtschaft und Statistik are issued.

Great Britain

1252.   Gt. Brit. Central Statistical Office. **Annual Abstract of Statistics.** no. 1 — 1840/53 — London. Title varies.

Every number contains statistics for each of the 15 preceeding years. Divided into 14 chapters, where suitable statistical data is arranged in tables giving annual, quarterly, or monthly figures. Includes indexes of sources and of tables.

1253.   Gt. Brit. Central Statistical Office. **List of Principal Statistical Series Available.** London, H.M. Stationery Office, 1945. 36 p.

A very valuable guide covering economic, financial and regional statistics of Great Britain, with annotations.

1254.   Gt. Brit. Central Statistical Office. **Monthly Digest of Statistics.** no. 1 — Jan. 1946 — London, H. M. Stationery Office.

Includes an annual supplement containing explanatory notes.

1255.   Gt: Brit. Interdepartmental Committee on Social and Economic Research. **Guides to Official Sources.** London, Statistical Office, 1953 —

A series of booklets on specific subjects: no. 1. Labor statistics, 1950; no. 2 Census reports of Gt. Britain, 1801-1931, 1951; no. 3. Local government statistics, 1953; no. 4. Agricultural and food statistics, 1958; no. 5. Social Security statistics, 1961; no. 6. Census of production reports, 1961.

1256.   Great Britain. Treasury. **Government Statistical Services.** 2nd ed. London, H.M.S.O., 1962. 34 p.

Presents the work of the British official statistical services, giving information about the methods of collecting and interpreting of statistical data, their organization, analysis, etc.

1257.   Kendall, Maurice George, ed. **The Sources and Nature of the Statistics of the United Kingdom;** Edited for the Council of the Royal Statistical Society. London, Published for the Royal Statistical Society by Oliver and Boyd, 1952-57. 2 v.

1258.   Mitchell, Brian R. **Abstract of British Historical Statistics.** With the collaboration of Phyllis Deans. Cambridge, University Press, 1962. 513 p.

Presents in tabular form time series of British economy from the year 1199 to 1950's; but most statistical data have their starting point in the beginning of the nineteenth century. The material has been arranged in sixteen chapters according to the subject. A general index is added.

Hungary

1259.   Hungary. Központi Statisztikai Hivatal. **Statisztikai Evkonyv.** Budapest, Kultura, 19 — Annual.

A Hungarian statistical year book. There are English and Russian edition of this publication.

Italy

1260.   Italy. Istituto Centrale di Statistica. **Annuario Statistio Italiano.** Rome, Istituto Poligrafico dello Stato, 1878 — Annual.

In sections, covering various aspects of nation's life, some tables give statistics for a five-year period. Analytical subject index.

Japan

1261.   **Japan.** Bureau of Statistics. **Japan Statistical Yearbook.** Tokyo, 1949 —

Contains basic statistical data on Japan's land, people, culture, civilization, economy, and other aspects of life. In Japanese and English; subject index. Supplemented by Monthly Statistics of Japan. This yearbook replaced the Statistical Yearbook of the Empire of Japan, which ceased publication in 1941.

Korea

1262.   **Korea Statistical Yearbook.** 16th ed. Seoul, Korea Information Service, 1969. 421 p.

Latin America

1263.   Inter-American Statistical Institute. **America en Cifras,** 1960 —
Washington, Pan American Union, 1961 —   Biennial.

Reports up-to-date detailed statistics of Latin America countries on
population, agriculture, industries, transportation, commerce, finances,
culture, education, etc. Published in Spanish, with a detailed index in English.

1264.   **Latin America in Maps, Charts, Tables.** Mexico, Center of Inter-
cultural Formation, 1963-1965.

Suspended after v. 3 (1965).

1265.   **Statistical Abstract of Latin America.** Los Angeles, Calif., Univ. of
California, Center of Latin American Studies, 1956 —   Annual. (irregul.)

Presents a comprehensive coverage of statistical information on
Latin America's countries. Includes bibliographical references.

1266.   United Nations. Economic Commission for Latin America. **Boletin
Estadistico de Americana Latina. Statistical Bulletin for Latin America.** v. 1 —
Mar. 1964 —   New York.

Supersedes the Supplemento Estadistico of the Boletin Economico de
America Latina and the Statistical Supplement to the Economic Bulletin for
Latin America, which started 1960 —   Text in Spanish and English.

Luxembourg

1267.   Luxembourg. Service Central de la Statistique. **Annuaire Statistique.**
Luxembourg, Statec, 19 —   Annual.

Divided into various subject sections, tables give annual figures for
the past years and monthly figures for the current year.

Netherlands

1268.   Netherlands. Central Bureau voor de Statistiek. **Jaarcifers voor
Nederland.** The Hague, 1882 —   Annual.

New Zealand

1269.   New Zealand. Dept. of Statistics. **Statistical Publications, 1840-
1960.** (mainly those produced by the Registral-General, 1853-1910 and
the Government Statistician, 1911-1960) Wellington, Govt. Printer, 1961. 66 p.

Includes a section "Select bibliography on early New Zealand."

1270.　**New Zealand Official Yearbook.** Wellington, Dept. of Statistics, 1892 —
Annual.

Presents a detailed statistical survey in numerous chapters on geography,
population, education, economic and cultural activity, and other phases of
country's life. Includes a select bibliography and an analytical index.

North Atlantic Treaty Organization

1271.　Mueller, B. **A Statistical Handbook of the North Atlantic Area.**
New York, Twentieth Century Fund, 1965. 239 p.

In English and French. Deals with various phases of economic life
in countries of the North Atlantic Treaty Organization (NATO).

Poland

1272.　Poland. Glówny Urzad Statystyczny. **Poland in Figures.** 1944 —
Warszawa. Annual. (irregular)

Each issue cumulating from 1944.

1273.　Poland. Glówny Urzad Statystyczny. **Rocznik Statystyki.** rok 1 —
1920/21 — Warszawa. Annual. Title also in French; Annuaire Statistique.

1274.　_____ . **Concise Statistical Yearbook of Poland.** v. 1 —
1930 — Warsaw. Annual (Irregular).

Publications suspended 1940-46.

Portugal

1275.　Portugal. Instituto Nacional de Estatistica. **Annuario Estatistico.**
Lisbon, 1877 — Annual.

Published in two parts: v. 1. Metrópole, v. 2. Ultramar. Includes
maps and a subject index.

Romania

1276.　**Statistical Pocket Book of the Socialist Republic of Romania:** 1960 —
Bucharest, Directia Centrala de Statistica. Annual. Title varies: 1960-65,
Romanian Statistical Pocket Book.

Designed as a statistical yearbook to provide data on various aspects
of economic, cultural, educational, political and social life of Romanian
people.

Russia (Soviet Union)

1277.   Narodnoe Khoziaistvo S.S.S.R.: v. 1948 — g. **Statisticheskii Ezhegodnik.** v. 1 —   Moskva, TSentral' noe statisticheskoe upravlenie, 1948 —
Statistical Yearbook of national economy of the U.S.S.R. provides statistical data of the whole country, of the national and autonomous republics, and economic regions from 1913 — to date. Included are all sectors of national economy, geography, climatology, population, education, health and welfare, etc. Index is added.

Scandinavia

1278.   Nordic Council. **Yearbook of Nordic Statistics.** Stockholm, 1963 — Annual.
Covers Denmark, Finland, Iceland, Norway and Sweden, going back for 5-10 years. Introduction and headings in English and Swedish.

South Africa

1279.   South Africa. Bureau of Statistics. **Statistical Year Book. Statistiese Jaarboek.** Pretoria, 1964 — Annual.
Supplemented by Monthly Bulletin of Statistics. In 1960 has been published Union Statistics for Fifty Years which is a jubilee issue covering 1910-60.

1280.   South Africa. Office of Census and Statistics. **Official Yearbook of the Union and of Basutoland, Bechuanaland Protectorate and Swaziland,** v. 1 — 1917 —   Pretoria, Govt. Printer, 1918 —   Biennial.
Presents detailed statistical data related to all important factors of country's national life (geography, history, population, education, civilization, economic and business conditions, etc.) Includes bibliographical references and government publications.

Southeast Asia

1281.   Ajia Keizai Kenkyujo, Tokyo. **Bibliography of the Statistical Materials on Southeast Asia.** Tokyo, 1960. 66p.
A valuable union list of holdings of statistical material in Japan's 24 leading libraries for: British Borneo, Burma, Ceylon, Cambodia, Laos and Vietnam, India, Indonesia, Malaya, Pakistan, Philippines, Thailand, etc.

Spain

1282.   Spain. Instituto Nacional de Estadistica. **Annuario Estadistico de Espana.** Madrid, 1913 —   Annual.
Pt. 1. Totales nationales; pt. 2. Detalle provincial. Subject index.

Switzerland

1283. **Schweizerische Bibliographie für Statistik und Volkswirtschaft.**
Bern, Schwizerische Gesellschaft für Statistik und Volkswirtschaft, 1937 —
Bibliographie Suisse de Statistique de d'Economie Politique, 1 — 1937 —
Annual.

Contains all publications (books, pamphlets, serials, periodical articles,
reports, etc.) on statistics and economics issued in Switzerland or in foreign
countries when related to Switzerland or the author is Swiss. The arrangement
is according to Dewey decimal system. The author index is included.

1284. Switzerland. Eidgenossisches Statistisches Amt. **Statistisches Jahrbuch
der Schweiz.** Basle, Birkhäuser Verlag, 1891 — Annual.

In German and French. Includes a comparative international statistics,
list of sources and of Swiss official statistical publications. Subject index.

United States

1285. **Guide to U.S. Government Statistics.** Arlington, Va., Document
Index, 1956 — (revised periodically).

The 3rd edition of this Guide gives the information how to find out
and how to use the statistics in U.S. Government publications. It consists of
two parts: 1. The Guide, arranged by departments and agencies listing publications with statistical data giving bibliographical information and annotation
regarding statistical contents; and 2. The Index which is a detailed subject
index indicating the frequency and type of data.

1286. U.S. Bureau of the Budget. Office of Statistical Standards. **Federal
Statistical Directory.** 1st — 1935 — Washington. Irregular.

Title varies: Directory of Statisticians of the United States Government;
Directory of Federal Statistical Agencies.

1287. _____. **Statistical Services of the United States Government.**
rev. ed. Washington,1964. 136 p.

1288. U.S. Bureau of the Census. **Bureau of the Census Catalog.** Washington,
D.C., Govt. Print Office, 1947 — Quarterly and cumulative to annual with
monthly supplements. Lists all publications of the Bureau.

1289. _____. **County and City Data Book.** 1949 — Washington,
U.S. Govt. Print Off. Supersedes its Cities Supplement, 1940, and its County
data book, 1947.

Supplements the Statistical Abstracts providing 1960 data on
agriculture, area and population, banking, city government finances and
employment, construction education and all the other vital statistics for cities
and counties of the United States.

1290.   U.S. Bureau of the Census. **Statistical Abstract of the United States.** 1st — 1878 — Washington, U.S. Govt. Print Office. Annual.

An excellent one volume annual giving a wealth of statistical information on the cultural, economic, political and social conditions in the United States. Emphasis is given to national data though individual states and many regions are also covered. Statistical tables include a period of several years, 15 or more, some tables go back to 1800. Includes a Guide to statistical reference sources and a detailed index.

1291.   _____. **Summaries of Biostatistics; Maps and Charts, Population, Natality, and Mortality Statistics.** Prepared in cooperation with the Office of the Coordinator of Inter-American Affairs. Washington: Govt. Print. Off., 1944-45. 17 v.

1292.   U.S. Library of Congress. Census Library Project. **Catalog of United States Census Publications, 1790-1945;** prep. by Henry J. Dubester. Washington, 1950. 320 p.

This annotated catalog has two sections: pt. 1, decennial census publications; pt. 2, other publications, arranged by subject; Subject index is added.

Yugoslavia

1293.   Yugoslavia. Savezni Zavod za Statistiku. **Statisticki Godisnjak FNRJ.** Belgrad. S.Z.S.E., 1954 — Annual.

The Statistical Pocket-book of Yugoslavia consists of extracts from the original and some factual information about the country. In Serbo-Croatian.

CHAPTER TEN

PERIODICALS

(A Selected List of Periodicals and Serials which have Research Reference Value; Most Contain Book Reviews)

1294.   **Administrative Science Quarterly.** v. 1 — June 1956 — Ithaca, N.Y., Cornell University, Graduate School of Business and Public Administration.

1295.   **Allgemeines Statistisches Archiv.** Bd. 1 — 1890 — Tübingen, etc., Deutsche Statistische Gesellschaft. Quarterly. Supsended between 1944-1948.

1296.   American Academy of Political and Social Science, Philadelphia. **Annals.** Philadephia. v. 1 — 1890 — Bimonthly.

1297.   **American Economic Review.** Cambridge, Mass., American Economic Association, 1911 — Quarterly.

1298.   **American Journal of Economics and Sociology.** v. 1 — 1941 — New York. Quarterly.

1299.   **The American Review of Soviet and Eastern European Foreign Trade.** v. 1 — Jan./Feb. 1965 — White Plains, N.Y., International Arts and Sciences Press. Bimonthly.

1300.   **American Statistical Association. Journal.** Washington, D.C. v. 1 — 1881 — Title varies: v. 1-16, 1889-1919. Publications; v. 17, 1920/21, Quarterly publications.

1301.   **American Statistician.** v. 1 — 1947 — Washington, American Statistical Association. 5 no. a year.

1302.   **Annals of Public and Co-operative Economy.** v. 1 — 19 — Liege, Belgium. Quarterly. Organ of the International Centre of Research and Information on Collective Economy. Title varies.

1303.   **Antitrust Bulletin.** v. 1 — Apr. 1955 — New York, Federal Legal Publications. Quarterly. Subtitle: The journal of American and foreign anti-trust and trade regulations.

1304.   **Asian Economic Review.** 1st — Nov. 1958 — Hyderabad, Indian Institute of Economics. Quarterly.

1305.   **Aussenwirtschaft: Zeitschrift für Internationale Wirtschaftsbeziehungen.**
1 — Jahrg; Marz, 1946 — Bern, A. Francke. Quarterly. Issued by the
Schweizerisches Institut für Aussenwirtschaft und Marktforschung at the
Handelshochschule, St. Gall.

1306.   Banco di Roma. **Review of the Economic Conditions in Italy.** Rome,
1947. v. 1 —

1307.   **Bank of England. Quarterly Bulletin.** London, Economic Intelligence
Dept. Bank of England, 1960 — Quarterly.

1308.   **Bankers Magazine.** v. 1 — 1846 — Boston, Warren, Gorham &
Lamont, inc. Quarterly.

1309.   **Bankers' Magazine.** v. 1 — 1844 — London, Waterlow, etc. Monthly.

1310.   **Barron's National Business and Financial Weekly.** v. 1 — 1924 —
New York, Barron's Pub. Co.

1311.   **Bentley Business and Economic Review.** v. 1 — Fall 1964 — Boston,
Bureau of Business and Economic Research, Bentley College. 3 mo. a year.

1312.   **Boletin Bibliografico Agricola.** no. 1 — Feb. 1948 — Madrid,
Ministerio de Agricultura, Servicio de Capacitacion y Propaganda. Bimonthly
(irregular).

1313.   **British Journal of Industrial Relations.** v. 1 — Feb. 1963 —
London, London School of Economics and Political Science. 3 no. a year.

1314.   **Business Cycle Developments.** Oct. 1961 — Washington, Bureau
of the Census; U.S. Govt. Print Office. Monthly. "Series ESI".

1315.   **Business History Review.** v. 1 — June 1926 — Boston, Mass.,
Harvard University Graduate School of Business Administration etc.
Quarterly.

1316.   **Business Literature.** v. 1 — Apr. 1928 — Newark, N.J., The Public
Library of Newark Monthly (except July and August).

1317.   **Business Week.** v. 1 — 1929 — New York, McGraw-Hill. Weekly.
Supersedes Magazine of Business.

1318.   **Canadian Farm Economics.** v. 1 — Apr. 1966 — Ottawa, Dept. of
Economics. Bimonthly. Supersedes Current Review of Agricultural Conditions
in Canada, and Economic Analist.

1319.   **Canadian Journal of Agricultural Economics.** 1 — 1952 — Ottawa. Canadian Agricultural Economics Society. Includes Proceedings of Canadian Agricultural Society. 2 nos. a year.

1320.   **Canadian Journal of Economics and Political Science.** Feb. 1935 — Toronto. University of Toronto Press. Quarterly.

1321.   **Cartel.** v. 1 — July 1950 — London, International Cooperative Alliance.

1322.   **Demography.** v. 1 — 1964 — Chicago, Population Association of America.

1323.   **The Developing Economics.** v. 1 — Jan./June 1963 — Tokyo, Semi-annually.

1324.   **Distribution Data Guide.** 195 — Washington, Office of Distribution, Business and Defense Services Administration. Monthly.

1325.   **Dun's Review and Modern Industry.** v. 1 — Aug. 5, 1893 — New York, Dun & Bradstreet. Weekly, 1893 — Mar. 1933; Monthly, Apr. 1933 — Title varies: 1893-Feb. 25, 1933, Dun's review. Apr. 1933 - 1936, Dun & Bradstreet monthly review; 1937-July, 1953, Dun's Review. In March 1933 absorbed Bradstreet's Weekly, and Aug. 1953 Modern industry.

1326.   **East African Economics Review.** v. 1 — July 1954 — Nairobi, Economics Club of Kenya. Semi-annually.

1327.   **Econometrica; Journal of the Econometric Society.** v. 1 — Jan. 1933 — Quarterly.

1328.   **Economia Internazionale.** v. 1 — 1948 — Genova, Camera di commercio, industria e agricoltura. Quarterly.

1329.   **Economic Development and Cultural Change.** v. 1 — Mar. 1952 — Chicago, University of Chicago. Research Center in Economic Development and Cultural Change. Quarterly.

1330.   **Economic Geography.** v. 1 — March 1925 — Worcester, Mass., Clark University.

1331.   **Economic History Review,** London, Economic Historical Society, 1927-1948; series 2. 1948/49 — Welwyn Garden City, England. Three times a year.

1332.   **Economic Journal,** v. 1 − 1891 − London, Royal Economic Society. Quarterly.

1333.   **Economic Record (Melbourne).** v. 1 − Nov. 1925 − Melbourne, Melbourne University Press. Quarterly.

1334.   **Economic Trends.** no. 1 − Nov. 1953 − London, H.M. Stationery Office. Monthly. Published for the Central Statistical Office.

1335.   **Economica.** London, London School of Economics and Political Science. 1921-1933 − New sec., v. 1 − no. 1 - Feb.. 1934 − Quarterly.

1336.   **Economisch en Social Tijdschrift.** v. 1 − Feb. 1947 − Antwerpen, Sint-Ignatius Handelshogeschool en A.L.S.I.

1337.   **Economist.** v. 1 − 1843 − London, Weekly.

1338.   **Economist.** v. 1 − Jaarg. 1852 − Harlem, etc., Erven F. Bohn, etc. Frequency varies. Organ of the Nederlandsch Economisch Instituut, 1933 −

1339.   **Economy and History.** v. 1 − Spring 1958 − Lund. Annual.

1340.   **Ekonomicko-Matematicky Obzor.** roc. 1 − 1965 − Praha, Ceskoslovenska akademie ved v Academii, etc. 4 no, a year. vols. for 1965-66 issued by Ekonomickomatematicka komise of Ceskoslovenska akademie ved. Summaries in English. Title translated: Review of mathematical economics.

1341.   **Ekonomika i Matematicheskie Metody.** t. 1 − ianv./fevr. 1965 − Moskva, Nauka. Title translated: Economics and mathematical methods.

1342.   **Ekonomika Radians'koi Ukrainy.** 1959 − Kyiv, Radians'ka Ukraina. Monthly. Issued byInstitut ekonomiky of the Akademiia nauk U.R.S.R. Transl. Economic conditions in Soviet Ukraine.

1343.   **Ekonomisk Tidskrift.** 1 − arg. 1899 − Stockholm H. Geber. Monthly.

1344.   **Far Eastern Economic Review.** no. 1 − 1946 − Hong Kong, Weekly with special supplements.

1345.   **Federal Economic Review.** v. 1 − Oct. 1954 − Karachi, University, Dept. of Economics. Semi annually.

1346.   **Federal Reserve Bulletin.** v. 1 − 1915 − Washington, Board of Governors of the Federal Reserve System. Monthly.

1347.   **Finanzarchiv.** Bd. 1 — 1884 — Berlin, etc. 3 no. a year. Suspended 1944-1947; resumed publication in March 1948 — Subtitle: Zeitschrift für das gesamte Finanzwesen.

1348.   **Food and Agriculture Organization of the United Nations. Economic Division.** Monthly Bulletin of Agricultural Economics and Statistics. v. 1 — May 1952 — Rome.

1349.   **Foreign Agriculture.** v. 1 — January 7, 1963 — Washington, U.S. Dept. of Agriculture, Foreign Agricultural Service; U.S. Government Print Office. Weekly.

1350.   France. Ministere de l'economie et des finances. **Statistiques et Etudes Financieres.** Paris, Imprimerie Nationale, 1949 — Monthly.

1351.   **The German Economic Review.** v. 1 — 1963 — Stuttgart, Wissenschaftliche Verlagsgesellschaft. An English Language Quarterly on German Economic Research and Current Developments.

1352.   **Giornale degli Economisti e Annali di Economia.** v. 1 — June 1886 — Bologna, Rome, etc. Supersedes Giornalo Degli Economisti, 1886-1909; and Giornale Degli Economisti' e Revista di Statistica, 1910-1938.

1353.   **Harvard Business Review.** v. 1 — Oct. 1922 — Boston, Mass., Graduate School of Business Administration, Harvard University. Bimonthly.

1354.   **Indian Economic Review,** v. 1 — Feb. 1952 — Delhi, Delhi School of Economics, University of Delhi. Semiannual.

1355.   **Indian Journal of Economics.** v. 1 — Jan. 1916 — Allahabad, Economics Dept., University; New York, Macmillan, etc. Quarterly.

1356.   **Industria. Rivista di Economia Politica.** 1886 — Milano. Quarterly. New series: 1946 — Subtitle varies.

1357.   **Industrial and Labor Relations Review.** v. 1 — 1947 — Ithaca, N.Y., State School of Industrial and Labor Relations, Cornell University. Quarterly.

1358.   **Industrial Management Review.** v, 1 — 1959 — Cambridge, Mass., Massachusetts Institute of Technology, School of Industrial Management. Semiannual.

1359.   **Institut International de Statistique. Revue de l'Institut International de Statistique.** 1 — 1933 —The Hague, etc. 3 no. a year.

1360. **Institute of Transport Journal.** v. 1 — 1920 — London. Bimonthly.
Formerly: Transport.

1361. **International Development Review.** v. 1 — Oct. 1959 — Washington,
Society for International Development. Quarterly. (irregular).

1362. **International Executive.** v. 1 — Winter 1959 — Hastings-on-Hudson,
etc., Foundation for the Advancement of International Business Administration.
Quarterly.

1363. **International Labour Review.** v. 1 — Jan. 1921 — Geneva, International Labour Office, 1921 — Monthly.

1364. **International Monetary Fund.** Staff Papers. v. 1 — Feb. 1950 —
Washington. 3 no. a year.

1365. International Statistical Institute. **Review.** v. 1 — Jan. 1933 —
The Hague. Quarterly; 3 no. a year. Supersedes Institute's Bulletin Mensuel.
Added title in French.

1366. **International Trade Reporter's Survey and Analysis of Current
Developments,** 19 — Washington, Bureau of National Affairs, n.d., Weekly.

1367. **International Trade Review;** a Business magazine for those who sell
ship-operate abroad. v. 1 — 1926 — New York, Dun & Bradstreet. Monthly.

1368. **Internationales Archiv für Verkehrswesen.** Bd. 1 — 1949 —
Frankfurt am Main, Tetzlaff-Verlag. Monthly. Subtitle: Zeitschrift für
Verkehrswirtschaft, Verkehrstechnik, Verkehrspolitik und Verkehrsrecht —
mit Sonderteil der Verkehrsingenieur.

1369. **Jahrbuch für Sozialwissenschaft.** Bd. 1 — 1950 — Göttingen,
Vandenhoeck & Ruprecht. 3 no. a year.

1370. **Jahrbücher für Nationalökonomie und Statistik.** Bd. 1 — 1863 —
Jena, Stuttgart. 5 no. a year. Suspended between Sept. 1944 — Sept. 1949.

1371. **Journal des Economistes.** Paris, Société d'économie politique,
1841-1940. Subtitle: Revue mensuelle de la science économique et de la
statistique.

1372. **Journal of Business.** v. 1 — 1928 — Chicago, Univeristy of Chicago
Press. Quarterly. Supersedes University Journal of Business.

1373. **Journal of Development Studies.** v. 1 — 1964 — London, F. Cass.
subtitle: A Quarterly Journal devoted to Economic, Political and Social
Development.

1374. **Journal of Economic History.** v. 1 — 1941 — New York, Economic History Association. Quarterly.

1375. **Journal of Farm Economics.** v. 1 — June 1919 — Lancaster, American Farm Economic Association. Quarterly.

1376. **Journal of Finance.** v. 1 — Aug. 1946 — Chicago, American Finance Association. Quarterly.

1377. **Journal of Finance (New York)** v. 1 — Aug. 1946 — New York, American Finance Association. Quarterly.

1378. **The Journal of Industrial Economics,** v. 1 — Nov. 1952 — Oxford, Eng., Blackwell. 3 no. a year.

1379. **Journal of Industrial Relations.** v. 1 — April 1959 — Sydney, Industrial Relations Society. Semi-annually.

1380. **Journal of Management Studies.** v. 1 — Mar. 1964 — Oxford, B. Blackwell.

1381. **Journal of Marketing.** v. 1 — July 1936 — New York, American Marketing Association. Quarterly.

1382. **Journal of Personnel Administration, and Industrial Relations.** v. 1 — Jan. 1954 — Washington, Personnel Research Publishers. Quarterly.

1383. **Journal of Political Economy.** v. 1 — 1892 — Chicago, University of Chicago Press. Bimonthly.

1384. **Journal of the Economic and Social History of the Orient.** v. 1 — Aug. 1957 — Leiden, E. J. Brill, 3 no. a year.

1385. **Journal of Transport History.** v. 1 — 1953 — Leicester, Eng., Leicester University Press. Semiannual.

1386. **Konjunkturpolitik. Zeitschrift für Angewandte Konjunkturforschung.** Bd. 1 — 1954 — Berlin. Bi-monthly.

1387. **Labour Gazette (Ottawa)** v. 1 — Sept. 1900 — Ottawa, Dept. of Labour. Monthly.

1388. **Labor History.** v. 1 — Winter 1960 — New York, Tamiment Institute. 3 no. a year.

1389. **Labor Relations Reporter.** Washington, D. C., Bureau of National Affairs. 1935 — Published three times a week in loose-leaf form; continuously revised.

1390. **Land Economics.** v. 1 — Jan. 1925 — Madison, Wis., University of Wisconsin, etc. Quarterly. Title varies: v. 1-23, 1925-47, Journal of Land & Public Utility Economics. Subtitle: Journal of planning, housing and public utilities.

1391. **Manchester School of Economic and Social Studies.** v. 1 — 1930 — Manchester, Dept. of Economics, University of Manchester. 3 nos/yr. Quarterly.

1392. **Marketing.** v. 1 — 1908 — Toronto, MacLean-Hunter Pub. Co. Weekly.

1393. **Der Marktforscher.** Bd. 1 — Feb. 1957 — Bad Wörishofen, etc., H. Holzmann, etc. Frequency varies. Title varies: 1957, Marktforscher in der Wirtschaft. Beginning with 1965 each issue is accompanied by separately paged supplement: Sonderdienst. Marktinformationen.

1395. **Metroeconomica; Rivista Internazionale di Economica.** v. 1 — luglio 1949 — Trieste, L. Cappelli. 3 no/yr. Text in Italian, French & English.

1396. **Monthly Bulletin of Agricultural Economics and Statistics.** v. 1 — May 1952 — Rome, F.A.O.

1397. **Monthly Labor Review.** v. 1 — July 1915 — Washington, D.C., Bureau of Labor Statistics.

1398. **Moody's Active Stock Reports.** Bergenfield, N.J., 1966 — 3 v. (loose-leaf). Updated four times every year.

1399. **Moody's Insurance & Financial Stocks.** v. 1 — Apr. 29, 1963 — New York, Moody's Investor Service. Biweekly (irregular). Title varies: Apr. 29, 1963 — Jan. 17, 1966, Moody's Insurance Stocks.

1400. **The National Banking Review.** v. 1 — Sept. 1963 — Washington, Comptroller of the Currency, United States Treasury. Quarterly.

1401. **National Tax Journal.** v. 1 — Mar. 1948 — Chicago. Quarterly.

1402. **Nationaløkonomisk Tidsskrift.** v. 1 — 1873 — Copenhagen, Nationaløkonomish Forening. 3 no. a year.

1403. **Ordo. Jahrbuch für die Ordnung von Wirtschaft und Gesellschaft.** Bd. 1 — 1948 — Godesberg, H. Küppner. Annual.

1404. **Osteuropa Wirtschaft.** Bd. 1 – Aug. 1956 – Stuttgart, Deutsche Gesellschaft für Osteuropakunde. Quarterly.

1405. **Oxford Economic Papers.** no. 1-8, October 1938-1947; new ser., v. 1 – Jan. 1949 – Oxford, Clarendon Press. Irregular. 3 no. a year, 1951 –

1406. **Oxford University. Institute of Economics and Statistics.** Bulletin. v. 1 – 1939 – Oxford, Blackwell, etc. Quarterly. Name of issued body varies: 1939-62. Institute of Statistics.

1407. **Planovoe Khoziaistvo;** ezhemisiachnyi politiko-ekonomicheskii zhurnal. Moskva, v. 1 – 1923 – Title translated: Planned economy; a monthly political-economic journal.

1408. **Population; Revue Trimestrielle.** 1 – Jan./Mars. 1946 – Paris, Presses universitaires de France. Quarterly. Issued by the Institut national d'etudes demographiques.

1409. **Population Bulletin.** v. 1 – Sept. 1945 – Washington, Population Reference Bureau. 6 no. a year.

1410. **Population Studies; a Journal of Demography.** v. 1 – June 1947 – Cambridge, University Press. Quarterly. Issued by the Population Investigation Committee.

1411. **Primenenie Matematiki v Ekonomike.** vyp. 1 – 1963 – Leningrad. Title translated: The application of mathematics in economics.

1412. **Public Finance. Finances Publiques.** v. 1 – 1946 – The Hague. Quarterly.

1413. **Public Relations Journal** v. 1 – Oct. 1945 – San Francisco, American Council on Public Relations. Monthly.

1414. **Quarterly Journal of Economics,** v. 1 – 1886 – Boston, Harvard University. Quarterly.

1415. **The Quarterly Review of Economics and Business.** v. 1 – 1961 – Urbana, Bureau of Economic and Business Research. College of Commerce and Business Administration. University of Illinois.

1416. **Recherches Économiques de Louvain.** t. 1 – Dec. 1929 – Louvain, Universite catholoque de Louvain. Supersedes the Bulletin de L'Institut de Recherches.

1417.   **Research Management.** v. 1 — Spring 1958 — New York; London, Industrial Research Institute. Bimonthly.

1418.   **Review of Economic Studies.** v. 1 — Oct. 1933 — Edinburgh, etc. Quarterly. Published for the Economic Study Society by Oliver and Boyd.

1419.   **Review of Economics and Statistics.** v. 1 — 1919 — Cambridge, Mass., Harvard University, Committee on Economic Research. Quarterly.

1420.   **The Review of Income and Wealth.** 1966 — New Haven, Conn., Yale University Press. Quarterly. Journal of International Association for Resources in Income and Wealth. Supersedes the Income and Wealth Series.

1421.   **Review of Social Economy.** v. 1 — Dec. 1942 — Milwaukee. Catholic Economic Association. Semiannual.

1422.   **Revista de Economia.** v. 1 — Mar. 1948 — Lisbon. Quarterly.

1423.   **Revista de Economia Politica.** v. 1 — enero/marzo 1945 — Madrid, Seccion de Economia of the Instituto de Estudios Politicos. Semi-annual. Publication suspended July 1945-Apr. 1950.

1424.   **Revista de Economia y Estadistica.** v. 1 — Jan. 1939 — Cordoba, Facultad de ciencias economicas, etc.

1424a.   **Revue d'Économie Politique.** 1887-1940; 1945 — Paris, Sirey.

1425.   **Revue d'Histoire Économique et Sociale,** 1 — 1908 — Paris, P. Geuthner, etc. Quarterly. Title varies slightly. Suspended Apr. 1914 — Sept. 1919.

1426.   **Revue de Science Financiere.** t. 1 — Jan. 1903 — Paris. Quarterly. Suspended April/Je 1940-Jan&Mr. 1946. Title varies slightly. Supplements accompany some volumes.

1427.   **Revue Economique.** Paris, Librairie Armand Colin, 1950 —

1428.   **Rivista Internazionale di Scienze Economiche e Commerciali.** anno 1 — sett./ott 1954 — Padova, C.E.D.A.M. Monthly, 1956 —

1429.   **Royal Statistical Society. Journal.** London, 1838 — Series A. General. v. 1 — Quarterly.

1430.   **Scandinavian Economic History Review.** v. 1 — 1953 — København. Semiannual. Issued by the Scandinavian Society for Economic and Social History and Historical Geography.

1431. **Schmollers Jahrbuch für Gesetzgebung, Verwaltung und Volkswirt-schaft.** v. 1 – 1877 – Berlin, Duncker and Humblot. Bi-monthly.

1432. **Schweizerische Zeitschrift für Volkswirtschaft und Statistik.** v. 1 – 1865 – Basel, Schweizerische Geselleshaft für Statistik und Volkswirtschaft. Quarterly.

1433. **Scottish Journal of Political Economy.** v. 1 – Mar. 1954 – Edinburgh, Oliver and Boyd. 3 no. a year. Published for the Scottish Economic Society.

1434. **Social Security Bulletin.** v. 1 – Mar. 1938 – Washington, Social Security Administration. Monthly. Supersedes publication with the same title.

1435. _____. **Annual Statistical Supplement.** 1956 – Both publications contain much useful information, statistical data and directories on social insurance.

1436. **South African Journal of Economics.** v. 1– Mar. 1933 – Johannesburg, Economic Society of South Africa. Quarterly.

1437. **Southern Economic Journal.** v. 1 – 1933 – Chapel Hill, University of North Carolina Press. Quarterly. (Irreg.)

1438. **Soviet Export.** no. 1 – 1957 – Moscow, Vneshtorgizdat. Quarterly.

1439. **Soviet Studies, a Quarterly Review of the Social and Economic Institutions of the U.S.S.R.** v. 1 – 1949 – Oxford, Blackwell. Quarterly.

1440. **Statsokonomisk Tidsskrift.** v. 1 – 1887 – Oslo, Statsøkonomiske forening.

1441. **Studi Economici.** v. 1 – Jan./Mar. 1946 – Naples, Universita. Facolta di economia e commercio.

1442. **Studia Demograficzne.** t. 1 – 1963 – Warszawa, Państwowe Wydawnictwo Naukowe. 3 no. a year.

1443. **Survey of Current Business.** v. 1 – 1921 – Washington, U.S. Office of Business Economics. Monthly with weekly statistical supplements.

1444. **Transport World; Road, Passenger & Freight Transport.** v. 1 – 1892 – London, Carriers Publishing Co. Monthly.

1445. **Transportation Journal.** v. 1 – Fall 1961 – Chicago, American Society of Traffic and Transportation. Quarterly.

1446.   El Trimestre Economico. 1934 — Mexico City. Quarterly.

1447.   Uchenye Zapiski Kafedr Politicheskoi Ekonomii Vysshikh Partiinykh Skkol. vyp. 1 — 1959 — Moskva, V.P.S.H.

1448.   Uebersee Rundschau. Bd. 1 — 1949 — Hamburg, Übersee Verlag. Semimonthly. Translated: Oversea Review.

1449.   United Nations. Statistical Office. Current Economic Indicators; a Quarterly Statistical Review of Developments in the World Economy. New York, United Nations, 1961 — v. 1, no. 1 — Quarterly.

1450.   U.S. Bureau of International Commerce. Overseas Business Reports. OBR 62 — Washington, For sale by the Superintendent of Documents, U.S. Govt. Print Off., 1962 —

1451.   U.S. Bureau of the Census. Summary of Foreign Commerce of the United States. Nov. 1866 — Washington, U.S. Govt. Print Off., Monthly, accompanied by annual issue in 1944, and by quarterly cumulative issues beginning in 1945. Title varies.

1452.   Vierteljahrshefte zur Wirtschaftsforschung. Jahrg. 1 — 1926 — Berlin, etc., Duncker & Humblot, etc. Issued by the Deutsches Institut für Wirtschaftsforschung. Quarterly. Title varies: 1926 — Vierteljahrshfte zur Konjunkturforschung. Also published are "Ergänzungsheft" (Supplements).

1453.   Vneshniaia Torgovlia. g. 1 — 20 Apr. 1931 — Moskva, Vneshtorgizdat, etc. Frequency varies. Supersedes in part Sovetskaia Torgovlia, published 1926-31. Title varies: Apr. - Aug., 1931, Nasha Vneskniaia Torgovlia. Translated: Foreign trade.

1454.   Voprosy Ekonomiki. Mar. 1948 — Moskva, Pravda, Monthly. Supersedes Mirovoe Khoziaistvo i mirovaia politika. Issued by Akedemiia nauk S.S.S.R. Institut ekonomiki. Title translated: Problems of economics.

1455.   Wall Street Journal. Jan. 1, 1899 — New York, Dow Jones. Daily.

1456.   Weltwirtschaft. Bd. 1 — Jahrg. 1950 — Kiel, Institut für Weltwirtschaft au der Universität Kiel. Semi-annual.

1457.   Weltwirtschaftliches Archiv; Zeitschrift für Allgemeine und Spezielle Weltwirtschaftslehre. Bd. 1 — Jan. 1913 — Jena, Hamburg, etc., G. Fischer. Quarterly. Frequency varies. Issued for the Institut für Weltwirtschaft, Universität Kiel. Suspended between 1945-1949.

1458. **Wirtschaftsdienst.** Bd. 1 − Aug. 1916 − Hamburg, Hamburgisches
Weltwirtschaftsarchiv. Merged into Deutsche Volkswirtschaft, May 1943-
Feb. 1945; resumed independent publication, June 1949.

1459. **Wirtschaftskonjunktur;** Berichte des I.F.O. Instituts für Wirtschaftsforschung München. 1 − Jahrg. 1949 − Berlin, etc., Duncker & Humblot, etc.
Quarterly.

1460. **Wirtschaftswissenschaft.** Jahrg. 1 − Juli&Aug. 1953 − Berlin, Verlag
Die Wirtschaft. Bimonthly.

1461. **Yale Economic Essays,** v. 1 − Spring 1961 − New Haven, Semiannual.

1462. **Zeitschrift für die Gesamte Staatswissenschaft.** Bd. 1 − 1844 −
Tübingen. Quarterly. Suspended between 1944-1948.

1463. **Zeitschrift für Markt- und Meinungsforschung.** 1 − 1957 −
Tübingen, Demokrit Verlag. Quarterly. Subtitle: Vierteljahresbeiträge zur
Theorie und Praxis.

1464. **Zeitschrift für Nationalökonomie.** Bd. 1 − Mai, 1929 − Wien,
J. Springer, 1930 − Frequency varies. Supersedes Zeitschrift für Volkswirtschaft und Sozialpolitik. Suspended between Sept. 1944- May 1948.

INDEX

Includes authors: personal and corporate; titles of works cited, and a selection of subject headings which are fully capitalized. Figures cited, after each item refer to the number designated to each entry and not to the pages.

ABC Goods Transport Guide, 979
Abstract of British Historical Statistics, 1258
Abstracts: Agricultural, Industrial and Economic Research, Territory of Hawaii, 478
Ackly, Gardner, 108
Ad Hoc Committee of Librarians for "Sources of Information in Transportation", 985
Adam Smith's Library, a Supplement to Bonar's Catalogue, 60
Adler, Max K., 701
Administrative Science Quarterly, 1294
Advertising Federation of America. Bureau of Research and Education, 660a
Advertising Research Foundation, 660b, 702-3
Ady, Peter, ed. See Scientific Council for Africa South of the Sahara
AFRICA
  Econ. condit., 306-6
African Bibliographic Center, 303
Agricultural Economic and Statistical Publications, 876
AGRICULTURAL ECONOMICS, 849-907
Agricultural Labor in the United States, 1054
Agricultural Rents in Theory and Practice, 875
Agricultural Statistics, 899
Ahmad, Jaleel, 218
Aide Amércaine à l'Europe, 1947-1956, 332

Aids to Geographical Research, 856
Ajia Keizai Kenkyujo, Tokyo, 95, 307, 1281
Akademiia nauk SSSR. Fundamental'-naia biblioteka obshchestvennykh nauk, 349, 414-18
Akademiia nauk SSSR. Institut ekonomiki, 109
Akademiia nauk SSSR. Sektor seti spetsiial'nykh bibliotek, 918
Alampier, P. M., 419
Alderfer, Evan B., 962
Alexander-Frutschi, Marian, 239, 1175
Allen, David E., 26
Allen, Frederick L., 455
Allen, George C., 963-4
Allen, Robert L., 927
Allen, Roy George D., 817
Allen, William R., 194
Allgemeines Statistisches Archiv, 1295
Almeida Sedas, J. G. de, 400
Alphabetical Index of Occupations and Industries, 1118
America en Cifras, 1232, 1263
American Academy of Political and Social Science, Philadelphia. Annals, 1296
American Agriculture (Mighell), 905
American Aid to Europe, 1947-1956, 332
American Arbitration Association, 1045
American Bankers Association. Dept. of Automation and Market Research, 497
American Economic Association, 94, 96, 110, 832

American Economic Development,
462
American Economic History, 460
American Economic Review, 1297
American Federation of Labor.
Dept of Education, 1046
American Finance Conference, 498
American Historical Association,
213
American Industries, 978
American Journal of Economics
and Sociology, 1298
The American Labor Force, 1133
American Labor in Journals of
History, 1078
American Labor Leaders, 1148
American Labor Union
Periodicals, 1026
American Labor Unions, What
they are . . . , 1108
The American Labor Yearbook,
1120
American Register of Exporters
and Importers, 774
The American Review of Soviet
and Eastern European
Foreign Trade, 1299
American Statistical Asso-
ciation, 1221
American Statistical Association
Journal, 1300
American Statistician, 1301
American University of Beirut,
Economic Research Institute,
402
American University, Washington,
D. C. Foreign Area Studies,
260
The American Workers' Fact
Book, 1109
THE AMERICAS
Statistics, 1231-4
America's Needs and Resources,
484
Anderson, Adam, 350
Anderson, I. G., 707

Andréades, Andreas M., 604
Andreano, Ralph L., 1
Andrews, H. T., 449
Andriot, John L., 1199
Angel, James W., 833
Angel, Juvenal L., 1097-9
Anglo-American Trade Directory,
775
Annals of Public and Cooperative
Economy, 1302
An Annotated Bibliography of
Industrial Relations, 1048
Annotated Bibliography of Materials
in Economic Education, 18
An Annotated Bibliography of the
Geography of Transportation, 998
Annotated Bibliography on Field
Sales Management, 668
An Annotated Index to the Pro-
ceedings of the American
Marketing Association Con-
ferences, 721
Annotirovanyi Ukazatel' Literatury
. . . po Aviatsii . . . , 999
Annuaire Statistique de la Belgique,
1238
Annuaire Statistique de la France,
1248
Annual Abstract of Statistics (Gt.
Brit.), 1252
Annual Bulletin of Transport
Statistics for Europe, 1016
Annual Economic Indicators for
the U.S.S.R., 443
Annual Report on Exchange
Restrictions, 581
The Annual Review of British
Industry, 950
Annual Survey of Manufactures, 958
Annuario del Mercado Espanol, 451
Annuario Estadistics de Espana,
1282
Annuario Statistico Italiano, 1260
Anstey, Vera (Powell), 372
Anstruy, Jacques, 220
Antitrust Bulletin, 1303

Antitrust Economics, 976
Antwerp. Institut Universitaire
des Territories d'Outremer,
219
Aplikácia Matematike v Ekonómii,
31
Approaches to Canadian Economic
History, 318
Arbitration Bibliography, 1045
Area Development Organizations,
254
Area Handbook . . . , series, 260
Argentine Republic. Ministerio
de Trabajo y Seguridad Social.
Departmento de Publicaciones
y Biblioteca, 1028
Ashley, Percy Walter L., 834
Ashley, Sir William James, 351
Ashton, Thomas S., 605
Ashworth, W., 835
ASIA
Econ. condit., 307-11
Asian Economic Review, 1304
Aspley, John C., 715a, 716, 1106
Assistance to Underdeveloped
Countries, 248
Associated University Bureaus
of Business and Economic
Research, 5, 468
Association française pour
l'accroissement de la pro-
ductivité, 1047
Auburn, H. W., 561
Aussenwirtschaft: Zeitschrift
für Internationale Wirt-
schaftsbeziehunger, 1305
Ausländische Adressbücher, 760
AUSTRALIA
Econ. condit., 312-4
Statistics, 1253-6
Australia. Commonwealth Bureau
of Census and Statistics, 1253-6
The Australian Economy, 312
Australian Public Affairs
Information Service, 313

AUSTRIA
Statistics, 1237
Austria. Statistisches Zentralamt,
1237

BLS Handbook of Methods for
Surveys and Studies, 1224
Badger, Ralph E., 562
Baer, Werner, 965
Balance of Payments and Economic
Growth, 839
Balance of Payments Yearbook, 821
Ball, Joyce, 757, 864
Balogh, Thomas, 606
Banco di Roma, 377
Banco di Roma. Review of the
Economic Conditions in Italy,
1306
Banco Espanol de Credito, 451
Bancroft, Gertrude, 1133
Bank for International Settlements,
575
Bank of America, 740
Bank of Canada, Ottawa, 315
Bank of England: a History, 608
Bank of England . Quarterly Bulletin,
1307
Bank-Lexikon, 538
Banken der Welt, 554
Das Banken-Ortslexikon für den
Zahlungsverkehr, 543
The Bankers' Almanac and Yearbook,
548
A Banker's Bibliography on Market
Research, 497
The Bankers Blue Book, 555
Bankers Magazine, 1308
Bankers' Magazine (London), 1309
BANKING
cover. by ch. 3 (491-639)
Banking and Monetary Statistics,
603
Banking and Monetary Statistics in
India, 596

Banking Systems, 607
Banks of the World, 630
Banks of the World; Brief
    Monographs, 554
Barcelona. Cámara Oficial de
    Comercio y Navagación.
    Biblioteka, 452, 661
Barclays Bank (D.C.O.), 803
Barnouw, Eric, 1021
Barron's National Business and
    Financial Weekly, 1310
A Basic Bibliography on
    Experiments in Marketing,
    675
A Basic Bibliography on Industrial
    Marketing, 688
A Basic Bibliography on Marketing
    in Canada, 679
A Basic Bibliography on Marketing
    Research, 693
Basic Bibliography on Mathematical
    Methods in Marketing, 664
Basic Insurance Books, 494
Basic Tables in Business and
    Economics, 563
Batson, Harold E., 27
Bauer, Peter T., 261
Baumol, William J., 110a
Bayitch, S. A., 388, 389
Bazhanova, Elena V., 865
Beale, Calvin L., 469
Beckhart, Benjamin H., 607
Beer, Max, 111
Beerman's Financial Yearbook
    of Europe, 576, 951
Behördenkatalog, 49
BELGIUM
    Stat., 1238
Belgium. Institut National de
    Stastique, 1238
    Ministère des affaires
    économiques. Bibliotheque,
    499
Bell, John F., 112
Benedict, Murray R., 900
Benjamin, Hazel C., 1080

Benko, E. de, 308
Benko, William J., 776-7
Bentham, Jeremy, 113
Bentley Business and Economic
    Review, 1311
BERLIN
    Stat., 1239
Berlin. Statistisches Landesamt.,
    1239
Besters, Hans, 252
Best's Insurance Reports, 577
Beutin, Ludwig, 114
Bevölkerungsentwicklung und
    Wirtschaftswachstum, 1172
Bibliografia da Ciencia Economica,
    34
Bibliografia de la Historia Monetaria
    de Espana, 514
Bibliografia Publikacyi Pracowników
    Naukowych . . . , 412
Bibliografia Sobre a Economia
    Portuguesa, 413
Bibliógrafia Sobre Economia
    Nacional, 7
Bibliograficheskie Ukazateli
    Sel'skokhoziaistvennoi Literatury,
    854
Bibliograficheskii Spravochnik
    Opublikovanykh Nauchnykh
    Rabot . . . , 420
Bibliograficheskii Spravochnik
    Pechatnikh Rabot . . . , 421
Bibliograficheskii Ukazatel' Knig i
    Statei po Politicheskoi Ekonomii,
    438
Bibliografie Ekonomicke Literatury,
    6
Bibliografie over het derde
    Wereldblok, 219
Bibliografiia Finansov, Promysh-
    lennosti, 918
Bibliografiia po Voprosam Raz-
    Politicheskoi Ekonomii (1917-
    1966), 419a
Bibliografiia po Voprosam Raz-
    meshcheniia . . . Promyshlennosti,
    918

Bibliografija Ekonomske Literatury, 25

A Bibliographic Guide to Population Geography, 1166

A Bibliographic Guide to the Economic REgions of the U. S., 849

Bibliographical List of References to Canadian Railways, 987

Bibliographie d'Economie Politique, 1945-1960, 62

Bibliographie der Amtlichen West-deutschen Statistik, 1945-51, 1250

Bibliographie der Kameralwissenschaften, 676

Bibliographie der Neueren Arbeitsund Betriebswirtschaftlichen Literatur, 1093

Bibliographie der Wirtschaftspresse, 13

Bibliographie des Études Démographiques, 1170

Bibliographie des Oeuvres de Karl Marx, 70

Bibliographie des Périodiques Statistiques Cataloguées . . . , 1212

Bibliographie des Sources de Documentation sur le Travail, 1059

Bibliographie Internationale d'economie Régionale, 222, 327

Bibliographie Internationale de Science Economique, 15

Bibliographie Konzetration, 923

Bibliographie Spéciàle Analytique. Inflation, 516

Bibliographie sur la Perou, 410

Bibliographie sur l'Iran, 376

Bibliographie sur les Transports, 989

Bibliographie über Entwicklungsländer, 215

Bibliographie Universelle de Securité Sociale, 509

Bibliographie zur Marktforschung, 672

Bibliographie zur Theorie und Praxis der Sozialistischen Wirtschaft, 345a

A Bibliography for Investment and Economic Analysis, 370, 521

A Bibliography for Students of Retailing, 662

A Bibliography in Economics for the Honour School of Philosophy, Politics, and Economics, 44

Bibliography in Public Finance, 519

Bibliography of Advertising and Marketing Theses, 667

Bibliography of Agriculture, 857

Bibliography of Basic Texts . . . on Statistical Methods, 1208

Bibliography of British History, 352

Bibliography of Current Publications on Canadian Economics, 1935-1952, 316

Bibliography of Economic Books and Pamphlets by Catholic Authors, 40

Bibliography of Economic Science, 65

Bibliography of Economics, 1751-1775, 46

A Bibliography of Finance, 515

Bibliography of Graduate Theses in the Field of Marketing, 684

Bibliography of Industrial and Distributive-Trade Statistics, 930

A Bibliography of International Business, 767

Bibliography of Nonparametric Statistics, 1213

A Bibliography of Personal Selling, 685

Bibliography of Publications of University Bureaus of Business and Economic Research, 5

Bibliography of Recent Official Demographic Statistics, 1179

A Bibliography of Reference
Materials on Consumer Installment
Credit, 498
Bibliography of Research Sources
on Labour Questions, 1059
A Bibliography of Resource
Materials, 235
Bibliography of Rural Land Economy,
866
Bibliography of Selected
Statistical Sources of the
American Nations, 1231
Bibliography of Statistical
Bibliographies, 1211
Bibliography of Statistical
Literature, 1210
Bibliography of Statistical
Textbooks, 1209
A Bibliography of Studies in
English on the Japanese
Economy, 384
Bibliography of the Collection
of Books and Tracts on
Commerce, Currency and
Poor Law. 681
Bibliography of the Published
Writings of John Stuart Mill,
59
Bibliography of the Statistical
Materials on Southeast
Asia, 1281
A Bibliography of Theory and
Research Techniuqes in the
Field of Human Motivation,
660b
Bibliography on Chinese Social
History, 323
Bibliography on Cooperation, 118
Bibliography on Cooperatives, 527
Bibliography on Income and
Wealth, 216
Bibliography on Industrial
Relations, 1060
Bibliography on Industrialisation
in Underdeveloped Countries,
929

Bibliography on Labor in Africa,
1067
Bibliography on Labour Law, 1061
Bibliography on Land Tenure, 868
Bibliography on Marketing to
Low-Income Consumers, 663
A Bibliography on New Product
Planning, 683
Bibliography on Peru, 410
Bibliography on Population, 1174
Bibliography on Productivity,
(OEEC), 1073
Bibliography on Productivity,
Project No. 233, 1047
Bibliography on Taxation in
Underdeveloped Countries, 505
Bibliography on the Analysis and
Projection of Demand and
Production, 869
Bibliothéque: Catalogue Analytique
de Fonds Plan Schuman, 12
The Big Change, 455
Biological and Agricultural
Index, 890
Black, John D., 901
Blaisdell, Ruth F., 985
Bloom, Gordon, 1134
Blum, Albert A., 1048
Bodnar, Artur, 326
Body, Alexander C., 3
Böhm von Bawerk, Eugen, 115
Bogue, Donald J., 469, 1190
Boiko, N. P., 439
Boletin Bibliográfico Agricola, 1312
Boletin Estadistico, 392
Boletin Estadistico de Americana
Latina, 1266
Bolletino Emerografico di Economia
Internazionale, 97
Books for the Advertising and
Marketing Man, 660a
Books on Soviet Russia, 1917-42,
428
Bordeaux. Chambre de Commerce.
Bibliothèque, 28, 29
Borisova, N. V., 420-1

Born, Karl Erich, 342
Bottin, 778
Bottin International: International Business Register, 778
Boulding, Kenneth E., 116
Bourque, Philip J., 470
Boyd, Harper W., 730
Bradford, Ernest S., 704
Braeuer, Walter, 117
Bremer Ausschuss für Wierschaftsforschung, 221
Breswick, William N., 766
Brewington, Ann, 500
A Brief Annotated Bibliography on Labor in Emerging Societies, 1084
Britain, an Official Handbook, 359
British & International Buyers & Sellers Guide, 779
British Commonwealth Year Book, 353
British Economic Statistics, 354
British Journal of Industrial Relations, 1313
British Labor Movement, 1153
British Public Finances, 620
British Rate and Data's Directories and Annuals, 705
British Tariff System, 840
Britt, Steuart H., 730
Brodskaia, A. B., 919
Bromley, D. W., 758
Brook, Warner F., 343
The Brookings Quarterly Econometric Model of the United States, 473
Brown, Emily C., 1135
Brown, Ernest, 1136
Brown, Lyndon O., 731
Bruchey, Stuart, 456
Brückmann, Kurt, 1049
Bruning, James L., 1220

Brussels. Université libre. Centre d'économie regionale, 222, 327
Bryce, Murray D., 966
Buckland, William R., 1208, 1218a
Buckley, K. A. H., 1243
The Budget of the United States, 600
Bücher, Karl, 118
Buenos Aires. Universidad Nacional. Instituto de Economia, 7
Bullock, Alan L. C., 328
Bureau of National Affairs, Washington, D. C., 793-5
Bureau of Railway Economics, Washington, D. C., 986
Bureau of the Census Catalog, 1288
Burgess, Norman, 501
Buros, Oscar K., 1204
Business and Technology Sources, 491
Business Around the World, 776
Business Books Translated from English, 26
Business Cycle Developments, 1314
BUSINESS CYCLES, 139-40, 184
Business Cycles (Schumpeter), 184
Business Cycles and National Income, 140
BUSINESS FINANCE
see PRIVATE AND PUBLIC FINANCE
Business Finance Handbook, 564
Business History Review, 1315
Business International Corporation, 724
Business Literature, 1316
Business Periodicals Index, 98
Business Service Check List, 658, 713, 914
Business Statistics; Statistical Supplement, 729
Business Week, 1317
The Businessman's Guide to Britain, 358
Buzzell, Robert D., 664

Caffé, Federico, 99
California. University. Giannini
Foundation of Agricultural
Economics. Library, 850
California. University. University
of Los Angeles. Institute of
Industrial Relations, 1050
California University. University
of Los Angeles. Latin America
Center. Statistical Abstracts,
1265
The Cambridge Economic History
of Europe, 329
CANADA
Econ. condit., 315-9
Stat., 1240-3
Canada.
Bureau of Statistics, 1240-1
Library, 987
Dept. of Agriculture. Economics
Division, 858-9
Dept. of Public Printing and
Stationery, 1029, 1242
Canadian Farm Economics, 1318
Canadian Government Publications;
Dominion Bureau of Statistics,
1242
Canadian Government Publications
Relating to Labour, 1029
Canadian Journal of Agricultural
Economics, 1319
Canadian Journal of Economics
and Political Science, 1320
Canadian Tax Foundation, 492
Canadian Trade Index, 780
Cannan, Edwin, 119
Cantillon, Richard, 120
Capital: a Critique of Political
Economy, 161
Capital and Interest, 115
Capital Formation & Foreign
Investment, 251
Capital in the American Economy,
625
Careers Encyclopedia, 1094
Carey, Richard, 404

Caribbean Economic Almanac, 489
Carpenter, Robert N., 640
Cartel, 1321
Carter, Charles F., 354
Carter Glass Papers, 511
Carter, Phyllis G., 1215
Cassel, Gustav, 121
Casselman, Paul H., 1095
Catalog of United States Census
Publications, 1790-1945, 1292
Catalogo Metodico (Buenos Aires), 8
Catalogue des Périodiques, 1966
(OECD), 64
Catalogue des Publications en Langue
Française du Bur. Intern. du
Travail, 1062-3
Catalogue of Periodicals (OECD), 64
Catalogue of Publications in English
of the Intern. Lab. Office, 1064
Catalogue of Social and Economic
Development Institutes and
Programmes, 255-6
A Catalogue of the Library of Adam
Smith, 72
A Catalogue of the Wage Studies of
the BLS., 1040
Catalogus van de Internationale
Verzekeringsbibliotheek te Leuven,
502
Census of Business, 728
Census of Manufacturers, 959
Census of Mineral Industries, 960
The Challenge of International
Finance, 632
Chalmers, Henry, 836
Chamber of Commerce of the
United States, 741
Chamber of Commerce of the United
States of America. Dept. of
Manufacture, 908
Chamber of Commerce of the United
States. State Chamber of Commerce
Service Dept., 909
Chamberlain, Neil W., 1051, 1137
Chamberlin, Edward, 30
Chamberlin, Waldo, 1052

Chambre de Commerce et d'Industrie, Paris. Biblioteque, 339
Chandler, Alfred D., 967
Chasteland, Jean C., 1167
Check List of Publications on American Railroads, 995
Chen, Nai-Ruen, 320
Chernevskii, P. O., 422
CHINA
    Econ. condit., 320-4
    Stat., 1244
China. State Statistical Bureau, 1244
Chinese Economic Statistics, a Handbook, 320
Chisholm's Handbook of Commerical Geography, 889
Chlebikova, M., 31
Chto Chitat' po Politicheskoi Ekonomii, 434
Chute, Aaron H., 666
City Finances, 601
Clapham, Sir John H., 355, 608
Clark, Donald T., 529
Clark, John B., 122-3, 968
Clark, Victor S., 968
Clarke, George T., 667
Classics in the Theory of Public Finance, 629
Clegg, H. A., 1143
Cleveland, Public Library. Business and Technology Dept., 491
Clough, Shepard Bancroft, 340, 378
Colbert and a Century of French Mercantilism, 125
Cole, Arthur H., 124, 471, 665
Cole, Charles Woolsey, 125-6
Cole, George D. H., 1138-40
Colegio de Doctores en Cièncias Económicas y Contadores Públicos Nacionales, Buenos Aires, 8
Collins, George W., 549
Coman, Edwin T., 32, 640a

COMMERCE, 640-739
Commerce and Industry and H.M.S.O., 670
Commerce Clearing House, 1107
Commerical Atlas and Marketing Guide, 723
Commerical Information; a Source Handbook, 641
Committee on Latin America, 390
Commodity Trade Analysis by Regions, 808
Commodity Trade Statistics, 826
Commodity Yearbook, 895
Common Market Antitrust, 915
Common People, 1746-1946, 1138
The Common Sense of Political Economy, 210
Commons, John R., 1141a
Commonwealth Development and Financing, 262
Commonwealth Economic Committee, 262
COMMUNICATION
    cover. by 2d pt. of ch. 7 (979-1024)
Comparative Banking in Australia, Austria, Belgium, 561
Compendium of Social Statistics, 1228
Compendium of Sources: International Trade Statistics, 759
The Complete Guide to Investment Analysis, 562
Complete Handbook of Labor-Management Relations, 1110
Complete Handbook on the Foreign Aid Policy, 259
A Comprehensive Classified Marketing Bibliography, 686
Computational Handbook of Statistics, 1220
Concise Guide to International Markets, 742
Concise Statistical Yearbook of Poland, 1274
Condliffe, John B., 405
Consumer Markets, 726
Consumers and the Market, 738

Contemporary Printed Sources for British and Irish Economic History, 363
The Contracting out of Work, 1053
Contracting Parties to the General Agreement on Tariffs and Trade, 753-4
International Trade Centre, 759
Contribution to Canadian Economics, 317
Conway, Hobart McKinley, 254
Cook, Roy Anthony P., 1141
COOPERATION, 219, 425, 508, 527
Cooperation (Bibliography), 508
Copeland, Morris A., 609
Coppieters, Emmanuel, 610
Cornell University. New York State School of Industrial and Labor Relations, 1030-1
Labor Management Documentation Center, 1025
Library, 1111
Corner, C. M., 536
Cornut, Paul, 341
Corporate and Business Finance, 503
Corporate Treasurer's and Controller's Encyclopedia, 531
Corporate Treasurer's and Controller's Handbook, 565
Cossa, Luigi, 33, 127, 379
County and City Data Book, 1289
Cours d'Economie Politique, 168
Cours de Documentation et de Methode Économiques, 42
Cox, Edwin B., 563
Crandall, Ruth, 105
The Creation and Development of an Insurance Library, 522
A Critique of Welfare Economics, 155
Croner's World Register of Trade . . . see Trade Directories of the World

Crowther, Sir Geoffrey, 611
Cruz, Salviano, 34, 35
A Cumulation of Selected and Annotated Bibliography of Economic Literature on the Arabic Speaking Countries, 304
Cumulative Bibliography of Economic Books, 9
Cumulative Index of N.I.C.B. Publications, 916
Currency and Credit, 619
Current British Directories, 707
Current Economic Indicators, 263, 1449
Current Economic Indicators for the U.S.S.R., 444
Current Industry Reports, 961
Current Literature in Traffic and Transportation, 982
Current Population Reports, 1188
Current Russian Bibliographies in Economics, 447
Current Sources of Information for Market Research, 669
Current Sources of Marketing Information, 671
Custodi, Pietro, 188
Custom House Guide, 1003
The Customs Union Issue, 845
Cutajar, Michael Z., 800
CZECHOSLOVAKIA Stat., 1245
Czechoslovakia. Statni Urad Statisticky, 1245

Danckwortt, Dieter, 223
Danckwortt, Helga, 223
Daniels, Lorna M., 922
Dartnell Corporation, 796
The Dartnell International Trade Handbook, 796
Davenport, Donald H., 720
Davids, Lewis E., 530
Davies, Antony H., 732

Davinson, Donald, 641
Davis, Ralph C., 969
De Francis, John, 323
Del Mar, Alexander, 612
Deliliz, Jean P., 224
Demographic Analysis, 1196
Demographic Training and
    Research Centre, Bombay,
    1168
Demographic Yearbook, 1186
Demographie: Bibliographie et
    Analyse . . . 1167
Demography, 1322
Denman, Donald R., 866
DENMARK
    Econ. condit., 325
    Stat., 1246
Denmark. Det Statistiske
    Dept., 1246
    Ministry of Foreign Affairs, 325
Desarrollo Economico . . . , 393
Deutsch-Englisches Glossarium
    Finanzieller und Wirtschaft-
    licher Fachausdrücke, 536
Deutsche Statistische Gesellschaft,
    1250
Deutsches Industrieinstitut,
    Cologne, 920
The Developing Economies, 1323
The Developing Nations, 236
Development Administration, 238
DEVELOPMENT ECONOMICS
    see ECONOMIC DEVELOPMENT
The Development of American
    Industries, 971
The Development of Economic
    Thought, 195
Devons, Ely, 356
Dewey, Davis Rich, 613
Dewhurst, J. Frederic, 334, 484
Dickinson, Henry D., 128
Dictionary of Banking, 546
Dictionary of Business and
    Fiannce, 529
Dictionary of Commercial,
    Financial and Legal Terms . . .,
    696

Dictionary of Development
    Economics, 253
Dictionary of Economic Terms, 78
A Dictionary of Economics, 89
Dictionary of Economics and Business,
    83, 700
A Dictionary of Economics and
    Commerce, 79, 698
Dictionary of Foreign Trade, 773
Dictionary of Insurance, 530
Dictionary of Modern Economics, 80
Dictionary of Occupational Titles,
    1096
A Dictionary of Statistical Terms, 1218a
Dictionary of Stock Market Terms,
    547
Dictionary Outline of Basic
    Statistics, 1217
Dictionnaire des Sciences
    Economiques, 75
Dievoet, Emilie van, 502
Digest of Current Economic
    Statistics (Australia), 1235
Dillard, Dudley D., 129
Direction of International Trade, 818
Direction of Trade, 592
Dimensions of Soviet Economic
    Power, 442
Directors' and Officers' Encyclopedic
    Manual, 938
Directory of Active Foreign Buyers,
    781
Directory of American Firms
    Operating in Foreign Countries,
    782
A Directory of BLS Studies in
    Industrial Relations, 1041
The Directory of British Exporters,
    783
Directory of British Market Research
    Organizations, 701
Directory of Business and Financial
    Services, 551
Directory of Economic and
    Statistical Projects, 257, 1222
A Directory of Foreign Advertising
    Agencies, 790

A Directory of Foreign Organizations for Trade . . ., 791

A Directory of Industry Wage Studies, 1042

Directory of Labor Organizations, 1102

Directory of Mailing List Houses, 647

Directory of National and International Labor Unions, 1103

Directory of Organizations which Conduct Motivation Research, 702

Directory of Railway Officials & Year Book, 1004

Directory of Research Organization Members, 703

Directory of Statisticians and Others in Allied Professions, 1221

Directory of United States Import Concerns, 784

Dirksen, Cletus F., 40

Dissertations in Demography, 1171

Distance and Human Interaction, 1194

Distribution Data Guide, 1324

The Distribution of Wealth, 122

Distributive Education Bibliography, 689

Dizionario Commerciale, 699a

Dmitriev, V.A., 988

Doctoral Dissertations in Labor and Industrial Relations, 1079

Documentacion Económica, 103a

A Documentary History of American Industrial Society, 1141a

Documentary Material in Asian Countries, 307

Documentation Economique, 100

Doig, Alison G., 1210

Doing Business Abroad, 761

Doing Business Abroad; Summary of Regulations . . ., 806

Dr. Gablers Verkehrs-Lexikon, 1000

Dr. Gablers Wirtschaftslexikon, 88

Dokuments und Berichte über Entwicklungspläne, 221

Donahue, Gilvert E., 1083

Donaldson, Gordon, 503

Donnithorne, Audrey G., 963-4

Donskaia, G. K., 434, 867

Dorfman, Joseph, 457

Doris, Lillian, 531, 564-5

Dougall, Herbert, 614

Douglas,Paul H., 130

Dubester, Henry J., 1247, 1292

Duesenberry, J.S., 472

Dulles, Foster R., 1142

Dun and Bradstreet, Inc., 552, 566, 642, 706, 743-4, 940-1, 1005

Dun & Bradstreet's Guide to Key British Enterprises, 357

Duncan, Otis D., 1196-7

Dunn, Albert H., 668

Dun's Reference Book of Corporate Managements, 940

Dun's Review and Modern Industry, 1325

Early British Economics . . ., 111

Early English Tracts on Commerce, 736

East African Economics Review, 1327

East-West Trade Relations, 765

Easterbrook, William T., 318

Econometrica; Journal of the Econometric Society, 1327

L'economia Degli Stati Italiani Prima dell' Unificazione, 36

Economia Internazionale, 1328

Economic Abstracts, 101

Economic Allemande Contemporaine, 344

Economic Almanac, 264

Economic Analysis, 116

Economic and Cultural Statistics of Communist China, 1244

Economic and Social Development of Modern China, 324

Economic and Social Development Plans, 241

Economic Areas of the United States, 469

ECONOMIC ASSISTANCE cover. by ch. 2 (213-490)

Economic Bulletin for Latin America, 399

ECONOMIC CONDITIONS IN VARIOUS COUNTRIES, 213-490

ECONOMIC DEVELOPMENT cover. by ch. 2 (213-490)

Economic Development and Cultural Change, 1329

Economic Development in Latin America, 401

Economic Development in the Nineteenth Century: France, Germany . . ., 331

The Economic Development of: Ceylon, 267; Communist China, 322; India, 372; Iraq, 268; Jamaica, 269; Jordan, 270; Kenya, 271; Kuwait, 272; Libya, 273; Malaya, 274; Mexico, 275; Morocco, 276ˆ Nicaragua, 277; Nigeria, 278; Spain, 279; Syria, 280; Tanganyika, 281; Thailand, 282; Papua and New Guinea, 283; Uganda, 284; Venezuela, 285

Economic Development of the British Overseas Empire, 364

Economic Developments in the Middle East, 403

Economic Forces in the United States in Facts and Figures, 485

ECONOMIC GEOGRAPHY cover. by ch. 6 (849-907)

Economic Geography (Quarterly), 1330

ECONOMIC HISTORY cover. by ch. 2 (213-490)

An Economic History of Modern Britain, 355

The Economic History of Modern Italy, 378

Economic History of the United States, 467

Economic History Review, 1331

Economic Indicators, 473

Economic Journal, 1332

The Economic Library of Jacob Hollander, 47

The Economic Literature of Latin America, 391

The Economic Mind in American Civilization, 457

The Economic Organization of Agriculture, 906

Economic Planning, 233

Economic Problems of Underdeveloped Areas, 245

Economic Record (Melbourne), 1333

Economic Report of the President to the Congress, 488

Economic Survey, 1919-1939, 289

Economic Survey of Denmark, 325

Economic Survey of Europe, 335

Economic Survey, Jamaica, 490

Economic Survey of Japan, 380

Economic Survey of Latin America, 398

Economic Surveys (OECD), 292

ECONOMIC THEORY, 1-212

Economic Theory and Operations Analysis, 110a

Economic Trends, 1334

Economica, 1335

Economics: a Select Book List, 43

Economics and Commerce, the Sources of Information . . ., 4, 649

Economics Department Publications, 1948-1966, 66-8

Economics for Agriculture, 901
Economics Library Selections,
New Books in Economics, 9
Economics Library Selections,
Series 1, 37
Series 2, 38
The Economics of Agricultural
Development, 904
Economics of Agricultural
Production, 902
Economics of American Industry,
962
The Economics of Crisis, 461
The Economics of Development,
227
Economics of Full Employment,
277
Economics of Inland Transport,
1023
The Economics of John Maynard
Keynes, 129
The Economics of Labor, (Brown),
1136
Economics of Labor, (Millis), 1151
The Economics of Labor and
Collective Bargaining, 1150
Economics of Labor Relations,
1134
The Economics of Location, 903
The Economics of Underdeveloped
Areas, 228
Economics of Underdeveloped
Countries, 261
Economics Selections: an Inter-
national Bibliography, 11
Economisch en Social Tijdschrift,
1336
Economist. (Harlem), 1338
The Economist (London), 358
Economist (London Weekly), 1337
The Economist's Handbook, 1202
Economy and History, 1339
Economy of Mainland China,
1949-1963, a Bibliography, 321
The Economy of Pakistan, 408
Edey, Harold C., 615

Edgerton, Harold A., 1219
Editor & Publisher, 643
Edwards, Charles M., 662
Ehlert, Willi, 92a
Eichhorn, Reinhart von, 76
Einführung in di Wirtschafts-
geschichte, 114
Einkommensverteilung, 523
Ekonomicheskaia Entsiklopediia,
77
Ekonomicheskaia Nauka i
Khoziaistvennaie Praktika, 423
Ékonomicheskaia Zhizn' SSSR, 424
Ekonomicheskoe Raionirovanie, 432
Ekonomicheskoe Raionovanie
SSR, 419
Ekonomicko-Matematický Obzor,
1340
Ekonomika i Matematicheskie
Metody, 1341
Ekonomika i Organizatsiia
Sel'skokhoziaistvennogo
Proizvodstva, 867
Ekonomika i Planirovanie
Sovetskoi Kooperativnoi
Torgovli, 425
Ekonomika Kapitalisticheskikh
Stran, 265
Ekonomika Radians'koi Ukrainy,
1342
Ekonomika SSR; Annotirovannyi
Perechen', 435
Ekonomika Sotsiialisticheskikh
Stran v Tsifrakh, 426
Ekonomika Zheleznodorzhnogo
Transporta SSR, 988
Ekonomisk Tidskrift, 1343
Eksportno-Importnyi Slovar', 771
Eldridge, Hope T., 1169
Elements of Pure Economics, 206
Ellis, Howard S., 131
Ellsworth, Paul T., 837
Elsevier's Banking Dictionary in
Six Languages, 532
Ely, J. Edward, 817
Employment and Earnings, 1125

233

Employment and Earnings Statistics for States, and Areas, 1126
Employment and Earnings Statistics for the United States, 1127
Employment and Wages in the U. S., 1159
Employment of Older Women, 1090
Employment Relations Abstracts, 1112
Encyclopedia of Advertising, 697
Encyclopedia of Banking and Finance, 539
The Encyclopedia of the Labour Movement, 1095a
Encyclopedic Dictionary of Business Finance, 542
Engineering-Economic Planning of Transportation, 990
English Banknote Circulation, 1694-1954, 610
Entwicklung der Gesetze des Menschlichen Verkehrs, 136
Entwicklungshilfe, Entwicklungsländer, 223
Entwicklungspolitik, 252
Enzyklopädisches Lexikon für das Geld, Bank- und Börsenwesen, 533
Essai sur la Nature de Commerce en General, 120
Essays in Economic Thought: Aristotle to Marshall, 194
Essays on Economic Policy, 148
Essays on Population, 1191
Essentials of Economic Theory as Applies to Modern Problems of Industry, 968
Europ Production, 712
EUROPE
Econ. condit., 326-7
Stat., 1247
The European Bibliography, 330

European Coal and Steel Community. High Authority, Bibliotheque, 12, 39
The European Common Market and European Free Trade Association, 336, 695
European Communities. Commission, 989
European Cultural Centre, 330
European Recovery Program, 333
Europe's Needs and Resources, 334
Europe's Postwar Growth, 1145
Evanston, Ill. Transportation Center at Northwestern University, 980
Everyman's Dictionary of Economics, 87
Evitt, Herbert E., 797
The Evolution of Wage Structure, 1155
Expectations in Economic Theory, 167
Export Shipping Manual, 794-5
Export Trade: the Law and Practice . . ., 843
Exporters' Encyclopaedia, 772
Exporter's Yearbook, 819
EXPORTS
cover. by ch. 5 (740-848)

FAA Statistical Handbook of Aviation, 1019
FAO Commodity Review, 897
FBI Register of British Manufacturers, 942
Facts and Figures on Government Finance, 573
Far Eastern Economic Review, a Yearbook, 309
Far Eastern Economic Review (Weekly), 1344
Farm Policies of the United States, 900

Farrell, David M., 1053
The Federal Antitrust Policy, 977
Federal Economic Review, 1345
Federal Reserve Bulletin, 599, 1346
Federal Reserve Chart Book on
Financial and Business
Statistics, 588-9
Federal Statistical Directory, 1286
Federation of British Industries,
942
Ferber, Robert, 693, 733
Ferguson, Elizabeth, 504
Field, James A., 1191
Filipetti, George, 970
FINANCE
see PRIVATE AND PUBLIC
FINANCE
FINANCE, PUBLIC
see PUBLIC FINANCE
Financial Handbook, 567
Financial History of the
United States, 613
Finanzarchiv, 1347
Finanzierungs—Handbuch, 570
Fine, Sidney, 458
FINLAND
Econ. condit., 338
Finland. Ministry of Finance,
Division for Eonomic Affairs,
338
First Essay on Population, 1193
Fishbein, Meyer H., comp., 692
Fisher, Irving, 132
FitzPatrick, Paul J., 40
Flanders, Allen, 1143
Flieger, Wilhelm, 1184
Flow of Funds in the United
States, 602
Fogel, Robert W., 1022
Folsom, Josiah C., 1054
Food and Agriculture Organiza-
tion of the United Nations,
820, 868-9, 896
Food and Agriculture Organiza-
tion of the United Nations
Commodity Division, 897

Economic Division. Monthly
Bulletin of Agricultural
Economics & Statistics, 1348
Forbes, F. Preston, 750
Forecasting and Estimation, 997
Foreign Agriculture, 1349
Foreign Aid: Theory and
Practice, 302
Foreign Commerce and Navigation,
829
Foreign Commerce Handbook, 741
FOREIGN EXCHANGE
cover. by ch. 5 (740-848)
Foreign Labor Publications of
the Bureau of Labor Statistics,
1088
Foreign Markets Report Service, 811
Foreign Statistical Documents, a
Bibliography . . ., 757, 864
Foreign Statistical Documents in
Stanford Libraries, 1214
FOREIGN TRADE, 740-848
Foreign Trade and Foreign
Exchange, 802
Foreign Trade Statistical Bulletins,
882
Forschungsarbeiten aus Agraröko-
nomik, 860
Forschungsgesellschaft für Agrar-
politik und Agrarsoziologie, 891
Foundations of Economic Analysis,
181
Fox, Ronald A., 1208
FRANCE
Econ. condit., 339-41
Stat., 1248
France.
Institut national de la
statistique et des études
economiques, 1170, 1248
Ministere de l'economie et
des finances, 590
Statistiques et études
financieres, 1350
France: a History of National
Economics, 340

Frank, Nathalie D., 644, 669
Frauendorfer, Sigmund von, 851
Free Trade, Tariff Legislation . . .,
768
French Bibliographical Digest,
Science, Economics, 41
French Mercantilism, 1683-1700,
126
Freund, John E., 1217
Frey, Albert W., 717
Friedberg, Robert, 568
Friedman, Milton, 616
Fuguit, Blenn V., 1171
Fundamentals in Marketing, 739

GATT Bibliography, 1947-1953,
753-4
GATT International Trade Centre,
see Contracting Parties to the
General Agreement . . .
Gallagher, Vincent L., 534
Gallatin Annual on International
Business, 798
Gardella, Roberta, 757
Gaynor Frank, 535
General Censuses and Vital
Statistics in the Americas, 1234
General Economic History, (Weber),
59
General Statistics. Statistiques
Générales, 1226
The General Theory of Employment,
Interest and Money, 149
Geografiia Naseleniia v SSR, 1173
Geographical Abstracts. C.
Economic Geography, 892
Geographical Distribution of
Financial Flows, 593
Geography: a Reference Handbook,
853
Georgievskii, P. I., 427
Gerloff, Wilhelm, 569
Germain-Martin, Henry, 42

The German Economic Review,
1351
German Economy, 1870 to the
Present, 345
GERMANY
Econ. condit., 342-8
Stat. 1249-51
Germany
(Democratic Republic)
Staatliche Zentralverwaltung
für Statistik, 1249
Zentralinstitut für Bibliotheks-
wesen, 345a
(Federal Republic, 1949-   )
Statistisches Bundesamt, 1251
Gide, Charles, 1345
Gilmour, S. Carter, 889
Gilpin, Alan, 78
Giornale degli Economisti e
Annali di Economia, 1352
Glasgow, Robert B., 475
Glass, David V., 1192
Glauber, Robert R., 627
The Globe World Directory for
Land, Sea and Air Traffic, 1006
Globus Jahrbuch des Deutschen
Verlages; die Welt und ihre
Länder, 1225
Glossary of Economics Including
Soviet Terminology, 92
Glossary of Financial Terms in
English, American, French,
Spanish and Germna, 537
Glover, John G., 971
Goldsmith, Raymond W., 617
Goldstein, Frederick A., 671
Goris, Hendrika, 225
Gospodarka Europejskich Krajów
Socjalistycznych, 326
Gossen, Herman H., 136
Gottfried, Bert A., 529
Government Securities Market, 635
Government Statistics for Business
Use, 725
Graham, I., 697

Gray, Sir Alexander, 137
GREAT BRITAIN
  Econ. condit., 349-71
  Stat., 1252-8
Great Britain
  British Council, 43
  Central Office of Inform., 359
  Central Statistical Office,
  1252-4
  Interdepartment Committee on
  Social and Economic Research,
  1255
  Ministry of Labour, 360
  Stationery Office, 670, 1252-4
  Treasury, 1256
The Great Economists, a History
  of Economic Thought, 160
Greenwald, Douglas, ed., 81
Grierson, Philip, 428
Gródek, Andrzej, 74
The Growth of World Industry,
  1938-1961, 956
Grubel, H. G., 574
Gruchy, Allan G., 138
Gsell, Donald, 1068
The Guaranteed Annual Wage, 1092
Guchek, T. S., 918
Guide de Recherches Documentaires
  en Démographie, 1165
Guide of Listings of Manufacturers,
  908
Guide to American Directories, 910
Guide to American Directories for
  Compiling Mailing Lists
  see Directory of Mailing List
  Houses, 647
A Guide to American Trade
  Catalogs, 1744-1900, 653
Guide to Area Employment
  Statistics, 1128
Guide to Asian Economic
  Statistics, 311
A Guide to Australian Economic
  Statistics, 314
Guide to Business History, 480
Guide to Current British Periodicals,
  8

Guide to Employment Statistics
  of BLS, 1129
A Guide to Foreign Business
  Directories, 749
Guide to Foreign Trade Statistics,
  752
Guide to Historical Literature, 213
A Guide to Keynes, 141
A Guide to Latin American
  Studies, 394
Guide to Listings of Manufacturers,
  908
Guide to Special Issues and
  Indexes of Periodicals, 655
A Guide to the Printed Materials
  for English Social and Econòmic
  History, 37
Guide to U. S. Government
  Statistics, 1285
Guidelist for Marketing Research
  and Economic Forecasting, 640
Guides for the Newcomer to World
  Trade, 750
Guides to Information Sources for
  Education in Distribution, 657
Guides to Official Sources
  (Gt. Brit.), 1255
Gulick, Charles A., 1055
Gunston, C. A., 536
Gunther, Edgar, 671
Gurley, John G., 618
Guyton, Percy L., 2

Haberler, Gottfried, 139, 838
Hacke, Sarah D., 994
Hald, Marjorie W., 226
Hall, Hubert, 361
Hall, Laura M., 44
Hamburg.
  Welt-Wirtschafts-Archiv., 13
  Bibliothek, 672, 760
Hamburger Jahrbuch für
  Wirtschafts und Gesellschafts-
  politik, 106
Hamilton, Henry, 362

Handbook of Airline Statistics,
1017
Handbook of Basic Economic
Statistics, 474
Handbook of Employee
Relations, 1106
Handbook of Financial Mathe-
matics, 572
Handbook of International
Marketing, 801
Handbook of Labor Statistics,
1130
Handbook of the American
Economic Association, 94
Handbuch der Finanzwissen-
schaft, 569
Handbuch der Wirtschafts-
wissenschaften, 107
Handbuch zur Geschichte der
Volkswirtschaftslehre, 117
Handwörterbuch des Finanz-
wesesn, 545
Hankins, Thomas D., 849
Hannay, Annie M. (Macgregor), 870
Hansen, Alvin H., 1401
Hansen, Gerald, 470
Hansen, Harry L., 736a
Hanson, John L., 79, 698
Hanson, Laurence W., 363
Haren, Claude C., 475
Harris, Seymour Ed., 142, 460
The Harry W. Bass Collection
in Business History . . ., 926
Harvard Business Review, 1353
Harvard University
Bureau of Economic Research
in Latin America, 391
Graduate School of Business
Administration, 214, 476
Baker Library, 45, 922
International Program in
Taxation, 505
Harvey, Joan M., 645, 1200
Hasse, Adelaid R., 477
Hausser, Philip M., 725

Hawaii. Industrial Research
Advisory Council, 478
Hawaii. University, Honolulu.
Industrial Relations Center, 1056
Hawtrey, Sir Ralph G., 619
Hax, Karl, ed., 107
Hayck, Friedrich A. von, 142a
Hazlewood, Arthur, 227, 228
Heady, Earl O., 902
Health Insurance Institute, New
York, 493
Heath, Gerald R., 534
Heilbroner, Robert L., 143
Heimann, Eduard, 144
Henderson, George P., 707
Heneman, Herbert G., 1163
Henius, Frank, 773
Herbst, R., 697
Hertfordshire, Eng. Country
Technical Library Service, 673
Hickok, Beverly, 998
Hicks, George L., 375
Hicks, John R., 1144
Hicks, Ursula Kathleen (Webb), 620
Higgs, Henry, 46
An Historical and Chronological
Deduction of the Origin of
Commerce, 350
Historical Catalogue of Dominion
Bureau of Statistics Publications,
1918-1960, 1241
The Historical Development of
Economic and Business
Literature, 124
Historical Statistics of Canada,
1243
Historical Statistics of the United
States Colonial Times to 1957,
479
History and Theories of Working-
Class Movements, 1055
A History of Banking Theory in
Gt. Britain and the United
States, 628
A History of Broadcasting in the
U. S., 1021

History of Economic Analysis, 185
History of Economic Doctrines
(Gide), 134
History of Economic Doctrines
(Heimann), 144
A History of Economic Ideas, 208
A History of Economic Thought,
(Bell), 112
A History of Economic Thought
(Roll), 178
HISTORY OF ECONOMICS
covered by ch. 1 (1-212)
The History of Economics, (Spann),
193
History of Labor and Unionism in
the United States, 1068
History of Labor in the United
States, 1137
History of Manufactures in the
U. S., 968
A History of Money in Ancient
Countries, 612
A History of Russian Economic
Thought, 109
History of the Bank of England,
604
History of the Homeland, 362
History of the Principal Public
Banks, 507
A History of the Theories of
Production and Distribution in
English Political Economy from
1776-1848, 119
History of Transport, 991-2
History of Wages in the United
States, 1131
Hollander, Jacob H., 47
Hollander, Stanley C., 674
Holloway, Robert J., 675
Holmes, Frank W., 404
Holzman, Franklyn D., 429, 621
Horecky, Paul L., 430
Horn, Stefan F., 537
Horowitz, Martin, 1075
Horton, Burne J., 80
Houghton, D. H., 450

How to Find Out About Banking
and Investment, 501
How to Find Out in Geography,
855
Huffschmid, Jörg, 923
Hughes, Jonathan, 459
Hulm, Mary W., 745
Human Resources and Economic
Growth, 239, 1175
Hume, David, 145
Humpert, Magdalene, 676
HUNGARY
Stat., 1259
Hungary. Központi Statisztikai
Hivatal, 1259
Hutchison, Terence W., 146

Illinois. University. Institut of
Labor and Industrail Relations,
1032, 1057
Images Economiques du Monde,
266
Important Sources of Information
for Work in Agricultural Econo-
mics, 850
Importation of Goods, 745
IMPORTS
cover. by ch. 5 (740-848)
Incentive Wage Systems, 1074
Income; an Introduction to
Economics, 170
Income and Welfare in the United
States, 465
The Income of Nations; Theory . . .,
295
Income Revisited, 171
Index of Canadian Tax Foundation,
492
Index of Economic Journals, 96
Index of Economic Material in
Documents of the States of the
U. S., 477
An Index to Business Indices, 720

Index to Catalog of Investment Information, 810

Index to Economic History, 105

Index to Labor Union Periodicals, 1113

INDIA
Econ. condit., 372-4

India
Dept. of Economic Affairs, 373
Government, 374

India Pocket Book of Economic Information, 373

Indian Economic Review, 1354

Indian Journal of Economics, 1355

Indice de Trabajos Publicados en Revista de Economia, 103

INDONESIA
Econ. condit., 375

The Indonesian Economy, 1950-1965, 375

Industira. Rivista di Economia Politica, 1356

The Industrial and Commercial Relations in Great Britain, 365

INDUSTRIAL AND LABOR RELATIONS, 1025-1164

Industrial and Labor Relations: Abstracts, 1111

Industrial and Labor Relations in Canada, 1065

Industrial and Labor Relations Review, 1357

Industrial Data Guide, 913

Industrial Democracy, 1161

Industrial Development; a Guide for Accelerating Growth, 966

Industrial Evolution, 118

Industrial Human Relations; a Select Bibliography, 1050

Industrial Management in Transition, 970

Industrial Management Review, 1358

Industrial Marketing, Media Marketing Planning Guide, 646, 911

Industrial Organization and Management, 969

Industrial Plants in the United States, 934

Industrial Psychology, 1158

Industrial Relations and Economic Development, 975

Industrial Relations Bibliographies, 1071

Industrial Relations in Germany, 1052

Industrial Revolution, 1750-1850, 368

The Industrial Revolution in the Eighteenth Century, 367

Industrial Statistics, 953

Industrialism and Industrial Man, 973

Industrialization and Economic Development, 246, 935

Industrialization and Economic Development in Brazil, 965

Industrialization and Labor, 1152

INDUSTRY, 908-78

Industry Surveys, 952

INFLATION, 516-7

Inflation (OECD), 517

Information System, 724

Innis, Harold A., 319

Input-Output Bibliography, 1955-1966, 931-3, 1085-7

An Inquiry into the Nature and Causes of the Wealth of Nations, 191

An Inquiry into the Principles of Political Economy, 196

Institut International de Statistique. Revue . . ., 1359

Institute of Asian Economic Affairs, see Ajia Keizai Kenkyujo, Tokyo

Institute of Transport Journal, 1360

Institutional Revenue, 128

INSURANCE
covered by ch. 3 (491-639)

Insurance Almanac; Who, What, When, and Where . . ., 578
Insurance Information Institute, 494
Insurance Principles and Practices, 633
Insurance Society of New York, Library, 506
Insurance Words and Their Meanings, 534
Inter-American Development Bank, 579
Inter-American Statistical Institute, 392, 1209, 1231, 1263
Interest and Prices, 639
Interindustry Economic Studies, 927
International Aid, 288
International Association for Research in Income and Wealth, 216
International Bank for Reconstruction and Development, 17, 267-85
International Bibliography of Agricultural Economics, 871
International Bibliography of Economics, 15
International Business and Foreign Trade, 770
International Business Dictionary in Five Languages, 535
International Business Publication Checklist, 756
International Committee for the Study of the History of Banking and Credit, 507
International Conference on Input-Output Techniques, Geneva, 286
International Cooperation and Programmes . . ., 249
International Credit Union Yearbook, 580
International Development Review, 1361
International Economic and Social Development, 769

INTERNATIONAL ECONOMICS, 740-848
International Economics Selections Bibliography. Ser. 1 New Books in Economics, 16
International Economy, 837
An International Economy; Problems and Prospects, 841
International Executive, 1362
International Financial Statistics, 591
International Guide to Foreign Commercial Financing, 556
International Importer's Trade Directory, 777
International Information Service, 746
International Institute of Agriculture. Library, 871
International Labor Directory and Handbook, 1100
International Labour Documentation, 1114
International Labour Office, 1058, 1121
International Labour Office. Library, 508, 1033, 1059-64
International Labour Review, 1363
International Market Guide: Continental Europe, 743
Inernational Market Guide; Latin America, 744
International Migration and Economic Development, 1178
International Monetary Fund, 17, 581, 804, 821
International Monetary Fund. Staff Papers, 1364
International Monetary Fund. Statistics Bureau, 592
International Monetary System, 763
International Payments, 764
International Population Census Bibliography, 1176-7

International Population Statistics
Reports, 1189
International Reference Handbook
of Services, Organizations,
Diplomatic Representation,
Marketing and Advertising
Channels, 747
International Reference Manual, 799
International Reports on Finance
and Currencies, 582, 805
International Social Security
Association. Documentation
Service, 509-10, 528
International Statistical Institute.
Review, 1365
International Telephone
Directory, 1007
International Trade, 847
International Trade Infromation,
740
International Trade Reporter, 793
International Trade Reporter's
Survey and Analysis of
Current Developments, 1366
International Trade Review, 1367
International Trade Statistics, 817
The International Yearbook and
Statemen's Who's Who, 286
International Yellow Pages, 785
Internationale Bibliographie der
Fachzeitschriften für Technik
und Wirtschaft, 14
Internationale Bibliographie des
Zollwesens, 755
Internationales Archiv für
Verkehrswesen, 1368
Interregional and International
Trade, 842
An Introduction to British
Economic Statistics, 356
Introduction to English Economic
History and Theory, 351
Introduction to Malthus, 1192
An Introduction to the Study of
Political Economy, 127
Introduction to Trade Unionism,
1139

Inventory of Economic Studies
Concerning Africa South, 306
An Inventory of Regional Input-
Output Studies, 470
Inventory of the Carter Glass
Papers, 512
Investigations in Currency &
Finance, 622
Investment Decisions, Economic
Forecasting and Public Policy,
627
Investment Information and Advice:
a Handbook and Directory, 553
INVESTMENTS
covered by ch. 3 (491-639)
IRAN
Econ. condit., 376
Isbester, A. Fraser, 1065
Isolated State, 907
Der Isolierte Staat, 907
ITALY
Econ. condit., 377-9
Stat., 1260
Italy. Istituto Centrale di
Statistica, 1260
Itogi Pervogo 10-letiia Sotsiialisti-
cheskogo Stroitel'stva SSSR,
446

Jaarcifers voor Nederland, 1268
Jahrbuch für Sozialwissenschaft,
1369
Jahrbücher für Nationalökonomie
und Statistik, 1370
Jamaica. Central Planning Unit,
490
Janberg, Hans, 570
Janeway, Eliot, 461
Janse, Renee S., 996
Janzen, Cornelius C., 83, 700
JAPAN
Econ. condit., 380-7
Stat., 1261
Japan. Bureau of Statistics, 1261

Japan Economic Yearbook, see
The Oriental Economist's
Japan Economic Yearbook
Japan Science Review: Economic
Sciences, 381
Japan Statistical Yearbook, 1261
Japanese Economic Statistics
Bulletin, 382
Japanese Economics, 386
Jenks, Elizabeth, 625
Jeremy Bentham's Economic
Writings, 113
Jevons, William S., 622
Jewkes, John, 972
John Creral Library, Chicago,
924-5
Johnson, Edgar A. J., 147
Joint Council on Economic
Education, 18
Joint Council on Economic
Education. Materials Evaluation
Committee, 48
Jones, Garth N., 237
Josephson, Aksel, G. S., 924
Journal des Economistes, 1371
Journal of Business, 1372
Journal of Development Studies,
1373
Journal of Economic Abstracts,
102
Journal of Economic History, 1374
Journal of Farm Economics, 1375
Journal of Finance (Chicago), 1376
Journal of Finance (New York), 1377
Journal of Industrial Economics,
1378
Journal of Industrial Relations,
1379
Journal of Management Studies, 1380
Journal of Marketing, 1381
Journal of Personnel Administration
and Industrial Relations, 1382
Journal of Political Economy, 1383
Journal of the Economic and
Social History of the Orient, 1384
Journal of Transport History, 1385

Kabir, A.K.M., 229
Kaldor, Nicholas, 148
Kaplun, S.I., 1066
Karataev, S. I., 431
Karey, Richard H., 404
Katz, Saul M., 230
Kawai, Saburo, 386
Keenleyside, Hugh L., 288
Keizagaku Bunken Kiho, 19, 383
Kelley, Eugene J., 677
Kelly's Directory of Merchants,
Manufacturers, 708, 943
Kendall, Maurice G., 1210, 1218a,
1256
Kerr, Clark, 973
Keyfitz, Nathan, 1184
Keynes, John M., 149, 623-4
KEYNESIAN ECONOMICS,
129, 141-2
Khungar, T. C., 786
Khungar's Directory of Trade
Directories of the World, 786
Kiel.
Universität. Institut für Welt-
wirtschaft, 301
Bibliothek, 49-55
Killinsworth, Charles C., 1077
Kincaid, Elbert A., 511-2
Kindleberger, Charles P., 1145
King, Robert L., 721
King, William R., 734
Kintz, B. L., 1220
Klein, B., 910
Klein (B) and Company, New
York, 647
Knisely, Verona B., 500
Knowles, Lilian C. A., 331, 364-5
Knox, Vera H., 513
Körperschaftenkatalog, 50
Kolpakov, B. T., 771
Koltun, M. I., 432
Komiya, Ryutaro, 384
Kompass, Register of British
Industry and Commerce, 709, 944
Konjunkturinstitutet, Stockholm,
453

Konjunkturpolitik. Zeitschrift
für Angewandte Konjunk-
turforschung, 1386
Koopmans, Tjalling, 150
KOREA
Stat., 1262
Korea Statistical Yearbook, 1262
Kress Library of Business and
Economics. Catalogue . . ., 45
Krestianskii Vopros v Rossii, 873
Krishnan, V. N., 308
Krooss, Herman E., 462
Kurtz, Albert K., 1219
Kuznets, Simon S., 151, 463, 625

Labor Development Abroad, 1116
Labor Dictionary, 1095
Labor Digest, 1132
LABOR ECONOMICS, 1025-1164
Labor Economics (Yodor), 1163
Labor Economics and Labor
Relations, 1156
Labor Fact Book, 1122a
The Labor Force under
Changing Income and
Employment, 1147
Labor History, 1388
Labor History in the United
States, a General Bibliography,
1083
Labor in America a History, 1142
Labor Relations Reporter, 1389
Labor Relations Yearbook, 1122
Labor Research Association, 1122a
Labor's Library, 1046
Labour Gazette (Ottawa), 1387
Lagai, Rudolph L., 971
Laissez Faire and the General
Welfare State, 458
Lancaster, Henry O., 1211
LAND ECONOMICS, 849-907
Land Economics (Quarterly), 1390
Land Ownership; a Bibliography . . .,
870

Land Use Planning and the Social
Sciences, 872
Landsberg, Hans H., 483
Landskron, William A., 305
Lanz, Karl, 554
Larson, Henrietta M., 480
LATIN AMERICA
Econ. condit., 388-401
Stat. 1263-6
Latin America: a Bibliographical
Guide, 388
Latin America and the Caribbean,
389
Latin America in Maps, Charts,
Tables, 1264
Latin American Economic & Social
Serials, 390
Lave, Lester B., 974
Lawrence, Richard M., 678
Lazer, William, 688
Leaders of Labor, 1141
Leamer, Laurence E., 2
Lebensbilder Grosser Nationalökono-
men, 174
Lebergott, Stanley, 1146
Le Clair, Marie J., 1067
Lectures on Political Economy, 209
Lee, Robert R., 990
Lees-Smith, Hastings B., 1095a
Legeard, Claude, 1165
LEISURE CLASS, 202
Leonard, William R., 725
Leontief, Wassily W., 464
The Less Developed Countries in
World Trade, 800
Letiche, John M., 839
Lewes, F.M.S., 366, 1201
Lewis, Howard T., 912
Lewis, William A., 152, 289
Li, Cho-Min, 322
Library Association. County
Libraries Group, 3, 648, 852
A Library of Public Finance and
Economics, 63
Life Insurance Catalog, 506
Life of Adam Smith, 173

Lifshits, I. A., 56
List Friedrich, 153-4
A List of Books on the History
of Industry . . ., 924
A List of Current Health Insurance
Books, 493
List of Institutions in the Field
of Applied Economics, 258
List of National Development
Plans, 225
List of Principal Statistical
Services Available, 1253
List of Statistical Series . . .,
1206
Liste Universelle des Périodiques
de la Sécurité Sociale, 510
Literatur für den Gewerkschafts-
funktionär, 1049
Literatur über Entwicklungsländer,
231
The Literature of Political
Economy, 57
Little, Ian M.D., 155
Litvak, I.A.., 679
Lloyd's Maritime Atlas, 1015
Lloyd's Register of Shipping, 1008
Local Government In-Service
Training, 1082
Lock, C. B. Buriel, 853
Löffelholz, Josef, 538
Lösch, August, 903
London. University. Centre for
Urban Studies, 872
London. University. School of
Oriental and African Studies,
304
Long, Clarence D., 1147
Looking for Employment in
Foreign Countries, 1097
Luck, David J., 735
Lundberg, Erik, 156
LUXEMBOURG
Stat., 1267
Luxembourg. Service Central
de la Statistique, 1267

Lybrand, Ross Bros. & Montgomery,
799

McCormich, Ernest J., 1158
McCoy, Ralph E., 1057, 1068, 1079
McCulloch, John R., 57, 626, 736
McGowan, Frank, 230
The McGraw-Hill Dictionary of
Modern Economics, 81
McGuire, Edward B., 840
Mackensen, Rainer, 1172
McNair, Malcolm P., 736a
McNicoll, Geoffrey, 375
MacRae's Blue Book, 710, 945
Macroconomic Theory, 108
MACROECONOMICS, 108, 203
Madison, Charles A., 1148
Madrid. Centro de Estudios
Sindicales, 1034
Main Economic Indicators (OECD),
293
Mainsprings of the German Revival,
347
The Making of Economic Society,
143
Mallen, Bruce E., 679
Maltby, Arthur, 4, 649
Malthus, Thomas R., 157, 1193
The Managed Economy, 466
Manchester School of Economics
and Social Studies, 1391
Manpower in Economic Growth,
1146
Manpower Planning and Utilization,
1089
Manpower Problems in Economic
Development, 1080
Manpower Research: Inventory,
1035
Mantoux, Paul J., 367
A Manual of Foreign Exchange, 797
Manuel Bibliographique des
Sciences Sociales et Economiques,
58

Marconi's International Register, 787

Marget, Arthur W., 158

Market Analysis: a Handbook . . ., 644

Market Guide, 643

Market Guide of Discounter and Mass Merchandisers, 642

Market Research and Scientific Distribution, 732

Market Research Society, 650

Market Research Sources, 656

Market Share Reports, 813

MARKETING, 640-739

Marketing (Toronto), 1392

Marketing and Distribution Research, 731

Marketing Handbook, 717

Marketing Information Guide, 651

Marketing Management: an Annotated Bibliography, 677

Marketing Management and Administrative action, 730

Marketing Maps of the United States, 691

Marketing Research, 735

Marks, Norton E., 680

Marksistko-Leninskaia Politicheskaia Ekonomiia, 414

Der Marktforscher, 1393

Marsh, Elsie A. G., 47

Marshall, Alfred, 159

Marshall, Howard D., 160

Marshall, M. Frances, 1117

Martinstetter, Hermann, 755

Marx, Karl, 161

MARX, KARL—BIBLIOGRAPHY, 70

MARXIAN ECONOMICS, 161, 414, 134

Mass Transportation. Directory, 1009

Massie, Joseph, 681

Massy, William F., 682

Master Directory for Latin America, 395

Masui, Mitsuzo, 515

Matematiko-Ekonomicheskie Metody i Modeli, 56

The Materials of Demography, 1169

Mateu y Llopis, Filipe, 514

Maunier, René, 58

Measures of Business Change, 471, 665

Median Family Income and Related Data by Countries, 475

Magathlin, Donald E., 683

Mellor, John W., 904

Menger, Anton, 1149

Menger, Karl, 162

Merchant Vessels of the United States, 1013

Merchants and Scholars, 737

Metastatics and Macroeconomics, 203

Metcalif, Kenneth N., 981

Methodisch-Theoetisches Schrifttum zur Wirtsch. Entwicklung, 240

Metroeconomica; Rivista . . ., 1395

Meyer, John R., 627

Meyers Handbuch über die Wirtschaft, 82

Mezhov, Vladimir, 1, 873-4

Michigan University. Bureau of Industrial Relations, 1070

Michigan. University. Survey Research Center, 465

Michl, H. E., 962

Microstatics, 204

MIDDLE EAST
Econ. condit., 402-3

Middle Market Directory, 706

Miernyk, William H., 1150

Mighell, Ronald L., 905

Mikheev, Nikolai M., 854

Mildner, H., 543

Mill, James, 163

Mill, Hohn S., 59, 164

Miller, Herman P., 481

Miller, Jerome S., 633

Million Dollar Directory, 552

Millis, Harry A., 1151

Milne, Alastair M., 1023

Minnesota. University. Library. James Ford Bell Collection, 737

Minto, S. C., 855
Mints, Lloyd W., 628
Mitchell, Brian R., 1258
Mitchell, Wesley C., 165
Mizuta, Hiroshi, 60
Modern Economic Growth, 151
Modern Economic Thought; the
American Contribution, 138
Modern Tariff History, 834
Moderne Deutsche Wirtschafts-
geschichte, 342
A Monetary History of the United
States, 616
Monetary Reform, 623
Monetary Theory and Policy, 636
MONEY
covered by ch. 3 (491-639)
Money (Robertson), 634
Money, Banking, and Economic
Welfare, 637
Money in the Theory of Finance,
618
Money, Interest, and Prices, 631
Montevideo. Centro de
Documentación Científica,
Técnica y Económica, 103
Montgomery, R. E., 1151
Monthly Bulletin of Agricultural
Economics and Statistics,
1348, 1396
Monthly Bulletin of Statistics,
1207, 1229
Monthly Digest of Statistics
(Gt. Brit.), 1254
Monthly Labor Review, 1397
Moody's Active Stock Reports,
1398
Moody's Bank & Finance Manual,
583
Moody's Insurance & Financial
Stocks, 1399
Moody's Municipal & Government
Manual, 571
Moody's Public Utility Manual,
1001
Moody's Transportation Manual:
Railroads, Airlines . . ., 1002

Moore, Justin H., 572
Moore, Wilbert E., 1152
Morgan Guaranty Trust Company of
New York. Intern. Banking Div.,
806
Morton, Arthur L., 1153
Moscow. Godudarstvennaia publich-
naia biblioteka, 434-5
Moscow. Publichnaia biblioteka, 61
Otdel spravochno-bibliograficheskoi
informatsionnoi raboty, 435
Mossé, Robert, 62
Mostecky, Vaclav, 761
Motivation and Market Behavior, 733
Motor Carrier Directory, 1005
Motta, Giuseppe, 699
Mueller, B., 1271
Müller, Gerhard, 538
Mulhall, Michael G., 290
Mundle, George F., 1071
Munn, Glenn G., 539
Musgrave, Richard A., 629
Myrdal, Gunnar, 841

Naas, Bernard G., 1026
Narodnoe Khoziaistvo SSR . . ., 415-6
Narodnoe Khoziaistvo SSR.
Statisticheskii Ezhegodnik, 436,
1277
National and International
Employment Handbook, 1098
The National Banking Review, 1400
National Censuses and Vital
Statistics in Europe, 1918-1939,
1247
National Economic Projection
Series, 482
National Income and its Composition,
1919-1938, 463
National Income and Social
Accounting, 615
National Industrial Conference
Board, 916

National Planning Association.
Center for Economic Projections,
482
National Research Council.
Highway Research Board, 983
NATIONAL RESOURCES,
334, 483-4
National Sales Executives, Inc.
New York, 652
National System of Political
Economy, 153
National Tax Journal, 1401
Nationalokonomisk Tidsskrift,
1402
Natsionalizatsiia i Problemy
Natsionalizirovanykh Otraslei . . .,
349
The Natural History of Population,
1195
Natural Resrouces in Low Income
Countries, 218
Natural Value, 211
The Nature of Capital and Income,
132
Nef, John U., 166
Nelson, L. T., 700a
Nemmers, Erwin E., 83, 700
NETHERLANDS
Stat., 1268
Netherlands. Central Bureau voor
de Statistiek, 1268
Neufeld, Maurice F., 1072
Neumark, Fritz, 569
A New Dictionary of Economics, 90
The New Economics: Keynes'
Influence . . ., 142
New York Times, 291
New York University. Graduate
School of Business Administra-
tion, 684
NEW ZEALAND
Econ. condit., 404-6
Stat., 1269-70
New Zealand.
Dept. of Statistics, 1269
Government, 406

New Zealand in the Making, 405
New Zealand Official Yearbook,
1270
1951 Union List of Economic and
Financial Services, 557
Nordic Council, 1278
Norges Økonomi Etter Krigen, 407
NORTH ATLANTIC TREATY
ORGANIZATION
Stat., 1271
Northrup, Herbert R., 1134
NORWAY
Econ. condit., 407
Norway. Statisk Sentralbyra, 407
Notes on Economic Theory, 91
Nouveaux Principes d'Economie
Politique, 190
Novaia Inostrannaia Ekonomicheskaia
Literatura, 20
Novaia Sovetskaia Ekonomichskaia
Literatura, 437
Novikov, N., 438
Novinkyliteratury. Spolecenske Vedy.
Rada II: Bibliografi Ekonomické
Literatury, 21
Novotny, Jan M., 63

Occupational Index, 1115
Occupational Outlook Handbook, 1104
Official Serial Publications Relating
to Economic Development in
Africa, 305
Official Yearbook of the Common-
wealth of Australia, 1236
Official Yearbook of the Union and
of Basutoland . . . (S. Africa),
1280
Ohlin, Bertil G., 842
Oklahoma. University. Library, 926
Okonomisk Utsyn over Aret, 407a
Olsson, Gunnar, 1194
Ordo. Jahrbuch für die Ordnung von
Wirtschaft und Gessellschaft, 1403

Organización Sindical. Consejo
Económico Sindical Nacional,
103a
Organization for Economic Coopera-
tion and Development, 232, 292-3,
593-4, 807-9, 822-5, 953, 1123-4,
1226
Development Centre, 255-6, 376,
410
Library, 64, 233, 234, 332, 516-7,
762-5
Organization for European Economic
Cooperation, 1212
European Productivity Agency,
1073
Library, 22
Organized Labor in American
History, 1157
The Oriental Economist's Japan
Economic Yearbook, 385
Orientamenti Nella Letteratura
Economica, 99
Orsinger, Roger, 630
Osaka Shoka Daigaku. Keizai
Kenkyujo, 65
Osnovy Politicheskoi Ekonomii, 61
Osteuropa Wirtschaft, 1404
Our International Monetary System,
638
Outline of Money, 611
Outstanding Books on Industrial
Relations, 1037
Overall Trade by Countries, 807
Overseas Business Reports,
(U. S. Bur. of Intern. Comm.),
1450
Overseas Development Institute,
London, 800
Overseas Marketing Survey, 748
Overseas Review, 294
Overseas Survey. (Barclays Bank),
294, 803
Owen's Commerce & Travel &
International Register . . ., 788
Oxford Economic Papers, 1405

Oxford University.
Institute of Statistics, 1154
Institute of Economics and
Statistics. Bulletin, 1406
Ozga, S. Andrew, 167

Paenson, Isaac, 84
PAKISTAN
Econ. condit., 408-9
Pakistan. Ministry of Finance.
Economic Adviser, 409
Pakistan Economic Survey, 409
Palgrave, Sir Robert H. I., 85
Palgrave's Dictionary of Political
Economy, 85
Palmer, George R., 314
Palmer, O. W., 732
Pan American Union, 1233
Pan American Union. Dept. of
Statistics, 1232
Panchenko, E. N., 439
Paper Money of the United
States, 568
Paperbound Books in Economics, 71
Papers in English Monetary History,
605
Pareto, Vilfredo, 168
Patinkin, Don, 631
Pauly, Paul E., 750
Payements Internationaux, 764
Peacock, Alan T., 629
Pearl, Raymond, 1195
Pehrsson, Hjalmar, 330
Pennance, F. G., 87
Periodicals for Latin American
Economic Development, 396
PERIODICAL IN ECONOMICS,
1294-1464
Personenkatalog, 51
Personnel Management and
Industrial Relations, 1164
PERU
Econ. condit., 410

Peterson, Florence, 1108
Petty, Sir William, 169
Phelps, Henry, 1136
The Philosophy of Wealth, 123
Physical Distribution and
Marketing Logistics, 680
Pick's Currency Yearbook, 584
Piettre, Andre, 344
Pigou, Arthur C., 170-1
Pinner, H. L., 937
Pitman's Business Man's Guide,
700a
La Planifications dans ley Pays
d'Economie Capitaliste,
224
Planification Economique, 233
Planning, Deveopment and
Change, 237
Planning in Marketing; a
Selected Bibliography, 682
Planovoe Khoziaistvo, 1407
Platt, Elizabeth T., 856
Point Four: Near East and Africa,
243
Pokrovskii, Ivan F., 440
Pokshishevskii, Vadim V., 1173
POLAND
Econ. condit., 411
Stat., 1272-4
Poland. Glowny Urzad Statystyczny,
1272-4
Poland in Figures, 1272
Political Economy, 135
Politique Régionale, 234
Polk's Bankers Encyclopedia, 540
Polk's Bankers Encyclopedia
(Purple Book) Foreign
Section, 541
Polski Instytut Spraw Mied-
zynarodowych, Warsaw.
Zaklad Informacji Naukowej i
Dokumentacji, 217
Poor's Register of Directors and
Executives, United States and
Canada, 711, 945a
POPULATION, 1165,1198

Population; Revue Trimestrielle, 1408
The Population and Manpower of
China, 1180
Population and Vital Statistics Reports,
1187
Population Bulletin, 1409
Population Index, 1183
The Population of the United
States, 1190
Population Reference Bureau,
Washington, 1174
Population Studies, 1185
Population Studies; a Journal
of Demography, 1410
Population Theory and Policy, 1197
Porch, Harriett, 66
Ports of the World, 1010
PORTUGAL
Econ. condit., 413
Statistics, 1275
Portugal. Instituto Nacional de
Estatistica, 1275
Postgate, Raymond, 1138
Potier, Michael de, 62
Power, Eileen E., 368
Predecessor of Adam Smith, 147
A Preliminary Bibliography of
New Zealand Economics and
Economic History, 404
Preliminary Inventory of the
Records of the Price Depart-
ment . . ., 692
Prentice-Hall, Inc., 542, 938
Pre-Soviet Bibliographies on
Economics, 448
Primenenie Matematiki v Ekonomike,
1411
Princeton University. Industrial
Relations Section, 1036-8,
1074-5
Principles and Practice of
Commerce, 718
Principles of Economics (Marshall),
159
Principles of Economics (Menger),
162

Principles of Economics (Taussig), 200

Principles of Political Economy (Malthus), 157

Principles of Political Economy and Taxation, 175

PRIVATE AND PUBLIC FINANCE, 491-639

Production and Distribution Theories, 197

Productivity: a Bibliography, 1081

PROFESSIONS covered by ch. 8 (1025-1164)

Progress of the World in Arts, Agriculture, Commerce . . ., 290

Projections to the Years 1976 and 200: Economic Growth, 78

Propaganda Literatury po Voprosam Konkretnoi Ekonomiki, 440

Prosperity and Depression, 139

Przeglad Bibliograficzny Pismien-nictwa Ekonomicznego, 23

PUBLIC FINANCE cover. by ch. 3 (491-639)

Public Finance. Finances Publiques, 1412

Public Finance. Information Sources, 513

Public Relations Journal, 1413

PUBLIC UTILITIES cover. by 2d pt. of ch. 7 (979-1024)

Publications Containing Recent Farm Enterprise Input-Output Data, 877

Publications of the U. S. Dept. of Labor. Subject Listing, 1043

Pugh, Ralph B., 369

The Pure Theory of Capital, 142a

Quantitative Analysis for Marketing Management, 734

Quantitative Japanese Economic History, 387

Quantitative Methods in Marketing, 687

Quarterly Bibliography of Economics, 19, 383

Quarterly Check-List of Economics & Political Science, 24

Quarterly Journal of Economics, 1414

The Quarterly Review of Economics and Business, 1415

Quellenverzeichnis zur Wirtschafts-statistik Iberoamerikas, 400

Quesnay, Francois, 172

The Quintessence of Capitalism, 192

Rae, Joh, 173

Railroads and American Economic Growth, 1022

Railway Economics, 986

Rand Corporation, 66-8

Rand McNally, 69, 723

Rand McNally International Bankers Directory, 555

Randall, C.R., 673

Rathmel, Hohn M., 685

Raw Materials in the United States Economy, 955

Razvitie Mirovoi Sotsiialisticheskoi Sistemy Khoziaistva, 417

Readers' Guide to Books on Agriculture, 852

Readers' Guide to Books on Economics, 3

Readers' Guide to Books on the Business World, 648

Readings in Marketing, 736a

Readings in Price Theory, 110

Readings in the Theory of International Trade, 832

Readings on the Soviet Economy, 429

Reagan, Michael D., 466

Recherches Economiques de Louvain, 1416

Recktenwald, Horst Claus, 174
The Records of the Colonial and
    Dominion Offices, 369
Reeves, Dorothea D., 214, 476
Referativnyi Zhurnal: Geografiia,
    861
Reference Book of Manufacturers,
    941
A Reference Guide to Metropolitan
    Transportation, 980
Regional Economic Development
    Institute, 235
Regionenkatalog, 52
Reid, Margaret G., 738
Reimann, Guenter, 556, 632
Les Rélations Commerciales
    Est-Ouest, 765
Remer, Charles F., 386
Remizova, E. S., 1076
Renooij, D. C., 1202
Répartition de la Fortune
    Privée en France, 341
Report on Transport Statistics
    in the United States, 1020
A Representative Bibliography
    of American Library History,
    1072
Re Qua, Eloise, 236
Research and Development, a
    List . . ., 948
Research Conference on Industrial
    Relations and Economic
    Development, Geneva, 1966,
    975
Research Index, 104, 722
Research Management, 1417
Research on Underdevelopment,
    298
Research Sources for South Asian
    Studies in Economic Develop-
    ment, 308
Reserve Bank of India, 596
Resources for the Future, 483
Resources for the Study of
    Economic History, 214, 476
Resources in America's Future, 483

Review of Economic Doctrines,
    1870-1929, 146
Review of Economic Studies, 1418
Review of Economics and Statistics,
    1419
The Review of Income and Wealth,
    1420
Review of Social Economy, 1421
Review of the Economic Conditions
    in Italy, 377, 1306
Revista de Economia, 1422
Revista de Economiea Politica, 1423
Revista de Economia y Estadistica,
    1424
Revue d'Economie Politique, 1424a
Revue d'Histoire Économique et
    Sociale, 1425
Revue de l'Institut International
    de Statistique, 1359
Revue de Science Financiere, 1426
Revue Économique, 1427
Revue Economique Internationale,
    69
Revzan, David A., 686
Reynolds, Lloyd G., 1077, 1155-6
Ricardo, David, 175, 176
Ricci, Julio, 532
Richter, Gerard R., 796
Riegel, Robert, 633
The Right to the Whole Produce
    of Labor, 1149
Riley, Vera, 927
The Rise of the National Trade
    Union, 1160
Rist, C., 134
Ristow, Walter W., 691
Rivista Internazionale di Scienze
    Economiche e Commerciali,
    1428
Roberts, Harold S., 939, 946, 1101
Roberts' Dictionary of Industrial
    Relations, 939
Robertson, Sir Dennis H., 634
Rocznik Bibliograficzny Polskich
    Wydawnictw Ekonomiznych, 411
Rocznik Statystyki, 1273

Rodbertus, Johann K., 177
Rogerson, I., 991-2
Roll, Erich, 178
Romaine, Lawrence B., 653
ROMANIA
    Stat., 1276
Romeuf, Jean, 75
Ronaghy, Hassan A., 527
The Roots of American Economic
    Growth, 456
Rosario, Argentine Republic
    (Santa Fe) Universidad
    Nacional del Litoral, 393
Roscher, Wilhelm G. F., 179
Rose, Fred D., 1078
Rosen, Ned, 1079
Rosovsky, Henry, 387
Roy, A. D., 354
Royal Statistical Society
    Journal, 1429
Rubel, Maximilien, 70
RUSSIA
    Econ. condit., 414-48
    Stat., 1277
Russia (1923-   U.S.S.R.)
    Tsentral'noe statisticheskoe
    Upravlenie, 1277
    Otdel statistiki sel'skogo
    khoziaistva, 898
Russia and the Soviet Union:
    a Bibliography, 430
Russian-English Glossary of
    Economic and Trade Terms,
    86

Sable, Martin H., 394-6
Sachkatalog, 53
Saggi Bibliografici di Economia,
    33, 379
Sakr, Carmelita S., 1026
Sales Manager's Handbook, 175a
The Sales Promotion Handbook,
    716
Samuelson, Paul A., 180-1

Sauter, Hermann, 397
Savage, I. Richard, 1213
Savings Banks Fact Book, 585
Say, Jean Baptiste, 182
Sayers, R. S., 605
Sayre, J. Woodrow, 71
La Scandale du Dévelopment, 220
SCANDINAVIA
    Stat., 1278
Scandinavian Economic History
    Review, 1430
Schaeffer, Winnifred E., 683
Scharf, Traute, 253
Schleiffer, Hedwig, 105
Schloss, Henry H., 766
Schmidt, Anny, 760
Schmitthoff, Clive M., 843
Schmollers Jahrbuch für
    Gesetzgebung, Verwaltung und
    Volkswirtschaft, 1431
Das Schrifttum der Bodenkultur,
    862
Schrifttum des Bank- und
    Kreditwesens von 1920 bis
    1960, 520
Schrifttum zum Marschall-plan, 337
Schultz, Henry, 183
Schultz, Theodore W., 906
Schumpeter, Joseph A., 184-7
Schwartz, Anna J., 616
Schwartz, Harry, 441
Schweizerische Bibliographie für
    Statistik und Volkswirtschaft,
    1283
Schweizerische Bibliographie über
    Geld, Währung und Notenbank-
    wesen, 518
Schweizerisch Nationalbank.
    Volkswirtschaftliche und
    Statistische Abteilung, 518
Schweirerische Zeitschrift für
    Volkswirtschaft und Statistik,
    1432
Scientific Council for Africa
    South of Sahara, 306

The Scope Year Book of
Industry, Trade and
Finance, 954
Scott, Frances V., 720
Scott, Ira O., 635
Scottish Journal of Political
Economy, 1433
Scrittori Classici Italiani di
Economia Politica, 188
Seldon, Arthur, 87
A Select Annotated Bibliography
on Population, 1168
A Select Bibliographical
Listing on Technical
Assistance in Africa, 303
A Select Bibliography for the
Study, Sources and Literature
of English Mediaeval Economic
History, 361
A Select Bibliography of Modern
Economic Theory, 27
A Select Collection of Scarce and
Valuable Tract on Money, 626
A Select Bibliography on
Computer Applications in
Commerce and Industry, 673
Select List of Books on European
History, 1815-1914, 328
A Selected and Annotated Biblio-
graphy of Economic Literature
on the Arabic-Speaking
Countries of the Middle East,
1938-1952, 402
A Selected and Annotated Biblio-
graphy of International Trade,
766
Selected and Annotated Biblio-
graphy of Marketing Theory,
690
A Selected and Annotated Biblio-
graphy of Retailing, 666
Selected Bibliographies on Labor
and Industrial Relations in
Burma . . ., 1056
Selected Bibliography for
Transportation Planning, 994

Selected Bibliography of Money,
Credit, Banking and Business
Finance, 526
A Selected Bibliography of Research
and Development, 247
A Selected Bibliography on Economic
Development and Foreign Aid, 226
Selected Bibliography on Monetary
Policy, 525
Selected Documents in Canadian
Economic History, 1497-1783,
319
A Selected List of Books and
Periodicals in the Field of
Personnel Administration, 1070
A Selected List of U. S. Readings
on Development, 230
Selected Readings and Source
Materials on Economic
Development, 250
Selected References for Labor
Attaches, 1044
Selected References on Equal Pay
for Women, 1091
Selected References on Industrial
Development, 925
Selka, K. R., 712
Sellien, H., 88
Sellien, R., 88
Sell's International Register, 788a
Sel'skoe Khoziaistvo SSSR, 898
Shaukat Ali, Dr., 237
Shaw, Edward S., 618
Sheparovych, Zenon B., 687
Sherman, Morton, 913
The Shippers Directory of
National and State Agencies . . .,
1011
Shipping World Yearbook and
Who's Who, 1012
Short History of the British
Workingclass Movement, 1789-
1947, 1140
Short History of the International
Economy, 835
Shoup, Carl Sumner, 519

Shumaake, Helen R., 1056
Sichtermann, L., 520
Siddall, William R., 993
Siddiqui, Akhtar H., 408
Sievers, Gale, 259
Silverman, Herbert A., 189
Simmons, George B., 767
Simonde de Sismondi, Jean, C. L.,
190
Simpson, Keith, 1080
Singer, Eugene M., 976
Singleton, Carey B., 875
Sivolgin, V. E., 435
Sloan, Harold S., 89
Small Industry; an Intern.
Annot. Bibliography, 928
Smith, Adam, 72, 191
Social and Economic History
of Germany, 343
Social Change and Nation
Building in the Developing
Areas, 229
The Social Concept. of Moeny, 500
Social Economics, 212
Social Reformers: Adam Smith to
John Dewey, 205
Social Security Abstracts, 528
Social Security Bulletin, 1434
_____ Annual Statistical
Supplement, 1435
The Socialist Tradition, 137
Society of Investment Analysts,
370, 521
Soltman, Theodore J., 994
Solutions to 3,500 Labor Problems,
1107
Sombart, Werner, 192
Source Book on Labor, 1051
A Source List of Selected
Labor Statistics, 1027
Source Materials for Business
and Economic History, 73
The Sources and Nature of the
Statistics of the U. K., 1257
Sources of Business Information,
640a

Sources of Commodity Prices, 654
Sources of Information for Industrial
Market Research, 678
Sources of Information for
Sales Executives . . ., 652
Sources of Information in
Transportation, 985
Sources of Information on
Foreign Trade Practice, 751
Sources of Insurance Statistics,
504
The Sources of Invention,
972
Sources of State Information, 909
Sources of Statistics, 1200
Sources of Statistics for Market
Research, 823
SOUTH AFRICA
Econ. condit. 449-50
Stat., 1279-80
South Africa.
Bureau of Statistics, 1279
Office of Census and Statistics,
1280
South Africa in the Sixties, 449
The South African Economy, 450
South African Journal of Economics,
1436
SOUTHEAST ASIA
Stat., 1281
Southern Asia Social Science
Bibliography, 310
Southern Economic Journal, 1437
Sovetskii Narod za Krutoi Pod'em
. . ., 865
Soviet Economic Growth, 445
The Soviet Economy; a Selected
Bibliography . . ., 441
Soviet Export, 1438
Soviet Studies, a Quarterly Review
of the Social and Economic
Institutions of the U.S.S.R., 1439
Soviet Taxation, 621
Soviet Trade Unions and Labor
Relations, 1135

Soviet Transportation and
Communications, 996
Soziale Briefe an von Kirchmann,
177
SPAIN
Econ. condit., 451-2
Stat., 1282
Spain. Instituo Nacional de
Estadistica, 1282
Spann, Othmar, 193
Spatz, Laura (Huyett), 1081
A Special Interest Bibliography
on Discount Selling . . ., 674
Special Libraries; a Guide for
Management, 175
Special Libraries Association, 1027
Business and Financial
Division. Committee on Sources
of Commodity Prices, 654
Committee on Insurance
Library Manual, 522
New York Chapter, 557
Advertising and Marketing
Group, 655
Social Science Group, 1027
Spectator Insurance Year Book, 586
Spencer, Vivian E., 955
Spengler, Joseph J., 194,
1196-7
Das Spezial-Archiv der Deutschen
Wirtschaft, 543
Spiegel, Henry W., 195
Spitz, Alan A., 238
Stamp, Laurence D., 889
Standard Advertising Register,
see Standard Directory of
Advertisers
Standard and Poor's Corporation,
544, 597
Standard Directory of
Advertisers, 712a
Standard Rate and Data Service, 726
Standard Register of National
Advertising, see Standard
Directory of Advertisers.
Standortskartei der Periodika, 54

Stanford Research Institute.
International Development Center,
238, 928, 1175
Stanley, Alexander O., 801
Stanton, William J., 739
The State of Food and Agriculture,
a Survey . . ., 896
The Statesman's Yearbook:
Statistical and Historical
Annual, 1227
Statham, Jane, 236
Statistical Abstract of Latin
America, 1265
Statistical Abstract of the United
States, 1290
Statistical Bulletin for Latin
America, 1266
Statistical Bulletins; an Annotated
Bibliography . . ., 1215
Statistical Bulletins: Foreign
Trade, 824
Statistical Compendium of the
Americas, 1233
Statistical Dictionary of Terms
and Symbols, 1219
A Statistical Handbook of the
North Atlantic Area, 1271
Statistical Methodology Reviews,
1204
Statistical Papers, 255
Statistical Pocketbook of the
Socialist Republic of Romania,
1276
STATISTICAL REFERENCES &
REPORTS, 1231-93
Statistical Services of the United
States Government, 1287
Statistical Sources for Market
Research, 650
Statistical Vocabulary, 1218
Statistical Yearbook. Annuaire
Statistique, 1230
Statistical Year Books, an
Annotated Bibliography . . ., 1216
Statisticheskii, Ezhegodnik, 1277
Statisticka Rocenka C.S.R., 1245

Statisticki Godisnjak FNRJ, 1293
STATISTICS, 1199-1293
Statistics-Europe: Sources for
    Market Research, 645
Statistics of Balance of Payments,
    1950-61, 825
Statistics of National Accounts
    1950-61, 594
Statistics of National Income and
    Expenditures, 297
Statistics of National Product
    and Expenditure, 595
Statistics of the British Economy,
    366, 1201
Statistics on Income, Prices,
    Employment & Production, 360
Statistics Sources, 1205
Statistics Sources, (Wasserman), 1203
Statistiques et Études Financières,
    590, 1350
Statistisches Jahrbuch Berlin, 1239
Statistisches Jahrbuch der Deutschen
    Demokratischen Republik, 1249
Statistisches Jahrbuch der Schweiz,
    1284
Statistisches Jahrbuch für die
    Bundesrepublik Deutschland, 1251
Statistisches Jahrbuch für die
    Republik Österreich, 1237
Statsokonomisk Tidsskrift, 1440
Statisztikai Evkonyv, 1259
Staudt, Thomas A., 688
Steneberg, Wilhelm, 545
Stepehnson, James, 718
Steuart Denham, Sir James, 196
Stewart, Charles F., 767
Stigler, George J., 197, 198
Stillman, Minna, 1214
Stobbe, Hanna, 240, 523-4
Stock Exchange; International
    Directory, 549
Stock Exchange Year Book, 587
Stock Market Encyclopedia, 544
STOCK MARKETS
    cover. by ch. 3 (491-639)
Stolper, Gustav, 345

Stonier, Alfred W., 199
Stout, Ronald M., 1082
Strategy and Structure, 967
Stroud, Gene S., 1083
Structural Interdependence and
    Economic Development, 286
The Structure of American Economy,
    1919-1939, 464
Stubbs, Carolyn, 503
Studenski, Paul, 295
The Student Economist's Handbook,
    1
Student's Guide to Occupational
    Opportunities, 1099
Studi Economici, 1441
Studia Demograficzne, 1442
Studies and Other Publications
    Issued . . . for Europe, 242
Studies in Enterprise, 922
Studies in Financial Organization,
    606
Studies in the Theory of Economic
    Expansion, 156
Studies in the Theory of International
    Trade, 846
Study Materials for Economic
    Education in the Schools, 48
A Study of Money Flows in the
    United States, 609
A Study of Savings in the United
    States, 617
Subject Index of Bulletins Purblished
    by the Bur. of Labor Statistics,
    1117
Substance of Economics, 189
Sufrin, Sidney C., 251, 1084
Suggestions for a Basic Economic
    Library, 2
Summaries of Biostatistics, 1290
Summaries of Trade and Tariff
    Information, 815
Summary of Foreign Commerce of
    the U.S., 1451
Sun, E-tu (Zen), 323
Survey and Directory of Marketing
    Research Agencies, 704

Survey of Abstracting Services . . .
in Agriculture, 851
A Survey of Contemporary
Economics, 131
Survey of Current Business, 486,
1443
Survey of International Trade
Theory, 838
SWEDEN
Econ. condit., 453
The Swedish Economy, 453
Swiss Credit Bank, 454
The Swiss Economy, 454
SWITZERLAND
Econ. condit., 454
Statistics, 1283-4
Switzerland. Eidgenössisches
Statistisches Amt, 1284
System der Volkswirtschaft, 179
The System of Industrial Relations
in Great Britain, 1143
Systematic Glossary English/French/
Spanish/Russian of Selected
Economic and Social Terms, 84
Systematischer Katalog der Bücher,
1952-1962, 39

Tabatoni, Pierre, 41
Tables of Contents of Selected
Advertising and Marketing
Publications, 659
Taft, Cynthia H., 1155-6
Taft, Philip, 1157
Tarriff History of the United
States, 844
Tarr, Raissa, 333
Taskier, Charlotte E., 931, 1085
Tate, George, 1153
Taussig, Frank W., 200, 844
Tax Foundation, New York, 573
Tax Foundation, New York.
Library, 495
Tax Institute Bookshelf, 496
TAXATION
cover. by ch. 3 (491-639)

Taylor, A.J.P., 328
Taylor, Philip A.S., 90
Taylor, Robert M., 680
Technological Change, 974
Ten Great Economists, 187
Teoria de Metodologia e Bibliografia
de Pesquisas Economicas, 35
Texas. University. Distributive
Education Dept., 689
Population Research Center,
1176-7
A Textbook of Economic Theory,
199
The Theory and Measurement of
Demand, 183
The Theory of Economic Develop-
ment, 186
The Theory of Economic Growth,
152
The Theory of Interest as Determined
by Impatience to Spend . . .,
133
The Theory of International Prices,
833
The Theory of Monopolistic
Competition, 30
The Theory of Price, 198
The Theory of Prices; a Reexamination
. . ., 158
The Theory of Social Economy, 121
The Theory of the Leisure Class, 202
The Theory of Wages, 130
The Theory of Wages (Hicks), 1144
Thomas, Brinely, 1178
Thomas' Register of American
Manufacturers, 947
Thompson, Ralph B., 690
Thomson, Thomas R., 995
Thomson, William, 546
Thorelli, Hans B., 977
Thorn, Richard S., 636
Three Essays on the State of
Economic Science, 150
Thünen, Johann H., 907
Tiffin, Joseph, 1158
Titelkatalog, 55
Tolfree, William R., 91

Trade and Securities Statistics, 597
Trade by Commodities, 809
Trade Directories of the World, 789
Trade of United States, Western
　Europe, Canada and Japan . . .,
　814
A Trade Union Library, 1075
Trade Union Publications, 1077
Trade Unions, 1162
Trade Yearbook (FAO), 820
Transport World; 1444
TRANSPORTATION, 979-1024
Transportation Geography, 993
Transportation: Information
　Sources, 981
Transportation Journal, 1445
A Treatise on Money, 624
A Treatise on Political Economy, 182
Trends in Economic Growth, 300
Trends in the Income of Families
　and Persons in the United
　States 1947 to 1960, 481
Trescott, Paul B., 637
Triffin, Robert, 638
El Trimestre Economico, 1446
Tropical Abstracts, 893
Tsenoobrazovanie v Narodnom
　Khoziaistve SSR, 418
Turgot, Anne R. J., 201
Tvorcheskaia Initsiativa, 1076
Twentieth Century Fund, 334,
　484, 1159
Types of Economic Theory, 165

Übersicht über Agrarpolitische und
　Agrarsoziologische Aufsätze, 891
Uchenye Zapiski Kafedr Politicheskoi
　Ekonomii Vysshikh Partiinykh
　Shkol, 1448
Uebersee Rundschau, 1448
Ukazatel' Liberatury . . . po
　Nauchnoi Ogranizatsii Truda, 1066
Ukazatel' Materialov dlia Istorii
　Torgovli, 422

Ukazatel' Rabot . . . Instituta
　Ekonomiki, 439
Ukazatel' Russkoi Ekonomicheskoi
　Literatury, 427
Ulman, Lloyd, 1160
UNDERDEVELOPED AREAS
　cover. by ch. 2 (213-490)
United Nations
　Dag Hammarskjold Library, 241
　Dept. of Economic Affairs, 257,
　1222
　Dept. of Economic and Social
　Affairs, 296, 403, 1185
　Economic Commission for Asia
　and the Far East, 311
　Economic Commission for Europe,
　242, 258, 335, 1016
　Economic Commission for Latin
　America, 398-9, 1266
　Library, 929
　Statistical Office, 297, 598, 826-8,
　930-3, 596-7, 1085-7, 1179,
　1186-7, 1206-7, 1223, 1228-30
　Statistical Office. Current
　Economic Indicators, 1449
United Nations Conference for
　Trade and Development, 762
United Nations Educations
　Scientific and Cultural Organization,
　1024
UNITED STATES
　Econ. condit., 455-88
　Stat., 1285-92
United States
　Agency for International
　Development, 299, 810
　Board of Governors of the
　Federal Reserve System, 599
　　Library, 525
　Bureau of Agricultural Economics,
　876
　Bureau of Customs, 1013
　Bureau of Foreign and Domestic
　Commerce, 656
　Bureau of Foreign Commerce,
　749, 750-1, 790-1

Bureau of International Commerce, 756, 811-2
Bureau of International Commerce. Overseas Business Reports, 1450
Bureau of International Labor Affairs, 1102
Bureau of Labor Statistics, 485, 727, 1039-42, 1088, 1103-4, 1116-7, 1125-32, 1224
Bureau of the Budget. Office of Statistical Standards, 1286-7
Bureau of the Census, 601, 728, 752, 829, 958-61, 1118, 1180, 1188-9, 1288-91
Bureau of the Census. Summary of Foreign Commerce of the U. S., 1451
Business & Defense Services Administration. Office of Distribution, 657
Civil Aeronautics Board, 1017
Civil Service Commission Library, 1089
Congress. Joint Economic Committee, 442-4
Dept. of Agriculture, 899
    Economic Research Service. Farm Production Economic Division, 877
Dept. of Commerce, 658, 713, 813-4, 914
    Library, 660
    Office of Technical Services, 244
Dept. of Labor, 1043-4, 1109
Dept. of State. Division of Library and Reference Services, 243
    External Research Division, 298
    Library Division, 934
    Office of Intelligence Research and Analysis, 245
Employment Service, 1096
Federal Aviation Agency, 1019
Federal Council on Aging, 1181

Federal Reserve System. Board of Governors, 602-3
International Cooperation Administration. Office of Industrial Resources, 246, 935
Interstate Commerce Commission, 1020
Library of Congress. Census Library Project, 1215-6, 1234, 1247, 1292
    Legislative Reference Service, 300, 445, 768
    Map Division, 691
    Reference Dept., 769, 996
National Agricultural Library, 863
National Archives, 692, 888
National Science Foundation. Office of Special Studies, 247
Office of Business Economics, 486-7, 729
President, 488
Small Business Administration, 948
Tariff Commission, 815
Women's Bureau, 1090-1
United States Department of Commerce Publications, 660
United States Government Statistics, 1199
United States Income and Output, 487
United States Overseas Loans and Grants, 299
University of Illinois Library Resources in Labor and Indus. Relations, 1057
University of Michigan Index to Labor Union Periodicals, 1119
Urquhart, M. C., 1243

Vance, Stanley, 978
Van Dillen, J. G., 507
Vaughan, F. L., 92
Veblen, Thorstein, 202

Velikaia Programma Stroitel'stva Kommunizma, 433
Verwey, Gerlof, 1202
Verzeichnis der Fest- und Denk- schriften von Unternahmunger . . ., 921
Verzeichnis der Kreditinstitute und ihre Verbände, 550
Ves' SSR; Ekonomichoskii, Finansovyi . . ., 445a
Vickrey, William S., 203-4
Vierteljahrshefte zur Wirtschafts- forschung, 1452
Viet, Jean, 248-9
Viner, Jacob, 846
Virginia Council of Highway Investigation and Research, 997
The Vital Few; American Economic Progress, 459
Vneshniaia Torgovlia, 1453
Vneshniai Torgovlia Soiuza SSSR, 830
Vo'f, R. A., 446
Volkswirtschaftliche Gesamtrech- nung, 524
Voprosy Ekonomiki, 1454
Voprosy Tekhnicheskogo Progressa, 919
Vradenburg, Juliet C., 1092

Waer, David Kent W., 915
Wages and Labour Mobility, 1123-4
Wagner, Donald O., 205
Wagner, Frank E., 1084
Walch, John W., 1110
Wales, Hugh G., 693, 733
Wall Street Journal, 1455
Wallich, Henry C., 347
Walras, Léon, 206
Walton, Leslie E., 802
War and Human Progress, 166
Warren, G. F., 153
Warsaw. Szkola Glówna Handlowa. Biblioteka, 74, 694

Szkola Glòwna Planowania i Statystyki. Biblioteka, 412
Washington, D.C., Economic Development Institute, 450
Wasserman, Paul, 1203, 654
Watkins, M. H., ed., 318
The Wealth of Nations, 191
Webb, Beatrice, 1161
Webb, Sidney J., 1161
Weber, Max, 207
Weidner, Edward W., 238
WELFARE ECONOMICS 155, 465
Wells, Jean A., 1090
Weltwirtschaft, 301, 1456
Weltwirtschaftliches Archiv., 1457
WEST INDIES Econ. condit., 489-90
Westerfield, Ray B., 526
Western Enterprise in Far Eastern Economic Development, 963
Western Enterprise in Indonesia, 964
Westminster Directory of the World, 792
Whale, Philip B., 847
What to Read on Exporting, 758
Wheeler, Lora J., 770
Where to Find It: Bibliography of Indus . . . Purchasing, 912
Whitney, Howard S., 527
Whittaker, Edmund, 208
Wholesale Prices and Price Indexes, 727
Who's Who in Banking, 558
Who's Who in Industrial Relations, 946, 1101
Who's Who in Insurance, 559
Who's Who in Labor, 1105
Who's Who in Railroading in North America, 1014
Wicksell, Knut, 209, 639
Wicksteed, Philip H., 210
Wieser, Friedrich von, 211-1
Wigglesworth, Edwin F., 556, 632
Wigham, Eric L., 1162

Wild, J. E., 336, 695
Wilhelms, C., 400
Williams, Frank J., 1217
Williams, Judith B., 371
Willmington, S. Clay, 259
Wilson, Fern L., 936
Wilson's Index of Publications
by University Bureaus of Bus.
Res., 936
Wirtschaft und Entwicklung
Lateinamerikas, 397
Wirtschaft und Statistik, 348
Wirtschaftsdienst, 1458
Wirtschaftskonjunktur: Berichte
des IFO-Instituts für
Wirtschaftsforschung, 1459
Wirtschaftswissenschaft, 1460
Wirtschafts-Wörterbuch, 76
Wisconsin. University. Center for
Studies in Vocational and
Technical Education, 1181
Wiser, Vivian, 888
Wish, John R., 401
Witte, Irene M., 1093
Wittkowski, Adolf, 337
Wörterbuch der Ökonomie.
Sozialismus, 92a
Wörterbuch der Volkswirtschaft, 93
Wolf, Charles, 251, 302
Wolfe, Roy I., 998
World Agricultural Economics and
Sociology Abstracts, 894
World Bibliography of Social
Security, 509
World Commerce and Governments,
848
World Economic Review and
Forecast, 291
World Economic Survey, 296
World Energy Supplies, 957
World List of Social Security
Periodicals, 510
World Monetary Reform: Plans
and Issues, 574, 816
World Population, an Analysis . . .,
1184

World Population and Production,
1198
World Radio and Television, 1024
World Trade Annual, 827
World Trade Data Yearbook, 714,
831
World Trade Directory Reports, 812
World Trade Policies, 836
World Unfair Competition Law, 937
World Weights and Measures, 1223
World Who's Who in Commerce and
Industry, 949
World Who's Who in Finance and
Industry, 715
World Wide Chamber of Commerce
Circetory, 560
Woytinsky, E. S., 848, 1198
Woytinsky, Wladimir S., 848, 1159,
1198
Wright, Chester, 467
Wright, John K., 856
Writings on Economics, 145
Writings Relevant to Farm
Management, 888
Wyckoff, Peter, 547
Wynar, Bohdan S., 447-8

Yale Economic Essays, 1461
Yamey, B. S., 261
Yearbook of International Trade
Statistics, 828
Yearbook of Labour Statistics, 1121
Yearbook of National Accounts
Statistics, 598
Yearbook of Nordic Statistics, 1278
Yoder, Dale, 1163-4
Yüan T'ung-li, 324
YUGOSLAVIA
Stat., 1293
Yugoslavia. Savezni zabod za
Statistiku, 1293

Zabreb. Ekonomski institut, 25
Zammit, Michael, 800
Zeitschrift für die Gesamte
  Staatswissenschaft, 1462
Zeitschrift für Markt- und Meinungs-
  forschung, 463
Zeitschrift für Nationalökonomie,
  1464

Zelinsky, Wilbur, 1166
Zemskii i Krestianskii Voprosy, 874
Zeszyty Bibliograficzne. Seria II,
  217
Zhabrov, A. A., 999
Zheleznodorozhnaia Literatura SSR,
  984
Zucher, Arnold J., 89